Praise for David Gerber and *The Lion Is You*

Lion tracking with David wasn't just about adventure—it was about learning how to stay present when everything in you wants to rush or control the outcome. That lesson has stayed with me in hockey and in life. This book reflects the same kind of work we've done together: slowing down, paying attention, and responding with intention.

JJ Moser, NHL Player

As CEO of Novus Global, I've worked alongside some of the best executive coaches in the world. What I can tell you is that very few have the depth, presence, and integrity that David Gerber brings into every room.

David has this incredible ability to slow people down enough to see what actually matters—and then challenge them to live it out with courage. He doesn't offer quick fixes. He invites real transformation.

That's what this book offers: an invitation to come alive again, to pay attention to what you feel, and to step into the life you already know you're meant for. If you're ready for that kind of conversation, David is the right guide.

Jason Jaggard, CEO of Novus Global and Cofounder of the Meta Performance Institute

I came to know David Gerber through our work together at Novus Global. What stood out immediately wasn't his ideas—it was his presence. As a captain, I learned that people don't follow words; they follow how you show up. David coaches from lived experience and hard standards. He creates space for honesty, challenges you without ego, and helps you lead in a way that's actually sustainable. This book reflects the same thing I experienced firsthand: clarity, courage, and accountability without pretense.

Blake Wheeler, Former NHL Captain

I've worked with a lot of people around the game, and David is different. He doesn't try to fix you or motivate you with noise—he helps you reconnect to what actually matters. The lessons in this book are the same ones he's helped me apply over the last three years, both on and off the ice. If you're someone who wants to grow without losing yourself in the process, this book delivers.

Dylan DeMelo, NHL Player

In *The Lion Is You*, David Gerber offers a brave and profoundly vulnerable account of his journey toward surrender and awakening. This book is a powerful invitation for men everywhere to follow the thread in their own lives—a trail that leads to a deeper, more fully alive existence. If you've ever felt there must be more, this book will guide you toward it.

Allison Trowbridge, Author, Founder and CEO of Copper Books

David is a true and fierce advocate for others and ever loyal to his mission; his book will invite you down the path to discovering your deepest inner roar.

Demore Barnes, Actor, *Law & Order: SVU*

In writing this book as well as regularly in our friendship, Gerber models something profound: true intimacy—with ourselves and others—begins with courageous vulnerability. By sharing his raw journey through heartbreak and rebirth in the African wild, he shows us how opening our full story awakens deeper connection and aliveness. A powerful, transformative telling of his journey so far.

Greg Foster, Friend

David embodies the deep, committed work of transformation moment by moment, day in and day out. He lives and breathes what he teaches. This is a man who has gone to hell and back and is consistently brave enough to advocate for his soul's freedom no matter the cost, all the while living a life of service to his family, community, clients, and the world around him. If you are in a season where you are stuck, your world has been flipped upside down, you're coasting, burned out, or you're tired of living by societal expectations, and are ready to discover the wild and free life you were meant for, *The Lion in You* is the book you need to read *now!* David's story will inspire you and challenge you to follow your unique path of aliveness in your life.

Kat Harris, Speaker, Executive Coach, Facilitator, and Author of *Sexless in the City*

My work with David came during a season where presence and self-belief mattered more than anything else. He helped me slow the game down internally and reconnect with who I was beyond hockey. This book captures that journey beautifully. It's for anyone navigating pressure, transition, or uncertainty—and learning how to stay grounded and whole through it.

Jack Campbell, Former NHL All-Star

The Lion Is You is an invitation to slow down and listen—to yourself, to your body, and to what's quietly asking for your attention. David Gerber weaves story, presence, and wisdom into a book that feels both steady and expansive. This is a guide for anyone who has achieved a lot but knows there's more life available when we stop rushing past ourselves.

Tina Wells, Entrepreneur and Author

David's coaching has helped me approach the game—and life—with more clarity and confidence. He doesn't give quick fixes or clichés. He helps you build trust in yourself and stay present when things get intense. This book is an extension of that work. If you care about growth, mindset, and showing up fully when it counts, this is worth reading.

Cole Perfetti, NHL Player

Working with David has pushed me to recognize where I was unknowingly limiting myself—especially in how big I allowed myself to think. He helped me challenge those internal ceilings and step into a broader vision for my career, leadership, and life beyond the game. This book reflects that same mindset work: expanding perspective, deepening awareness, and choosing growth intentionally.

Wil Trapp, MLS Player and Former Player for U.S. Men's National Team

THE LION IS YOU

THE LION IS YOU

LESSONS FROM THE WILD ON COMING ALIVE AGAIN

DAVID GERBER

WITH A FOREWORD BY ANDREW LADD

FORMER NHL PLAYER AND TWO-TIME STANLEY CUP CHAMPION

The Lion Is You:
Lessons from The Wild on Coming Alive Again

Published by Copper Books, Nashville, Tennessee.

Distributed by Simon & Schuster.

Printed in the United States of America.
First edition 2026.

Book design by George Stevens, G Sharp Design, LLC.

ISBN: 978-1-9717-9500-3 (paperback)
ISBN: 978-1-971795-01-0 (ebook)

Library of Congress Control Number: 2025926418

To Mom, Dad, Tim, and Beth.

You loved me through the unraveling and trusted I would find my way home.

You honored the wildness it took to become whole.

You believed the lion was still alive, even when I could not feel him.

TABLE OF CONTENTS

FOREWORD

DAVID GERBER IS the kind of coach who leaves people meaningfully changed. Not because he has all the answers, but because he's done the work—deeply, consistently, and with uncommon integrity. That work has created tremendous value for his clients, colleagues, and friends. And perhaps most of all, David's vulnerability builds trust. It invites honesty. It creates the conditions where transformation becomes possible.

I came to know David through our work together at Novus Global, an executive coaching firm that helps leaders around the world elevate their performance and expand their impact. As one of our top coaches, what I most admire about David is his steady commitment to growth. He repeatedly places himself in situations that demand more of him—and he meets those moments with humility, courage, and a willingness to evolve. He doesn't hide his process. He's honest about what he's learning, and in doing so, he gives others permission to do the same.

We often think courage is something you either have or you don't. This book offers a different perspective: courage is something you can build. Something you can practice. Something you can redefine—on your own terms, in your own life.

This book is an extension of who David is: grounded, thoughtful, open, and honest. I'm grateful for his friendship, and I'm excited for readers to experience the story—and the invitation—contained in these pages.

Andrew Ladd

Former NHL Player and Two-Time Stanley Cup Champion

THE DARK WITHIN
MY DARK IS WHERE
I FOUND MY LIGHT.

TREVOR HALL[1]

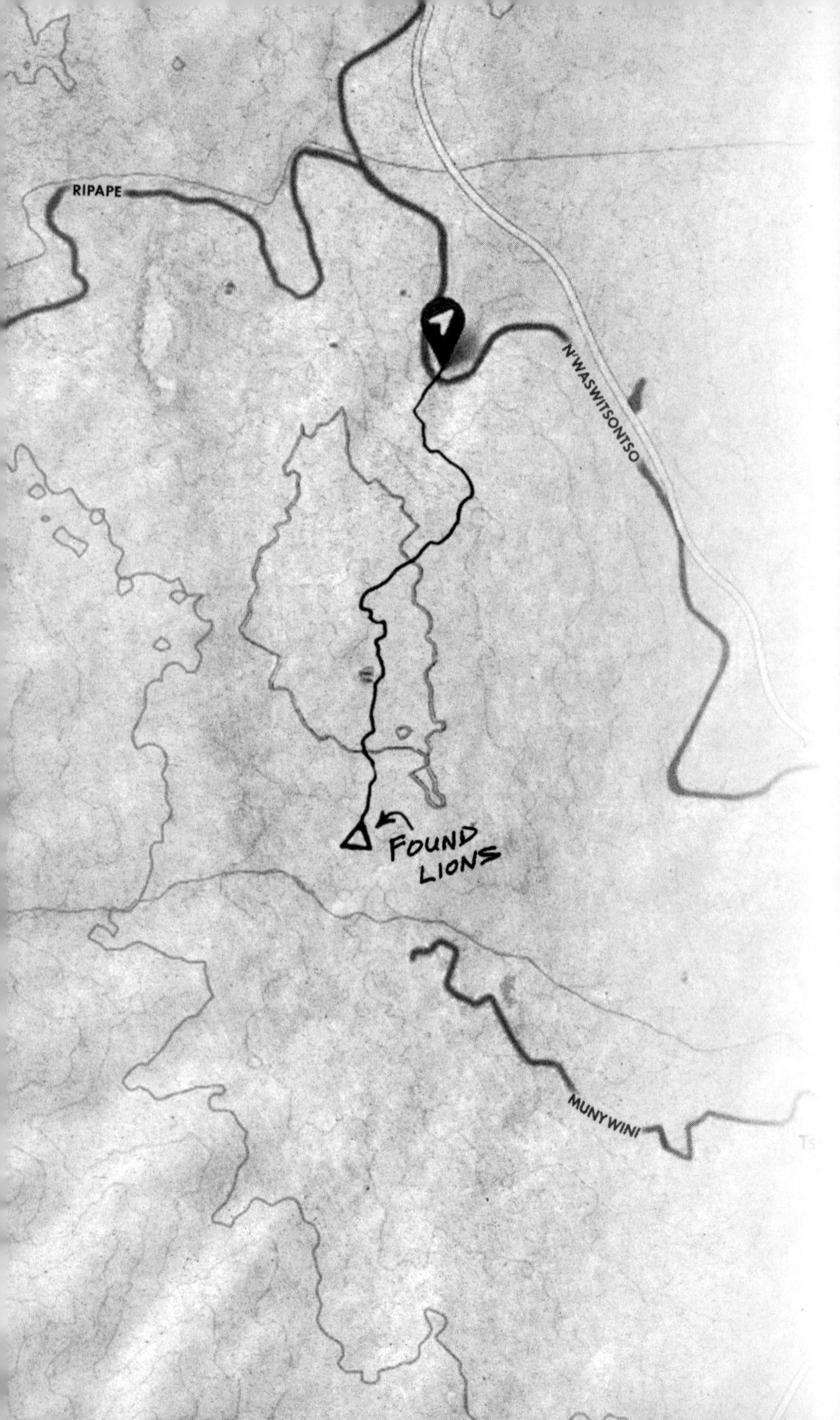
RIPAPE
N'WASWITSONTSO
FOUND LIONS
MUNYWINI

INTRODUCTION

A DEEP GROWL was the only warning.

I turned my head just in time to see a raging lioness leap from the African bush she'd been hiding in. Her enormous paws thundered on the plains as she raced toward us at fifty miles per hour. Her ears were flat against her head. Her teeth were bared. She was in absolute command, and we were at her mercy.

Every muscle in my body tensed as I desperately fought the instinct to run.

"Do not run, David," my guide cautioned, his voice calm and reassuring.

Thirty yards.

"Do not move."

Twenty yards.

"Steady."

Ten yards.

"Wait."

The lion stopped suddenly, six feet away from me, close enough that the sand she kicked up when she stopped sprayed across my exposed forearm.

Sizing us up, she growled again—a growl I could feel reverberate through my body. If we took one more step toward her cubs, which, our guide assumed, must have been somewhere nearby, she'd be forced to take swift action to defend her babies from a perceived threat: *us*.

I held my breath as I turned toward her, suddenly aware that this wasn't just *her* moment. It was also mine. I wasn't observing the wild anymore; I was standing inside the story itself.

We made eye contact, her amber eyes wild with fury. The wilderness itself looked straight back at me.

She stared us down for a few seconds, which felt like an eternity. Once she was convinced we'd gotten the message, she turned and leaped away, disappearing back into the bush.

Our small group of explorers let out a collective sigh of relief. We'd spent the day tracking lions through South Africa's magnificent Kruger National Park and were just about to break for lunch, disappointed that our search had come up empty. After four and a half hours, we'd seen nothing, not even a trace of a lion in the area.

We're not going to find any lions today, I thought, turning back toward camp.

But then, as often happens in life, the lion found *us*. So often, when we just let go, we find our way. Life becomes more about receiving what God has for us rather than *efforting* our way to it, trying to force an outcome that wasn't meant for us.

Things happen fast in the wild. One second, you are sipping your morning coffee around the fire, and then forty-five minutes later, you're standing your ground as a lion runs straight at you. The contrast is stunningly beautiful and awe-inspiring. A lion appears out of nowhere, in all her otherworldly majesty and power, and your life flashes before your eyes. Then she's gone, and you go and change your pants.

When you're out tracking lions on foot, you have absolutely no protection. No trucks to jump into. No windows to roll up. No fences to hide behind. You're just exposed. Defenseless. Vulnerable. Some of you know this feeling outside the African bush. Not because you're tracking lions, but because you're living in a season with no guarantees. A season where the old ways of operating aren't working anymore, where what used to protect you isn't protecting you. Maybe it's grief that you're facing. Maybe it's the end of something you thought would last.

Maybe you look fine on the outside but feel disoriented on the inside. If that's you, you're not broken. You're just in territory that requires a different kind of skill.

Trust me, there is a way to be in the wilderness and feel more alive than you have ever felt.

I can't think of a better way to describe the journey I've been on the past several years—the journey from being a little kid with big dreams; to having life tell you to play it safe; to sleepwalking through life; to reaching total terror and devastation; to finally becoming fully, freely, fantastically *alive*.

Maybe you're in the middle of that journey yourself. Maybe you're wandering around in a daze, lost and all alone. Maybe you feel like you've been tracking a lion of your own who refuses to be found. Maybe you feel a faint hint of wildness trapped within you, yearning to be set free.

Wherever you are and whatever you've been through, I invite you to join me on an expedition. Together, we'll track the lion that's lurking just out of sight. We'll find the magnificent creature that's creeping on the faint edges of your periphery. And we'll discover the wild, untamed, uncaged life you've always dreamed of.

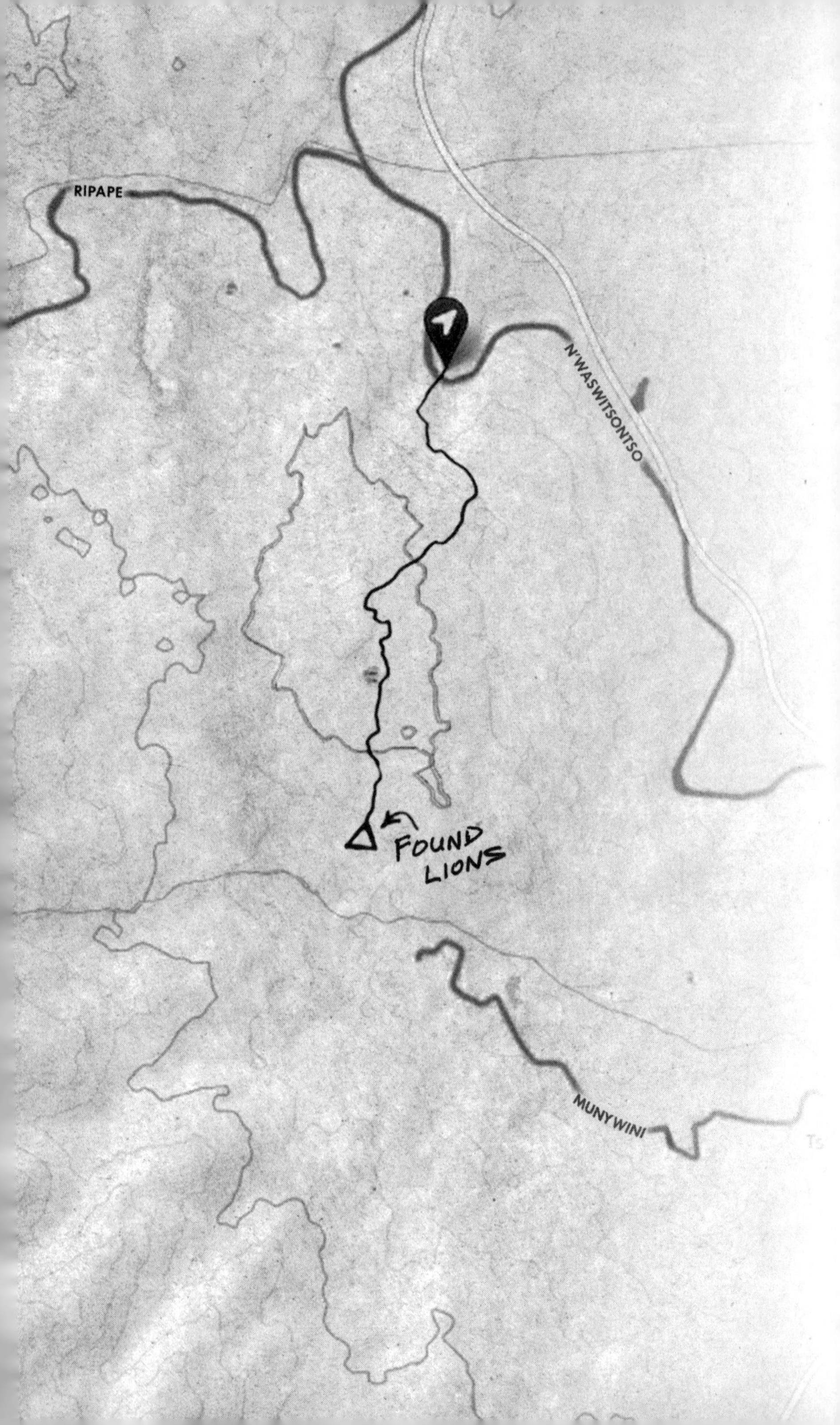
RIPAPE
N'WASWITSONTSO
FOUND LIONS
MUNYWINI

CHAPTER 1

BREAK FREE OF 1–10 LIVING

The first track is the end of a string. At the far end, a being [creature] is moving; a mystery, dropping a hint about itself every so many feet, telling you more about itself until you can almost see it, even before you come to it. The mystery reveals itself slowly, track by track, giving its genealogy early to coax you in. Further on, it will tell you the intimate details of its life and work, until you know the maker of the track like a lifelong friend.

TOM BROWN JR.,
NATURALIST AND WILDERNESS TRACKER[2]

MOST PEOPLE THINK the "9–5 grind" will be the death of them.

They fight through the morning commute, get to their desk at 8:58 a.m., and spend the next eight hours watching the clock. Then, they're out the door at 5:01

p.m., they fight the same traffic on the way home, and they spend a few hours with the family until bedtime. Rinse and repeat. Every day. For forty years.

At the executive coaching firm I'm a part of, Novus Global, we have found that this can also be true for our clients who are entrepreneurs, professional athletes, or have other non-traditional jobs outside a 9–5. As executive coaches, we've talked to business owners who feel stuck in the same rut. But for them, it feels more like a 24/7 grind. We've worked with professional athletes who, even though they are the best in the world at what they do, have felt the same sense of malaise going from practice to practice and game to game. A routine-driven existence leaves many searching for something more.

None of this exactly screams *life of adventure*.

There are a million alternatives to the traditional 9–5 grind that so many people are stuck in. My business partners and I pulled ourselves out of that rut a long time ago, building and growing an executive coaching firm that allows us to work whenever we want and, more importantly, *wherever* we want. There are already countless books and training programs designed to solve the 9–5 problem. You don't need my take on that well-worn topic.

What bothers me infinitely more than the 9–5 is the 1–10—the clear, tidy, predictable scale we're given to rate pretty much everything in our lives. You know what I'm talking about:

On a scale of 1 to 10, how would you rate your __________?

Pain. Experience. Attractiveness. Mood. Communication. Energy level. Career fulfillment. Leadership ability. Level of satisfaction. Enjoyment of a book. Ease of a service. Progress toward a goal. Physical health. Emotional health. Mental health. Intensity during a workout. Competence. Preparedness. Depression. Happiness. Likelihood to recommend *this* doctor, *this* business, *this* product, or *this* movie.

These days, we can't even buy toilet paper without getting an email asking us to rate our experience on a scale of 1–10. It's everywhere. And every time we see it, it reinforces a lie that is baked into the modern American experience—a lie that is stealing the kind of life we *really* want to live.

Society, business, and even faith communities constantly teach us, both implicitly and explicitly, that life itself exists on some easily quantified scale of 1–10. Whatever you think a 10 looks like in your life is the absolute peak of human existence—*for you*. But we're also conditioned to tamp down our expectations. When we're kids, a 10 may look like a career in the NBA or piloting the first manned mission to Mars. But that's not *reasonable*, is it? The world around us tells us that setting our sights that high is unrealistic, so we gradually downgrade our expectations as we get older. Or, as Søren Kierkegaard put it, "People settle for a level of despair they can tolerate and call it happiness."

Before we know it, we've redefined 10 to mean a safe and stable cubicle job, a path up the corporate ladder, and a 401(k) that we *hope* will let us have some fun and excitement . . . when we're in our seventies. Without realizing it, we're trading our prime decades of health, freedom, income-earning, and vitality—our twenties, thirties, forties, and fifties—for some dream of what our life might look like much, much later. Assuming, of course, we live long enough and are healthy enough to enjoy it by then.

All hail the American Dream.

Have you ever noticed that so many of our favorite books and movies tell the stories of people who dared to break free of this 1–10 box they had gotten too comfortable in? Think about it. If our favorite characters stayed blissfully ignorant and content in their little 1–10 lives:

- Luke Skywalker would have spent his whole life as a moisture farmer on a backwater planet in the Outer Rim.
- Frodo Baggins would never have left the Shire.
- Marty McFly would never have changed his family's small, dull history.
- T'Challa would have kept the wonders of Wakanda hidden away from the rest of the world instead of opening himself and his nation up to responsibilities outside its borders.
- Katniss Everdeen would never have become the catalyst and rallying cry that disrupted an entire system built on fear.
- Ray Kinsella would have kept plowing rows of corn instead of building a "field of dreams" where heaven literally touched earth.
- Harry Potter would still be living under his aunt and uncle's staircase.
- Tony Stark would have died in captivity, lost in a cave somewhere in the Middle East.
- Simba would have *hakuna-matata*-ed his way through a selfish, guilt-ridden, and ultimately meaningless life.
- Neo would have stayed willfully blind and lived a fake, useless life inside the Matrix.

- Moana never would have left the island of Motunui to sail across the sea and restore the heart of Te Fiti.

In these examples and thousands more, the hero felt a call to something more. They looked around at what everyone else had settled for and realized it wasn't big enough. They yearned for a life *beyond* the 1–10.

As a coach, I talk to people all the time who are moving fast, often faster than everyone around them. They're producing. They're achieving. Some are even wildly successful. And yet, somewhere underneath the motion, something feels strangely caged. Not because their life is objectively small, but because they've quietly narrowed what they believe is available to them, and they don't realize it's happened.

I've found that most people aren't choosing limitation. The problem is that they're unaware of the limits they've put on their lives. They don't realize how much of their life has been constructed around old fears, inherited expectations, and unconscious rules. They're living inside a cage they never meant to build because the bars are made of beliefs, not steel.

One of my clients, a professional hockey player, came to me in a season of transition. He was already talented, already successful, but he was playing from inside a narrow story about who he was and what was possible. As he started doing the work, he began seeing the walls of that story for the first time. And as he woke up, his actions changed. He took bigger risks. He made bolder decisions. He played freer.

Over time, his results changed dramatically, and he ended up tripling his lifetime earnings. That wasn't because growth is a formula, but because aliveness changes what you're willing to go for. And when you stop living inside a story you didn't write, you start writing a different one.

I had two experiences as a kid that knocked the luster off the 1–10 kind of life I was taught to expect. The first was when I noticed a mismatch between what I thought a 10 *should* look like and what I felt in my bones a 10 *would* look like.

I grew up in the church. My Christian faith was a huge part of my family life throughout my childhood and well into adulthood. I remember looking at the pastor up in the pulpit when I was young. He looked enormous. So powerful and confident. So close to God. So well-respected and well-loved. He was *the man*, and I always just assumed *that's* what a 10 looked like.

I felt the same about the professional athletes I idolized. Those guys were my heroes. I mean, they were paid millions of dollars a year to play their favorite game! They looked so strong and masculine. They represented who I wanted to be and the type of energy I wanted to radiate. Surely, *those* guys had level-10 lives.

Unless I went into ministry or got signed to a pro sports team out of high school, I figured I'd never be at a 10 myself, but at least I had a clear picture of what it looked like. By my mid-teens, I had a fixed reference point for understanding how big my own 1–10 life could be. I knew I wouldn't hit a Michael Jordan–level 10, but that still left plenty of room for me to have a fulfilling 7 or 8.

Around that same time, something happened that changed everything for me. I had an experience that blew a hole through the 1–10 way of life I'd been raised to expect.

I came face-to-face with a lion.

I was fifteen years old, my family had just moved from Minnesota to Nebraska, and I was struggling. I was so shy that I'd gone two months at my new school without saying a word. I didn't know how to make friends. I shuffled around from class to class with my shoulders slouched and head down, doing my best to be invisible in a crowded hallway full of jocks, geeks, skaters, cheerleaders, goths, preps, nerds, and stoners—the full assortment of late '90s cliques and trends.

I was frozen by fear and terrified of the world around me. I felt powerless, timid, alone, and depressed. Before long, that wasn't just how I felt; it became *who I was.* I took on the identity of someone who was breathing but barely alive. I was trapped in a cage that hid in my psyche and imprisoned my whole being from the inside out.

My parents were (and still are) amazing. They loved me, and they loved each other. Their happy marriage and our stable home have been foundational blessings of my life. One summer day, in an effort to lift my spirits, my parents loaded my brother, my sister, and me in the car for a fun family day at the zoo. It was a sweet thought, but it felt like the wrong day for a long outdoor suburban adventure. It was hot. And humid. I could feel the thick, muggy air pushing against me as we walked through the exhibits. Sweat poured off my face. My clothes stuck to me in all the wrong places. The stale summer air felt heavy in my lungs. I loved my parents, but I was *over* this attempt to cheer me up. I pressed on, but only because I had no choice.

Late in the afternoon, we wandered unsuspectingly toward the lion enclosure, and I saw him the moment I came around the corner. His large amber eyes found mine. His presence was immense and otherworldly. Mesmerized, I moved closer until there was just a surprisingly thin pane of glass between us.

I stood there, face-to-face with the king of the jungle as we looked deeply into each other's souls. The large, noisy crowd of onlookers, strollers full of screaming babies, children crying over spilled popcorn, and kids whipping balloons around. In the midst of the chaos, it was like the hand of God pulled out a remote control and hit *mute* on all of it. It all faded into the background as this majestic creature and I shared a moment of mutual recognition that I felt more than I understood.

I'd spent months becoming effectively invisible to everyone around me, but here, this regal, untamed beast saw me—*truly saw me.* I felt more seen in that moment than I'd ever felt in my life.

He was wild, but he was forced to exist in captivity—a four-hundred-pound apex predator trapped in a cage and put on display. He'd rubbed parts of his fur off with his constant, agitated pacing against the walls of his enclosure. I could see in his eyes that his spirit yearned to be free.

And yet, even if he was the saddest lion in the world, his presence was immense. Powerful. Wild. Forceful. The connection we shared was real, and it unlocked something inside me. Something I never knew was there. Something that made the 1–10 way of thinking look… small. Unfulfilling. Silly, even.

I didn't have the words at the time to explain or even fully understand the electricity I felt in my veins that day. I do now, in hindsight. I realized that afternoon that I, like the lion, was stuck in a cage. But it was a cage of my own making. I was both the predator *and* the prison guard; the creature *and* the cage.

That lion opened my heart and placed a question inside it: "What is this sensation inside me, and why do I feel a deep calling to it?"

FULLY ALIVE

I spent the next twenty-five years seeking an answer to that question, and I only figured it out after living through the absolute implosion and total devastation of my life. I'll spoil the ending for you, though. That feeling I felt standing eye to eye with a lion in the Henry Doorly Zoo in Omaha, Nebraska, in 1998? It was *alive*. I felt completely *alive* in that moment. All my worries, sadness, depression, anxiety, and loneliness were still there, and still something I knew I needed to deal with. But even with all that going on in my life, even when I thought my life could never get any worse than it was in that moment (boy, was I wrong), I felt this overwhelming sense of being *alive*. My senses were heightened. My brain exploded with endless possibilities, if only for a moment. Despite the horrible year I'd had, I didn't feel like a victim; I felt like I was the hero of some grand adventure. It was awesome. It was active and electric. It was *aliveness*. There's just no better word to describe it.

It's funny how, once you recognize this feeling, you can remember other times when you got a glimpse at what *fully alive* felt like. Experiencing that awakening at the zoo at fifteen reminded me of a similar experience I'd had when I was six. I'd been crammed in the back seat of our gold two-door Buick Somerset with my brother and sister for two days, making the twenty-seven-hour, 1,700-mile drive from Phoenix, Arizona, to small-town Ada, Minnesota, to visit my grandparents. I loved spending time with them. They were the type of grandparents who made you feel like you could do no wrong, like you were their favorite person in the world. The closer we got to their house, the more my whole body vibrated with anticipation.

Three blocks from their house, my dad pulled off on the side of the road. "I've got an idea," he said. "How would you guys like to ride your bikes the rest of the way to Grandpa Don and Grandma Verona's house?"

Our little-kid brains exploded, and we all three yelled an excited, "YES!"

Dad helped us unstrap our three bicycles from the back of the Buick, and we were off! I'm convinced that if I'd pedaled any faster, my bike would have flown through the sky, just like Elliott and his friends at the end of *E.T.* Even though my wheels were still on the ground, my spirit was soaring. The brisk Minnesota spring air in my face, my eyes watering, my little feet pedaling as hard and as fast as they could. I vividly remember seeing Grandpa Don standing in the driveway waiting for us. Our eyes found each other even though I was at the other end of the street. Pure joy was beaming off his face. I don't know that I have ever seen a more perfect picture of absolute joy than I saw in that moment. I felt so free, so happy, so fully *me*—the most alert, excited, authentic, joyful, and utterly alive version of myself possible.

That's what I felt staring into the lion's eyes at the zoo when I was fifteen.

That's what I felt when a lioness charged and stopped six feet from me on the South African plains when I was forty-two.

These were the precious few times in my life when I felt like there was a bigger life out there for me, a life beyond the 1–10 I had resigned myself to so long ago. At some point along the path of growing up, I lost that sense of wild and uninhibited living that sent me flying through the streets of Grandpa Don's neighborhood. I started riding my bike more cautiously. I put myself in my own little cage, just like the lion at the zoo. I ever so slowly began living a tame life: cautious, fearful, and passive. And ultimately, I traded "anything's possible" for "be realistic"—*realistic* meaning anything I could squeeze inside the little 1–10 box I'd made for myself.

But now, after going through (and surviving) an agonizing, unexpected journey to hell and back, I have a renewed perspective on life—and on *living*. I believe we are custom-built to experience the kind of wild, unbridled aliveness I tapped into at six and at fifteen. I think our nervous systems are wired for thriving on much higher highs than we usually dare to dream, and for surviving much lower lows than we ever want to have.

That last part is a lesson I learned the hard way.

The *really* hard way.

LIFE IN A NICE CAGE

In the spring of 2020, my life was pretty good. A solid 7 out of 10.

Well, at least as far as I knew.

I had checked all the boxes. I had done all the "right" things. I was a good person. I went to church. I graduated from high school and college. I got married. I had friends. I had a career I loved. I'd bought a house in California.

Would I call it a 10? No. Was everything in my marriage, career, and personal life perfect? No. Would I call it the peak of *aliveness*? No. But it was livable. Enjoyable. Stable. Predictable.

Like I said, a solid 7.

Until it wasn't. Until the day when, through a series of events in my late thirties, life as I knew it fell apart. I'd very quickly plummeted from a comfy 7 to a *negative* 10, curled up in a ball on the floor of an Airbnb because my wife had asked for a divorce. In the following days, weeks, and months, my joy died. My faith withered. My sex drive, my vitality, and any sense of masculinity I had completely disappeared. And the vision I'd always had for my life—marriage, kids, grandkids, retirement—evaporated.

How could this happen after I'd done all the "right" things?

It was a moment that shattered every illusion I'd been living in for decades. Beneath the surface of my "fine" life was the reality that I was just like that lion sitting in the zoo: caged, frustrated, disillusioned, and wasting the best years of my life pacing along the walls of my enclosure. Mine was a glass cage. I couldn't see the walls until they cracked. My ex-wife asking for a divorce was just the tip of the iceberg. It was then followed by everything you are about to read about how my life came crashing down and shattered the invisible walls of my 1–10 life.

Once I knew the truth, I wanted so badly to break free.

But I didn't know if I could.

Worse, I didn't know if I could even *survive* outside the walls I'd always lived in.

TRACKING LIONS . . . AND LIFE

As I healed from the heartbreak of my divorce, I gained a new perspective on life—the life I'd always lived, and the life I *wanted* to live from then on. I realized that, despite doing everything we're taught we should do to build a happy, healthy, emotionally stable life, I had only been going through the motions. I had a fine life, but

I wasn't *alive*. Not really. Not fully. And except for those rare glances here and there, I probably never had been.

It was a horrifying revelation to have halfway through what were supposed to be my prime years. It did, however, put me on the path toward a new life, an *alive* life, and that started when I did the most anti-1–10 thing possible: I decided to book a trip to go be in the wild. I followed a call within me to venture to Africa to track wild lions on foot. My first tracking expedition changed my life in every way that a life can be changed. It showed me how small I'd always lived, and it made me realize how silly it was to live a life that topped out at 10 when the scale actually went to 100 and beyond.

When I returned home from my first safari, I realized my craving for adventure, for doing something risky and putting myself in a situation where all my senses were firing, was never just about tracking lions. It was about reconnecting with my nervous system. It was about feeling alive. It was about tracking something even more mystical and elusive than the lions I'd been looking for my entire life. It was about tracking *myself*.

As I studied more and more about the art of lion tracking, I came across a wonderful parallel between tracking lions and tracking life. As naturalist and wilderness tracker Tom Brown Jr. wrote:

> The first track is the end of a string. At the far end, a being [creature] is moving; a mystery, dropping a hint about itself every so many feet, telling you more about itself until you can almost see it, even before you come to it. The mystery reveals itself slowly, track by track, giving its genealogy early to coax you in. Further on, it will tell you the intimate details of its life and work, until you know the maker of the track like a lifelong friend.[3]

To put it more succinctly, there's a clear, three-step process for tracking a lion in the wild:

1. Discover the first track.
2. Follow the string.
3. Find the creature in the wild.

Those are the same three steps we can take to track the wild, untamed, uncaged life we secretly yearn to live. Of course, every tracker knows that the creature you *find* is not always what you expected, and sometimes, you find nothing at all. But if you're really paying attention, even "nothing" can be something.

When we keep our eyes open, we can discover "first tracks" in our lives when we least expect it. Take my trip to the zoo at fifteen, for example. Now, imagine a string connecting that first track to my passion for tracking lions in the wild. I let more than twenty-five years pass between discovering that first track and following the string to something I now realize I was born to do.

For me, "finding the creature in the wild" meant *literally* finding exotic animals out in the wild. That's my passion. It's what I found at the other end of the string I was following. But that's *my* thing, and my thing might not be your thing. The "creature" you find might be a career change into an area you always loved but never thought you could make money doing. Maybe it'll be a love for dancing or playing golf or finding fulfillment being a parent. I remember hearing a well-known speaker tell the story of having a life-changing emotional and spiritual experience experimenting with mushrooms. Once, when he described to an audience how he felt during his "trip," an elderly woman approached him afterward and said she knew exactly how he felt. He assumed she'd tried mushrooms too, but she explained that was the same kind of euphoria she felt while crocheting!

That is one of the great beauties of life: The "creature" you find at the other end of the string could be literally anything. The world is filled with endless jobs, interests, activities, objects, people, and relationships that could be *your* thing. What I might see as mundane could light a fire under you, unlike anything you have ever experienced! That's what makes each of our journeys so special: They are uniquely *ours*. And here's what I wish I'd figured out sooner: We live our lives in the gap between discovering the first track and finding the creature in the wild. As long as we're following the string, we aren't just living; we're *alive*-ing. That's why, although we might enjoy crashing on the sofa after work and binge-watching TV shows until bedtime, we'll never feel fulfilled doing that. That's an example of spending our time zoning *out* instead of tuning *in* to the thing that will give our lives meaning. It's simply living when we could be, when we *should* be, alive-ing.

A CALL TO ADVENTURE

Now, I should mention here that life tracking, like lion tracking, is not for the uninitiated. You must be diligent, and you must be prepared. You must be ready for hard work, serious risk, real uncertainty, and intense emotions. Then, at the end of your greatest efforts, you must come to a place of surrender, where you welcome whatever life, whatever passion, whatever "creature" you find waiting at the end of the string. And maybe, somewhere along the way, perhaps even when you feel like giving up, the lion will find you first.

This book is your field manual for a new life of exploration. I will teach you what I've learned about tracking lions, and I will show you how to adapt it to tracking your own life. I'll illustrate these principles using the best case study I know: my life.

In the pages ahead, I'm going to share my story with you, and I'm going to hold nothing back. I'm going to tell you about the first tracks I discovered and the creatures I found moving on the other side. Some of them were wonderful. Others I wished remained hidden.

I'm going to share parts of my story that I'm terrified to put into print, because I realize I can never take them back. The part when I went to bed each night silently hoping I'd never wake up again. The part when I finally opened my eyes to sexual trauma that I'd never allowed myself to see. The part when my parents sat on the floor with me and held me like a little child as I wept uncontrollably for several hours. The part when the only thing getting me through the day was a handful of naps between work appointments and three ice-cold showers a day to shock my system back into the land of the living for a few hours at a time.

I wish I could say this depth of pain is rare. What I've learned from my clients and my colleagues at Novus Global is that many people carry it quietly, especially the ones others rely on the most.

This book dives into the depths of pain, grief, depression, trauma, lies, and the "what the hell?" moments of life to unravel the tangled web of *life stuff* that most of us stay stuck in. But don't get the wrong idea: This isn't a how-to book on managing trauma recovery or depression, and it's not a thinly veiled excuse for me to write a memoir. Instead, this book is about discovery, curiosity, and wonder. It's about finding the way back into the light while realizing that even the darkness is an essential part of your journey. It's about discovering the first tracks in your life and following the string to whatever is waiting on the other side.

As we journey together, I'm going to share several lessons I've learned while tracking lions and other magnificent creatures in the wilderness of Africa. I'll weave these stories into the chapters ahead, mixing them with my journey through the wilderness of grief and recovery.

For the more detail-conscious readers, I should point out that the tracking stories bounce around chronologically. I've peppered them in based on the lesson I learned and how each one related to each stage of my healing journey. I've done my best to provide a clear chronology of my recovery, but don't try to match that to my safari stories. Just sit back and enjoy them.

Now, with all that out of the way, I want to invite you to join me on this expedition. As you hear a bit about my life, maybe the frustrations in your own life will start to bubble up to the surface. Maybe you're already wrestling with the sense that your life is not "as good as it gets." Maybe you'll dream with me about what your life can look like beyond the frustrations and the darkness and all the heartbreak you have been through. Maybe you'll finally break free of the 1–10 way of life that never asked what your soul truly wanted.

If you've ever had the sense that more was waiting beyond the 1–10, if you're ready to leave what you know and follow the call of adventure, the following pages are an opportunity to step into the kind of life you've always hoped was possible—a life of courage, wildness, and the strength of vulnerability. It's a journey we've coached thousands of clients to discover. It's a journey back to the truest parts of who you are, the experience of being fully alive.

This book is an invitation to track a lion.

And that lion is you.

TRACKER MANUAL

Step 1: Break Free of 1–10 Living

- How would you rate your current life on the old scale of 1–10?
- How well does that number *really* reflect who you are and the type of life you want to have?
- In what ways have you let circumstances fool you into a tame, caged life?

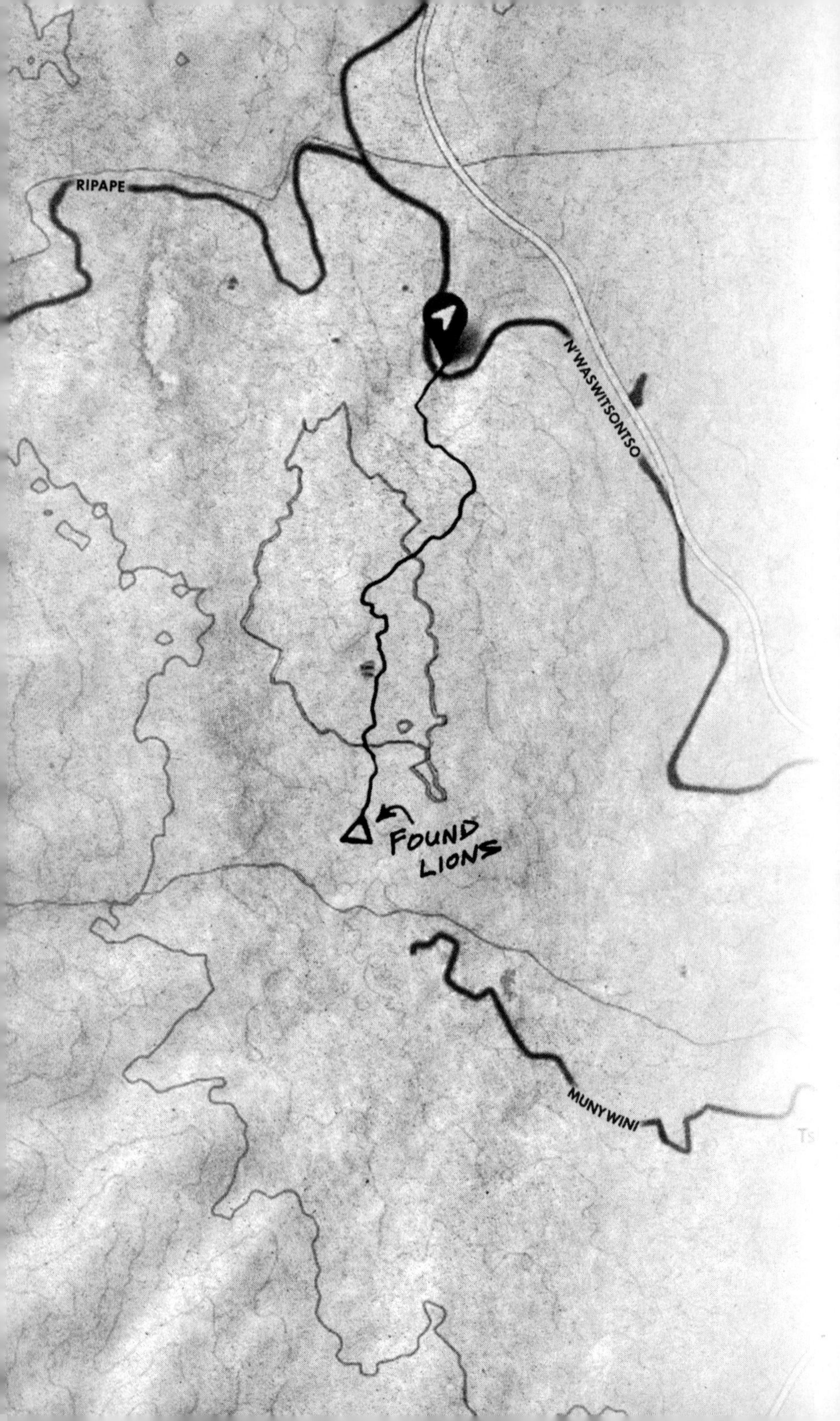
RIPAPE
N'WASWITSONTSO
FOUND LIONS
MUNYWINI
Ts

CHAPTER 2

DECIDE TO START TRACKING

The cave you fear to enter holds
the treasure you seek.

JOSEPH CAMPBELL[4]

"I DON'T THINK your wife likes you."

My friend's comment left me speechless. It was a phone call that only lasted a few minutes, but one that changed the entire course of my life from that moment on.

As far as "first tracks" go, hearing someone who knew my wife and me well say he didn't think she liked me very much was about as unmistakable as you can get. There's no way I could have overlooked that one. The only way I could get *that* clear of a first track while tracking lions in the wild would be if I tripped on a tree root and fell onto a sleeping lion's back. Once I discovered this particular first track about my marriage, I had no choice but to follow the string to see where it led.

But man, how I didn't want to.

THEY'RE AFRAID OF YOUR COURAGE

Zimbabwe, October 2022

It was my first trip tracking lions in the wild. No walls. No safety fences. Nowhere to run. Saying I was out of my element would be an understatement. And yet, ever since that incredible moment at the zoo when I was fifteen, when I'd stood eye to eye with a lion through a pane of safety glass, I had dreamed of seeing lions in the wild, outside the confines of a zoo exhibit. I wondered, *What will it feel like to see them with nothing separating us but air? Will I panic? Will the lion notice me as much as the one at the zoo did? Will it feel threatened by me, or will it welcome me into the wild?*

These thoughts had run through my head for at least two decades. Some people want to go cage diving with great white sharks or climb Mount Everest. Some want to hike the Camino de Santiago in Spain. Some want to swim through the Great Barrier Reef. But for me, it was and always has been tracking wild lions on foot. And to be clear, when I say *tracking*, I mean finding and observing. This is absolutely not about hunting. It's just the opposite, in fact. I don't want to end their lives; I want to watch them live their lives!

That experience at the zoo when I was a kid unlocked something in me. It revealed a deep, almost spiritual connection I had with lions—their power, their posture, and their presence. How they walk with such confidence, unbothered by what anyone thinks. The way you can feel their growl vibrating in your bones. The tenderness they have with each other as they lounge with their pride in the shade of a tree in the heat of the day. In my mind, a lion was the epitome of living wild, fierce, and free—everything I had always wanted to be.

And now, after dreaming of this moment for most of my life, I, along with my fellow explorers, had touched down at Zimbabwe's Mana Pools airstrip. By *airstrip*, I mean a small patch of dirt and gravel where wild animals meander until seconds before a plane lands. We were picked up in a 1960s Land Cruiser and driven to Goliath Camp, perched along the Zambezi River, which flows through six countries in southern Africa and is filled with wonderfully noisy hippos and crocodiles.

The small camp was completely outdoors. It consisted of just six tents for guests, areas for eating and sitting by the fire, and accommodations for the staff. The tents were traditional safari tents, big enough to stand and walk around inside. Each tent even had an actual bed, so we could rest in comfort each night but still get the full outdoor camping experience. Thankfully, they also had a running toilet and shower, and the tents could be completely zipped up to keep out unwanted guests. Coming from the relatively safe American Midwest, I probably didn't take that feature as seriously as I should have at first—a lesson I learned the hard way when I returned one afternoon to find a snake relaxing in my tent.

Snakes and bugs weren't the only dangers, of course. There were no fences, so the camp was completely open to wildlife. We were required to stay aware of our surroundings at all times, whether we were out tracking or not. It was especially critical to stay inside our fully zipped tents after dark, when many animals freely wandered through camp looking for their next meal.

I'd signed up for a six-day, on-foot safari that offered the chance to see a wide variety of African wildlife, including leopards, elephants, hyenas, hippos, African wild dogs, crocodiles, Cape buffalo, impalas, and many types of birds. But the primary goal of the expedition, and the reason I was there, was to track and find lions in the wild.

Our guide was a gangly, bearded Zimbabwean who went by the name Stretch because of his long, lanky six foot seven inch frame. When we arrived at camp, Stretch gathered our group for what he called "training." Given how dangerous our surroundings were and how many safety waivers we'd had to sign before reaching this point, I was prepared for a thorough and detailed session on how to ensure we'd all make it back alive from each day's trek.

But Stretch's entire training lasted all of thirty seconds and basically came down to this: "When you see a lion, stand completely still. Do not move unless instructed. Whatever you do, don't run."

That was it—the shortest TED Talk in history, yet one that my life would literally depend on. I'd gotten a more thorough safety briefing before boarding a rollercoaster at Disneyland! I wanted more answers, but Stretch exuded a quiet confidence that put me at ease. I knew this whole experience was going to push the limits of my comfort zone, and I had already resolved to try not to overthink everything for once in my life. After all, I was here for an adventure; Stretch and his crew were already delivering!

Still, over the next few days, I spent a lot of time with Stretch, peppering him with questions as we walked and tracked lions. When I asked him to elaborate on his brief training session, he reiterated: When you come face-to-face with a lion, you have to force yourself to do the exact opposite of everything your body will instinctively tell you to do. It's natural to want to run when you see an apex predator in the wild, but in this case, that is what you *cannot* do.

He explained that when you stand completely still and face the lion confidently, it will view you as a human to be cautious of. Lions in the wild don't see many humans, especially humans walking around the jungle on foot, so they aren't quite sure what to make of us. Out of an abundance of caution, a wild lion will see a confident human as a threat to avoid. However, if you run, the lion will see you less as a potential threat and more as a prey animal like a gazelle, and you can imagine what lions do to gazelles.

Stretch also told me that lions will sometimes charge, and even though it feels scary in the moment, the whole event is quite predictable, as long as the sun's up. Lions hunt at night, so all bets are off when the sun goes down. But during the day, if a lion charges at you, you absolutely cannot move. You have to will yourself to stand your ground and face it, no matter what your fear is screaming at you to do. As long as you stay still, the charging lion will stop some distance in front of you, potentially as close as a few feet, growl, paw at the ground, attempt to intimidate you, and then turn around and walk away.

When I heard this, I practically laughed out loud because it sounded like a joke. To think that a four-hundred-pound apex predator, the king of the jungle, would stop charging at me, just because I held my ground, sounded absolutely ridiculous. But this was no joke. When we got back to camp that evening, Stretch shared this excerpt with me from expert lion-tracker Boyd Varty's book:

> Often it will stop only yards in front of you. On these occasions, you must under all circumstances stand your ground and face up to the lion. "It's afraid of your courage"... Lions aren't used to other creatures staring them down.[5]

The words "It's afraid of your courage" pierced my heart. I knew Varty was just talking about lions, but there was something else behind those words for me. Like when you hear a new song with lyrics that are exactly what you needed to hear at that very moment, like the song was written for you.

As I lay in my bed that night listening to the sounds of the untouched wilderness of Zimbabwe (struggling to sleep thanks to the hippos' thunderously loud chewing and elephants snapping and chomping branches right on the other side of my tent wall), I repeated to myself, over and over again, "They're afraid of your courage." I began to think that this whole thing—my dream of tracking and experiencing lions on foot—might not really be about the lions after all. I suspected that the lions were trying to teach me something about life.

BUILDING A CAGE AROUND MYSELF

I didn't grow up tracking lions through the African wilderness. In fact, I grew up about as far from that as you can get. I was born in Crookston, Minnesota, in the early 1980s, but we didn't stay there long. We were a military family, and my dad's career always kept us on the move. I lived in eight different cities before I turned sixteen. I spent my entire childhood as "the new kid" at school, moving every two or three years. We'd usually pack up and move just as I started to settle in. As you can imagine, that made it hard for me to make friends and build any meaningful relationships as a kid outside of my family.

Fortunately, my family was (and still is) awesome.

My parents have been married for nearly fifty years, and I'm blessed to call them not only Mom and Dad but also my dear friends. The same goes for my brother and sister, their spouses, and their kids; I'm probably the proudest uncle in the world. Despite all the moves and new schools, I always knew I was loved and accepted by the people who really knew me. I absolutely adore my family. They are my foundation. I have no idea who I'd be without them in my life.

I went to college and then grad school, where I earned a master's degree in theological studies, though I've never actually used that degree professionally. My Christian faith and spirituality are still a significant part of my life, but I view it a bit differently now than I did when I was younger.

I kept bouncing around even after moving out of my parents' house. During the sixteen months I lived in Los Angeles, for example, I moved five times. These moves were never exactly upgrades, either. I was so broke that one of my new "homes" was a three-hundred-square-foot studio apartment that I shared with two other guys. I slept on a futon, piled everything I owned in the corner, and used the trunk of my car as a closet.

In my early twenties, I hadn't really figured out what I wanted to do with my life, so I had a string of jobs I wasn't passionate about but that paid the bills. I worked full-time at Trader Joe's during the day, then spent my nights working a second full-time job from home as an IT support representative. I had no idea what I was doing—neither in tech support nor in life.

I had just finished seven and a half years of school and had a master's degree. Working at Trader Joe's for $12 an hour and an IT job I hated for $25 an hour was not at all what I had thought I would be doing at this point in my life. I felt so far from the life I dreamed of living. I was floundering. I was broke. I was so afraid of living a miserable life that it became a self-fulfilling prophecy, leaving me with little ambition, no focus, and no sense of stability. By my mid-twenties, I was incredibly frustrated.

I've always been an emotional guy. Even as a kid, I felt things deeply. I didn't know what to do with all those big emotions, so I cried a lot. In my twenties and thirties, those tears turned to anger. I developed a bad anger problem from trying to bottle up all those powerful emotions I felt. Eventually, I discovered breathwork, meditation, nervous system work, somatic therapy, life/

executive coaching, and the work of Byron Katie, all of which have helped me immensely.

Now, in my forties, I've learned how to embrace all the powerful emotions I never knew what to do with as a kid. I cry a lot, because I know it's okay to feel emotions, to experience them however they need to come out. It's funny, the thing I was most ashamed of as a kid (being connected to my emotions) is the thing I am most proud of today as an adult.

During the last couple of years of my twenties, my career, finances, and personal life all sprang to life. I was fortunate enough to discover my life's work at twenty-eight and began building a business as an executive coach. A few years later, I joined my longtime friend Jason Jaggard and a few others in building the executive coaching firm Novus Global, in what would become one of the best decisions of my life. This gave me a sense of purpose and direction, and it provided an income that enabled me to live like I'd never lived before. It has given me a comfortable lifestyle and the opportunity to travel whenever and wherever I want. I grew up hating being on the move all the time, but weirdly, it's one of my favorite things as an adult. I've traveled to twenty-one countries (so far), and I'm actually writing this chapter from a friend's home in Johannesburg, South Africa, just a few days away from another lion-tracking safari!

I also had a blossoming romance to accompany my growing career. Her name was Lisa, and I was absolutely in love with her. She was vibrant, fun, beautiful, and everything I'd ever hoped to find in a partner. Every interaction with Lisa felt so easy. Considering the fact that I didn't even know how to talk to girls for the first thirty years of my life, I knew I had hit the jackpot. The best part was that she loved me back! We dated for a year and a half, I popped the question, and we got married.

So, let's see . . . Beautiful wife? Check. Fulfilling career? Check. Stability? Check—especially after we bought a home together, which had been a lifelong dream of mine. After so many years moving around, struggling with loneliness, dealing with big emotions, not knowing what the heck I was doing, I was somehow now living an awesome life.

A solid 7.

Until, of course . . .

"I DON'T THINK YOUR WIFE LIKES YOU"

It was March 2020. I was thirty-seven, had been married for nearly ten years, and was now an experienced executive coach at Novus Global working with Fortune 500 executives and professional athletes. I was living the life I used to dream about, but I was blind to how *tame* I'd become. As difficult as it feels to admit, I can see that I was essentially living on autopilot. And I sure didn't anticipate what was about to happen.

I was in Oakland, California, about to walk into a large event to connect with potential clients. I didn't know it at the time, but this would be my last big networking event for a while, as the pandemic lockdowns were just days away.

My phone rang. It was my friend Jared. I had a few minutes to kill, so I answered, and we caught up for a few minutes. It was good to hear from him, but his voice sounded . . . off. He seemed nervous, which was unusual. The reason became clear, though, when he transitioned from our initial chitchat into the reason for his call.

"David," he said in a slightly sharper tone, "can I share something with you?"

"Of course," I said.

"You know I love you and Lisa both." Taking a deep breath, he continued, "But it just seems like she doesn't like you."

My heart sank. I was speechless.

"Honestly," he said, "I've been thinking about this for a couple of years, but I just didn't know how to tell you."

I felt dizzy. I'm sure I turned white as a ghost, as though all the blood had been drained from my body—taking my energy, passion, vitality, confidence, and joy with it.

It would be years before I felt all those things return.

I tuned back in to the phone call just as Jared was saying, "I finally just had to check in and talk to you about it. Is everything okay with you two? Is there something going on?"

I sat down on the nearest bench to absorb what he'd said.

"Hey, man," I eked out, summoning false confidence and steadiness. "Thanks so much for calling and for caring about me. I'm sure this was a hard call for you to make. But I'm afraid I've got to run. I'm about to be late for this event."

But I never even walked inside the venue. I needed to think. Jared's words had hit me hard. I sensed deep down that they might be true, like I'd been willfully ignoring several red flags in my relationship for the past few years. Sure, things had been off lately, but isn't that just how marriage is sometimes?

I went home and lay on my couch, wondering how and where things had started to go wrong. What had I done? What had I *not* done? How did we end up here? Was it really that obvious to other people that things were off in my marriage? What should I do with this information now?

The way Jared had phrased his concerns bothered me, too. He didn't say Lisa didn't seem to *love* me; he said she didn't even seem to *like* me. That felt worse, like it wasn't just that the spark had died down a bit, but that she probably couldn't stand being around me at all.

The rest of that day was torture. I was stuck in this weird in-between state where I was both happily married and also worried I was heading for divorce. I paced the floor of our condo for hours with my stomach tied in knots, counting the hours until she got home from work.

I tried to play it cool when she walked in, going through the motions of a normal evening. We cooked dinner together like we usually did, and we chatted about our day while we ate. Finally, before we got up to clear the dishes, I swallowed the lump in my throat and started the conversation.

"Hey, so Jared called me today . . . ."

I told her what he'd said, praying the whole time for her to have a strong reaction of surprise, disagreement, or even outrage.

But that wasn't what I saw in her eyes.

She stammered a bit, looking for the right words, but I knew. I knew before she said anything. I saw the rest of my life flash before my eyes before she spoke her first word.

"Well, yeah. There's . . . there's some truth to that."

I could tell from her long pause and hesitation that she was trying to be gentle with me, but it didn't matter. It was clear that this wasn't when or how she wanted to start having this conversation, but it was a conversation she knew we'd have to have eventually.

In bed that night, I couldn't turn off my brain. My body felt achy, like I had the flu. I had a pit in my stomach—the kind you get when you're equal parts nervous and scared—where you sense something awful is about to happen, but it hasn't yet. So you're stuck in the anticipation of misery.

I refused to entertain the idea of divorce. There had to be a way forward together. But how do you stay in a marriage with someone who doesn't even like you? How could this even be? Had I been living inside an illusion—a façade of a happy marriage—this whole time?

My mind kept flooding with moments I had missed over the last ten years—hints, signs, and signals that my marriage had been on the rocks a lot longer than I wanted to admit. It was like Jared had put words to what my body and heart knew deep down, and now I couldn't hide from it. I couldn't suppress those emotions any longer. I had to face them.

I felt the walls of my little cage slowly starting to crack.

FIRST TRACK: "I WANT TO GO ON A SAFARI"

All hell broke loose after that night. Everything in my life changed, and I was brought down lower than I ever thought I could go as my marriage came to a painful end. I'll share more about that later. For now, I'll jump ahead sixteen months to August 2021. By that point, it's no exaggeration to say I felt dead inside. There was no light at the end of the tunnel. Life felt utterly hopeless, joyless, and like a cruel joke. I'd been lost in a cloud of depression for over a year, and I had begun worrying that I might feel like this for the rest of my miserable life.

But life, such as it is, goes on.

One warm summer afternoon, I had forced myself to attend a networking event at a scenic winery in the Napa Valley region of Northern California.

Between wine and food tastings, we were walking from one building to the next when one of the men from the group asked me one of the best questions I've ever heard:

> "David, what is something you've wanted to do for a long time but haven't done yet?"

As soon as he said it, the answer appeared fully formed in my mind—although I wasn't sure if I was ready to say it out loud yet. I took this fantasy so seriously that I felt that just by saying it, I'd be committing to it—and in the state I was in at the time, I was terrified of committing to anything.

However, the answer burned in me too brightly to ignore. It *demanded* to be spoken into existence, to be recognized as a real and valid desire, rather than a childish daydream.

"I want to go on a safari," I said. "I want to be out in the wild."

For the first time in a year, I felt the tiniest spark of anticipation—that awesome feeling you have when you're looking forward to something. It wasn't much. Barely perceptible. But after going so long without it, I noticed it. That small flicker of light was all I needed. It represented something I thought I'd lost: hope.

That little spark grew into a flame over the next few months—enough to get me Googling "African wildlife expeditions on foot." From there, I graduated to travel planning. Eventually, that wine-tasting conversation led me to my fully zipped-up and snake-free tent in the middle of Zimbabwe's Mana Pools National Park.

Noticing that first track at the wine-tasting event and making the decision to follow that string had led me to the adventure of a lifetime—what would be the first of many.

"THAT'S A LION"

Zimbabwe, October 2022

It was 9:00 a.m. The heat from the sun had begun to warm my body, and I felt a bead of sweat roll down the side of my face—partially from the heat, partially from the anxious tension I was feeling. The only sound was our own footsteps as we walked through the African bush following huge paw prints in the dirt. We had discovered the first track, and we were following the string.

Stretch scanned the landscape through his binoculars. He paused, pointed, and whispered, "There, about a hundred yards out. An animal just lifted its head in the bushes and put it back down."

Every cell in my body flooded with anticipation. The hair on the back of my neck stood at attention. I'd never felt so alert in my life. I'd never felt so fully aware of my surroundings. I'd never felt all my senses firing at the same time like this. I'd never felt this *wild*.

And then, I had another realization: I felt many things—anticipation, energy, exuberance, even joy. I was surprised to realize that, even though I felt fear, it wasn't the *dominant* emotion. Instead, the biggest thing I felt in that moment was the incredible rush of being alive.

I felt my heart pumping and the blood rushing through my veins. I could taste the gritty dust from the earth. I could smell the sweet scent of the acacia trees. I was about to see a lion in the wild.

And I *finally* felt alive again.

We took two more steps toward the bushes where Stretch had seen the animal move.

This was it!

This was what I'd been dreaming about!

This was . . . *not* a lion.

A startled hyena popped her head out of the bushes, desperately trying to wake up from the nap we'd just disturbed. I didn't move, just like Stretch had taught me. But then a second hyena appeared. Then a third, a fourth, a fifth . . . and before we knew it, we were trying to keep track of *nine* wild hyenas scurrying back and forth around us.

This could have been a very bad situation. Hyenas have one of the strongest bites on the planet. A safari guide can usually tell immediately if a pile of animal droppings came from a hyena because the droppings are actually *white*. White because hyenas can literally eat the *bones* of whatever carcass they stumble upon. They can be vicious animals, and you sometimes find them traveling in packs, which is exactly how we found them.

Would they surround and attack us? There was absolutely nowhere for us to run or hide. Not that we would have had even the slightest chance of escape if they *did* decide to attack.

My euphoric high downshifted into nervous caution.

"Are we in danger?" I asked Stretch, trying hard to keep my voice steady.

"No, it's okay," he replied. The calm in his voice was reassuring. "See the way they're scampering away from us so quickly? They want nothing to do with us."

That was good news, but what he said next was *great* news.

"Finding nine hyenas in one place in the middle of the morning tells us one thing," he said. "They're waiting for something else."

Hyenas hunt occasionally, but most of the time, they are scavengers. They wait for larger predators, like lions or leopards, to finish eating, and then they pick the bones of what's left. Hyenas are even known to steal prey from cheetahs—the fastest land animal—and get away with it because they're so ferocious and they're larger than most cheetahs. If a predator has made a kill and is enjoying his meal, you can bet there are some hyenas anxiously waiting nearby for scraps.

The string that began as a lion's paw print in the dirt earlier that morning had led us to a pack of hyenas. My heart was bursting out of my chest with excitement about where the string would lead us next.

I didn't have to wait long.

When the hyenas scattered, I noticed a large, thick vine-like bush about a hundred yards in front of us. Stretch directed us to head that way—slowly, carefully, and as quietly as possible. About forty yards from the bush, I saw something moving—an animal's tail.

Oh great, I thought. *More hyenas.*

But then I looked to my left, where I knew the pack of hyenas we'd encountered was standing by, waiting for their next meal. *Wait a minute*, I thought, as my eyes focused on the hyenas' tails. *Their tails are different than what I just saw ahead.*

Turning back to the bush, I held my breath and squinted my eyes, sharpening my focus on the animal's hindquarters as they came more clearly into view.

Then it hit me. *That's not a hyena. That's a lion.*

Just as that realization struck me, I heard the most intimidating sound I'd ever heard. It was coming from the bush—a loud, deep-throated growl that rumbled like an approaching Harley-Davidson. The sound shook the earth and reverberated through my body. He was letting us know his displeasure.

Stretch motioned for us to stop advancing and to stand perfectly still. He realized we'd found the lion at an inopportune time. The beast was standing over a fresh kill, guarding it from the hyenas he sensed nearby. He was alone, so he was much more defensive than he would have been if his pride were with him. When several lions are together, scavengers don't bother trying to steal their kill. But when it's a lone lion, they might risk it. So, a single lion over a fresh kill is always on guard.

That changed the dynamic between us and the lion, too. If we'd just found him resting or walking through the jungle, Stretch told me later, he wouldn't have wanted anything to do with us. He'd have avoided us and eventually wandered off. However, with a fresh kill on the line, the lion saw us as just as much of a threat to his meal as the hyenas.

His agitation was apparent as he sized us up and evaluated his options.

His growling paused for a moment, so we risked a few more steps toward him. He didn't react, so we took a few more, each step giving us a clearer view of this magnificent creature. He was radiating pure, raw, wild energy. The closer we got, the more I could literally *feel* his power and presence.

This is why I'm here, I thought. *To get out of my world and experience this lion in his world.*

The ground rumbled. He began growling again, this time louder.

Then, without warning, he charged at us.

My heart jumped into my throat. I felt my stomach tie itself in knots. Every nerve in my body crackled with electricity. It was like I was aware of *everything* all at once. It was both terrifying and life-giving.

I instinctively took a half step back. It was almost as though an energy field around the lion was pushing me back. My body flooded with adrenaline. Thankfully, one of the guides grabbed my elbow and simply whispered, "Stay." I took a deep breath and stood perfectly still.

The lion bolted straight at us. We held our ground, facing the lion as he charged right toward us.

He was pissed. I could see it on his face. I saw it rippling through his body. He just wanted to enjoy his lunch, but now, he had to deal with us.

Suddenly, just like the guides said he would, he stopped a few yards from us, giving us a fierce look to emphasize his irritation. Then, remembering the hyenas, he turned around and ran back to guard his carcass.

We didn't move. He charged at us two more times, trying to intimidate us into leaving. Both times we stood our ground, just as we'd been instructed.

After the third attempt, he gave us one final look of displeasure and then ran off. He kept his distance and eventually returned to his meal as we left.

That experience changed me, deeply and unmistakably, forever.

I felt a whole new level of courage welling up from deep within me. I had tapped into some wild energy I'd never felt before, and I knew at that moment: *This is how I survive. This is how I truly live.*

I had barely felt a flicker of life for nearly two years at that point, but now . . . I was more fully *alive* than I'd ever felt. I'd spent most of my life sleepwalking, but now, I was wide awake. Best of all, I had gotten my first taste of what living life to its fullest felt like. And I wanted more.

MAKE THE CHOICE

I've had several "first track" moments in my life. Racing my bicycle toward my grandparents' house to surprise them. The lion at the zoo when I was fifteen. The phone call with my friend Jared. The conversation with a colleague at a wine-tasting event. The paw prints in the dirt one morning in Zimbabwe. Every time I discovered a new track, I had to decide if I'd ignore it or if I'd follow the string and see where it led.

That's the decision we all face. Wherever you are and whatever you do, you stumble upon first tracks all the time. Do all of them change your life? No. But can some of them? Absolutely. It comes down to the decision you make in that moment: *Will I ignore this track and stay comfortably in my status quo, or will I investigate this track and follow the string to see where it leads?*

Only one path leads to that *fully alive* version of you . . . but you've got to choose whether or not to follow the tracks.

TRACKER MANUAL

Step 2: Decide to Start Tracking

Every journey begins with a decision—the decision to commit to the journey and, more importantly, to take the first step.

Find the First Track:

- What is something you want to do that you haven't done yet?
- What is it you're looking for? Allow yourself to look for it, even if it scares you . . . especially if it scares you.
- What's the first step you can take?

Enter the Wilderness:

- What emotions do you feel when facing the unknown?
- Remember the Joseph Campbell quote from the beginning of this chapter: "The cave you fear to enter holds the treasure you seek." What caves are you afraid to enter right now?

Pay Attention and Become Aware:

- What are you avoiding? What are you afraid to look at?
- How might becoming more aware of yourself and your surroundings help you on this journey?

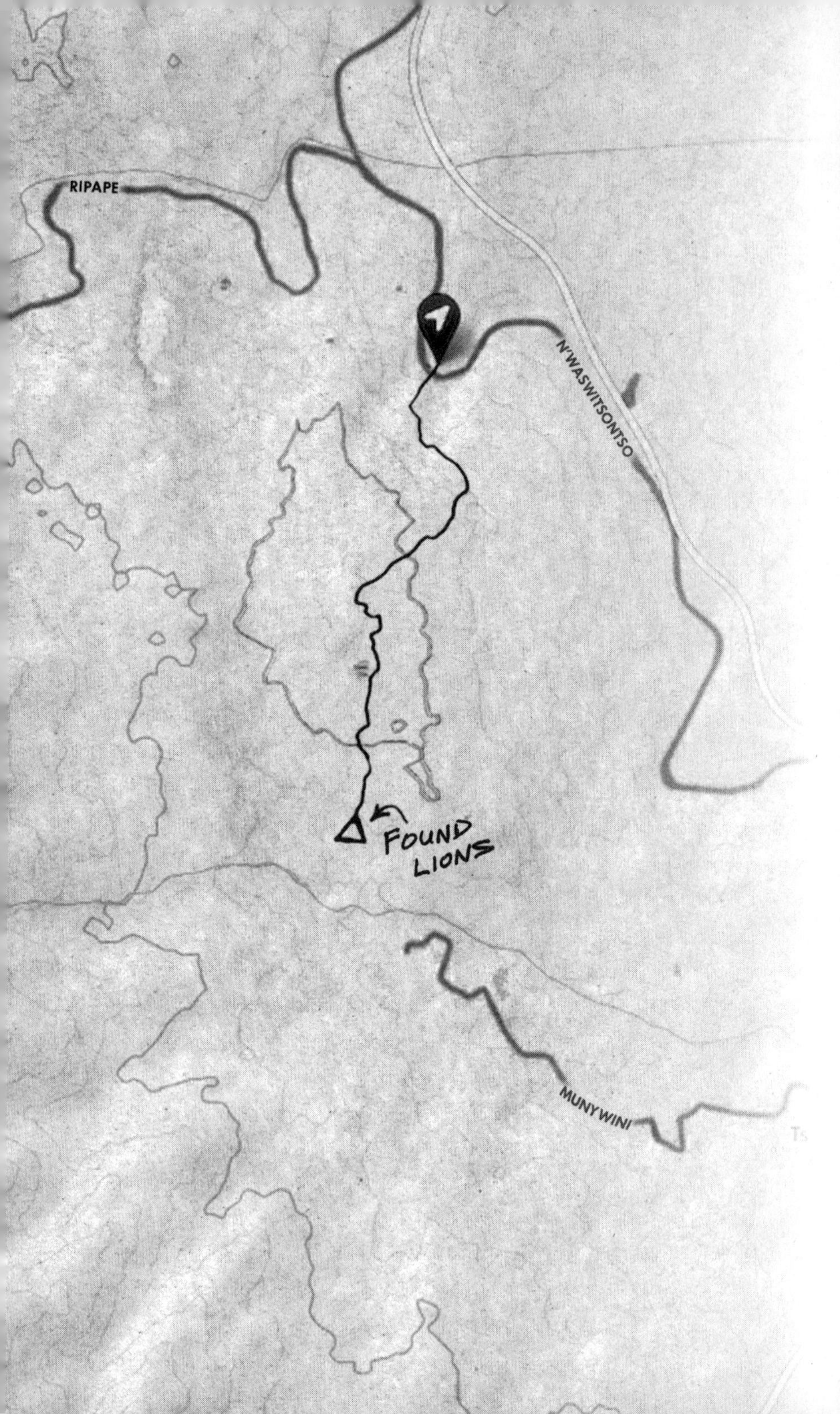

RIPAPE
N'WASWITSONTSO
FOUND LIONS
MUNYWINI

CHAPTER 3

GET UNCOMFORTABLE

All commas, no periods
All stops, no stays
The pleasure's for rent
And so is the pain.

MATTHEW MCCONAUGHEY[6]

IF YOU COULD sum up the phrase "out of your comfort zone" in a single experience, it'd have to be a four-hundred-pound lion charging at you, roaring, and flashing his enormous teeth and claws while you stand perfectly still right in front of him. For 99.99 percent of the world, that would be the single most terrifying moment of their life. When I talk about tracking lions in the wild, most people say something like, "I could never do that," or "I'd be way too scared to do that." And yes, it is scary. It can be *really* scary. I feel it too. I'm not immune to the sudden surge of adrenaline or the self-preservation instinct that makes people want to run in the face of danger. I feel it every single time I'm on a safari and find a lion, hyena, hippo, or other wild creature that most people only see in zoos or children's books. Trust me, there's nothing comfortable about it.

However, one of the most important lessons I've learned over the years of tracking lions is to get comfortable being uncomfortable. Standing six feet away from an angry apex predator who is clearly trying to decide whether she wants to eat me is anything but comfortable! But it is also the most *alive* I've ever felt. I realized—much later in life than I would have liked—that leaning into my fear can leave me feeling like every cell in my body is lit up with energy and excitement that I could never experience within the safe confines of my "comfort zone."

Your comfort zone can be a cage. As long as you keep yourself safely locked away, you'll deny yourself the opportunity to experience life on an infinitely more exciting and fulfilling scale than you can find crammed into the 1–10 way of life.

If you really want to find the wild and free version of yourself at the end of the string, you must first understand that there are going to be a lot of uncomfortable moments. You will come to the end of everything you think you know about yourself many times over. So, you must decide right now—at the start of the journey—whether you are up for it. Are you willing to face your greatest fears in order to live the life your soul truly longs for?

FINDING COMFORT IN THE DISCOMFORT

July 2025

We were on our third day of tracking lions, and we were excited. After following what we knew was a short string from the track to the lions waiting for us at the other end, we'd come upon some very fresh, very recent tracks.

Fresh tracks have a unique energy about them. It's like the lions leave a tiny bit of their power and magnificence in each track that lingers. Those paw prints seem to leap up at you from the soil when you know what to look for—and my friend and tracking mentor, Renias Mhlongo, definitely knew what to look for.

We could tell there were four or five lions traveling together, at least one male and a few females. Their tracks wove together in the dirt in a familiar figure-eight pattern that indicated the lions were likely hunting. That always comes as good news when you're tracking lions. If you come upon a pride of lions after a fresh kill, especially if they haven't finished eating yet, they are less willing to run away from you. They don't want to leave their kill, and they are more confident in their numbers that scavengers won't try to steal their meal, so you have a better chance of observing them for longer.

We inched closer through the brush, and Renias signaled for us to stop. Our little group froze in place, trying not to make a sound. Even the subtle sound of a twig snapping beneath your feet can be enough to send a pride of lions running.

"Listen," Renias said. "Do you hear it, David?"

I leaned forward and turned my ear toward the brush ahead, taking in the raw, primal sounds of a lion banquet. They had taken down their prey, and the pride was enjoying their meal. We still couldn't see them, but we could tell they were no more than thirty or forty yards directly ahead of us. We could hear the sounds of their teeth pulling the flesh off the bones, the wet smacks of their chewing, and the deep breaths they took between bites. It was thrilling, but it was also a powerful reminder of just how dangerous these creatures were. A single lion in the wild is nearly unstoppable, and here we were, sneaking up on four or five, with nothing between us but thirty yards and some thickets.

After listening for a minute or two, I slowly twisted my upper body to try to get a new angle through the brush. As I moved, a thin branch next to me lightly grazed the canvas strap of my backpack. It was hardly a sound at all, but that was all it took. The lions heard it and darted off in different directions. One of the lionesses spotted us through the bushes as she ran, but fortunately she decided not to charge at us. We knew they wouldn't have gone far from their kill, but it was clear they weren't going to let us listen in any longer. Respecting the lions and the kill they'd worked so hard for, our group slowly backed away and left them to their meal.

Having tracked for several years now, I've learned one of the keys to tracking lions and other creatures in the wild is to maintain a certain level of comfort in uncomfortable situations. You never want to get so comfortable that you forget where you are and ignore the dangers all around you. But you also don't want to be so nervous and uncomfortable that you fail to take in the wonder of nature as you walk through parts of the world most people never experience. It's a balancing act—respecting what makes the experience uncomfortable without allowing that discomfort to control your actions.

It's funny what kind of crazy scenarios we can get used to once we're willing to lean into our discomfort. If only I'd realized that five and a half years earlier, when my happy little "7 out of 10" life was about to fall apart.

MY LIFE BLOWS UP

Despite my many lion-tracking expeditions, Africa isn't where I had to face my biggest fears. In 2020, all my greatest fears tracked *me* down in what used to be the safest place in the world to me: my home.

My friend Jared had lobbed a grenade into my life that March with his "Hey, your wife doesn't like you" phone call. That—plus Lisa's admission that it was partially true—was an eye-opener. I'll admit I didn't think our relationship was fully dialed in, but I had no idea we were as far apart as we were. After that devastating conversation with Lisa, we committed to working through things as best we could. We attended counseling together, talked openly about where we were emotionally and relationally, and in time got back into a familiar rhythm.

That summer, pandemic shutdowns gave us a lot of time together. We both worked from home, took afternoon walks, cooked, and binge-watched TV series like most people did that year. Not to downplay the seriousness of the pandemic, but I was glad to have so much unexpected time with her at such a critical time in our marriage. Work picked up for both of us in the fall, though. That, plus some traveling and a lot of Zoom meetings, cut into the time we were spending together. The closeness and reconnection I had started to feel over the summer gave way to increasing distance. The busier we got, the further she seemed to be. I had started to worry, and the shock and fear I'd felt back in March, when she'd said there was "some truth" to what Jared said, had come flooding back.

After what felt like an especially awkward Thanksgiving that year, I was on the outer edge of a first track I prayed I'd never find—one so clear, though, that I couldn't ignore it. It would be a string I'd *have* to follow.

"Is everything okay?" I asked hesitantly.

She was packing a bag for a work trip to Santa Cruz. I sat on the bed, hoping the conversation sounded more casual than desperate.

"I want to check in with you," I continued. "I know life and work have been super busy for both of us, but I've just been feeling like you're really distant lately. Maybe I'm just having old worries come up, but I just wanted to talk to you about what I've been noticing and check in. Is everything okay? I mean . . . are *we* okay?"

"Everything's fine, David. We're good."

Her dismissive tone wasn't very convincing.

She caught herself and softened. "Things have just been really busy with work and that's been taking a lot of my focus. We're *fine*, really." She went on to explain that she had been having some good sessions with her therapist but wasn't ready to tell me about it, so that might be why she had appeared a bit distant. "But we're good," she reiterated.

"Okay," I said. "Thanks. I love you."

I kissed her on the forehead and went back out to the living room.

I felt like I was going crazy. Everything she was saying told me we were fine, but everything I was feeling told me that we were in serious trouble. She'd been traveling more, and she had developed a pattern of ignoring my texts and not answering my calls while she was gone. She certainly never seemed sad to leave or happy to get back home. And when we were home together, it felt like she was a million miles away—even if she was just on the other end of the sofa.

All these fears and insecurities reached the breaking point a few days into her trip. She had never betrayed my trust before, but I was convinced that either something was going on or I was losing my mind. All the signs were there, and I couldn't just keep waiting around to be blindsided. So, I did something I'd never even considered doing at any point in our ten-year marriage: I logged into her computer and read her text messages.

I won't linger on whether this was right or wrong. I'll just say that in the moment, I felt like I had no choice. And, as I very quickly discovered in her messages, my fears and mistrust had been justified after all.

I found several messages that proved undeniably that, despite her pre-trip protests, Lisa and I were neither *fine* nor *good.* Not by a long shot. I found some texts between her and a man she worked with. Part of me knew as soon as I saw those messages that my marriage was over. The funny thing is that, as horrifying as this was, I still felt validated. It was good to at least know that I wasn't crazy.

That said, I was scared. Scared she didn't want me anymore. Scared I was about to be abandoned by the person I loved most in the world. Scared about my future. Scared that one of my worst nightmares—*divorce*—was now a clear possibility.

Now that I knew how serious things were, what was I going to do about it? After all, this wasn't exactly a subtle track that I'd stumbled onto. This wasn't a faint paw impression or a broken twig; I'd practically been thrown into a den full of starving lions! This string was pulling me along whether I wanted to follow it or not.

THE TALK

I called Lisa that afternoon. The call didn't go well. I admitted that I'd looked at her text messages, and I told her what I'd found. She offered no apologies, no explanation, and no denials. She told me we'd talk it out when she got back from her trip *four days later*. I had to just sit in our empty home for another four days, scared to death about what was happening.

Being alone with my thoughts during that time wasn't great. I just kept thinking, *Do I really have to wait four days to find out if my marriage—my whole life—is over? I'm just supposed to sit here and wait for her to get home and tell me if she's leaving me?*

But what other options did I have?

So, I waited.

Lisa and I had been together for more than a decade, and we'd had our fair share of tough conversations. I had been proud of how we had both showed up and worked through things in the past. In those moments, I had felt how much Lisa had loved me. Even in some of our most challenging moments, I had still felt connected to her, like we were a team fighting through hard times together. That is not what I felt when she stepped back into our home this time. From the moment she walked in, the tension was so heavy I could *feel* it, like someone had dropped a weighted blanket on top of me. I swear, the thick fog of tension even made the room seem strangely dim, even though all the lights were on.

Neither one of us wanted to be the one to start the conversation, so we both tried to act normal. We sat down to dinner and made idle small talk for half an hour, talking about her trip and the weather and nothing that was remotely important. I so desperately wanted to stay married. I acted like tiptoeing around the six-ton elephant in the room would prevent it from crushing me. Looking back on who I was at that time, I see a guy who had no idea how fragile and tame he was. No adventure. No passion. No alive-ness. Just a half-empty shell of a man who had completely lost track of who he was—who he longed to be—in order to maintain some fantasy of what an ideal life looked like. He didn't think he could survive in the wild, so he did everything he could to stay in his safe and predictable little cage.

After dinner, we moved into the living room to talk. She took her journal off the coffee table, opened it to a predetermined spread full of notes, and slowly pressed down along the center binding to keep the pages from flipping.

I got a pit in my stomach. She'd been writing about this moment, this conversation we were about to have, trying to find her words. This was another track, another clue, as to where this was all headed. My intuition could sense this was not going to go in the direction I'd hoped it would.

"I'm sorry you found out this way," she said. "This isn't how I wanted all of this to happen. I was going to tell you, David. I've just been trying to figure all this out."

Lisa let out a deep sigh as she adjusted her body to sit cross-legged, and our eyes found each other's from across the room.

"I'm strongly considering divorce," she said.

There it was. The first time in ten years of marriage that *divorce* was brought up. After I found those texts, I knew it was there below the surface—but now, here it was staring me in the face, taunting me.

She went on, "All I know is that version 1.0 of 'David and Lisa' is over, and I'm not sure if there is a 2.0 version."

I felt like I couldn't breathe—like the elephant in the room was now sitting on me. My mind was bouncing all over the place, trying to process and make sense of what Lisa was saying. She kept talking, giving me explanations and platitudes she'd scripted for herself in her journal. But all I could hear was, "It's over."

She'd clearly been thinking about this for a while. I'm sure she'd been processing her own emotions about all of this for months, but this was all brand-new to me. I was standing at ground zero, and the bomb had just gone off. My reality was suddenly spiraling out of control. I didn't know what to do. I lay down on the couch and stared up at the ceiling—completely numb, saying nothing.

The conversation lasted thirty minutes, but it somehow felt both endless and instantaneous at the same time. In that one conversation, everything I'd ever thought about my life over my entire thirty-eight years shifted. My foundation was shattered, and I didn't know how to get my bearings. All I knew was that I had to get out of that room. I had to make the conversation stop.

Lisa and I agreed we needed some space that night, so I threw some clothes and my toothbrush in a bag, grabbed my keys, and headed to my friends Justin and Kelly's house. I called them on my way to make sure they were home and give them a heads-up, and just like good friends do, they showed up for me that night. They welcomed me in, listened, made me dinner, and even gave me a key to their front door.

By the time I collapsed onto their living room couch that night, I was in total shock. I never in a million years would have believed I'd be facing a likely divorce. But as reality sank in, my mind flooded with all the things I would lose—not just now, but in the future. Lisa and I would never celebrate the moment of seeing those two pink lines on a positive pregnancy test together. We'd never raise children together. We'd never spend the holidays together again. We'd never crawl into bed at night and wake up next to each other the next morning. We'd never again travel together. We'd never see each other's families again. We'd never grow old and gray together. All these *we'd never* moments weighed heavily on my soul.

And then there was the rejection and abandonment, which kept washing over me like incessant waves thrashing against coastline cliffs. It was relentless. My mind flashed back through all the times in my life when I'd felt different, unknown, disliked, misunderstood, rejected, embarrassed, outcast, and abandoned. If I couldn't even convince my own wife that I was worth her time, maybe all those people throughout my life who I believed thought I wasn't good enough, smart enough, or cool enough were right after all.

ONE FINAL SWING

I sat up on my friends' sofa the next morning with a flicker of hope I hadn't felt the night before. Lisa hadn't said she *wanted* a divorce; she had said she was *considering* a divorce. She'd talked about version 1.0 of our relationship being over, but she mentioned the possibility of version 2.0, even though she wasn't sure if it would come together or not. I clung to that faint possibility of a new phase of our marriage. I did not want to lose her or the life we'd built together. So, I gathered my resolve to give whatever was left of our marriage everything I had.

We made plans to make dinner together at home that night. I spent the day trying to reset my heart and brain so I could bring my A-game. I wanted to walk into the house exuding confidence and strength. I wanted her to remember why she had fallen in love with me in the first place. I pushed back on the terror I was feeling, and I hyped myself up for what I felt would be the most important dinner date of my life.

If I'm going down, I thought, *at least I'll go down fighting.*

She was in the kitchen washing vegetables when I walked in and handed her a bouquet of flowers. She thanked me and went to work cutting the stems and arranging them in a vase while I started chopping the vegetables. Lighthearted Italian dinner music played in the background, a desperate attempt to fill the immediate awkward silence between us. The vibe felt so uneasy. I had come in filled with so much hope and confidence that I had failed to note just how uncomfortable Lisa was. I can see now that we both approached that dinner filled with resolve. The problem was that we'd come up with vastly different resolutions. It's like I was trying to alter reality through sheer force of will.

We prepared our dinner mostly without speaking, as neither of us knew what to say. Our bodies were on autopilot, doing a task we'd done together countless times over the past ten years. It was the epitome of "going through the motions." But the room swirled with unasked and unanswered questions. We were both so emotionally charged—me, with fear, anxiety, shock, and a sense of betrayal, and Lisa, with whatever she was feeling at that moment. I was there looking for a solution, while she seemed to want to just get it all over with as quickly as possible.

Despite the discomfort, though, we were there together, doing something familiar. Something we'd always enjoyed. Something that had always felt romantic. Something that had long been a staple of our married life. I was trying not to overthink every move I made, so I went with what felt right and natural in the moment.

I leaned over to kiss her. Just a small, simple, gentle kiss.

She recoiled. I felt a flash of embarrassment that I'd even tried.

"What are you doing?" she shot back. "I told you I'm still trying to figure this out!"

I stepped back. "I'm confused," I said. "I thought you said you were open to exploring what version 2.0 of us could look like."

As the words came out of my mouth, I realized our versions of "exploring" were extremely different. All the hope and confidence I had tried to build up throughout the day evaporated in an instant, and the ocean of despair and rejection I'd been trying to hold at bay crashed over me like a tidal wave.

She reiterated, "I said I *wasn't sure* if there would be a 2.0 version of us. I still need some time to process all of this."

And that was it. That was the moment I knew it was over. David and Lisa were done. The way she responded when I leaned in for the kiss said it all.

We looked at each other, neither of us finding our words, and allowed the weight of what was unfolding between us to settle in. We shared so much history. So much life. So much comfort and trust—the kind that comes only from years and years of companionship. Yet, as we stood there in our kitchen, it all felt so incredibly uncomfortable, distant, and confusing.

I pressed in. "Lisa, will you just tell me? Is there anything left of us moving forward? I don't want this to be over, and I'm willing to put in the work. But I need to know where you're at."

"I know, David. You deserve to know. I've just been trying to figure out what I'm feeling . . . without making a rash decision," she said, slowly stumbling through her words. "But if I'm being honest with myself… I want a divorce. I just feel like we got married too young and have grown apart. I don't think we have the chemistry I'm looking for and that I want in my future."

Just as she'd done the previous night, she kept talking, offering explanations and being painfully honest with herself and with me. There was no mistaking the certainty in her voice, though. It was clear she had already been mentally and emotionally preparing for divorce. She was weeks, months, maybe years ahead of me in processing all the emotions, because she'd been making this decision for a while. But I was getting hit with it all at once, and the impact was soul-crushing.

At some point, my brain stopped processing what she was saying. I had gotten the answer I needed. It was over. *We* were over. And I was heading into more pain than I'd ever imagined a person could endure.

I got up to move around because the emotions were overwhelming. I couldn't just sit there. I began pacing around the room, but I couldn't stand upright. I felt weak. My mind felt like mush. I couldn't seem to gather any sound, logical thoughts. My heart was literally shattering. My knees were buckling. The weight of what I was feeling became a physical burden, like it was strapped to my back, pulling me down to the ground.

I collapsed onto the living room floor, curled up into a fetal position, and began weeping uncontrollably. My mind was overtaken by an image of Lisa slowly disappearing, like an evaporating mist, from my life. The thought utterly tormented me, hitting harder and deeper with every wave of grief that swept over me. I had always imagined we'd be married forever—"until death do you part." Yet here I was, just another guy going through a divorce, crying on the floor while his soon-to-be-ex-wife looked on.

When I was finally able to pull myself together enough to stand up, I made my way to our spare room. That was the first of many nights I slept on our sleeper sofa, a guest in my own home as we sorted out how to bring our marriage to a close over the next few months. I cried myself to sleep that night as the early stages of grief consumed me.

Over the next few months, I moved everything I owned to Denver—two suitcases at a time. I'd book a flight to visit my family in Colorado and cram as much of my stuff in two suitcases as I could. It took a long time, but that's as much as I could do and as quickly as I could move. It was so hard to let go, to fully surrender to what was happening, that moving out two bags at a time was about as much as my broken heart could handle.

Sometimes the tracks that life leaves for us are like this. We know we are about to go down a track that we have a sense we must follow without any idea of where it is going to lead, if we will make it through the dense thickets, or, if we do make it, who we will be on the other side. I've learned that this is simply a part of life sometimes. We just keep following the tracks, one at a time, trusting that it will all work out.

TRACKER MANUAL

Step 3: Get Uncomfortable

If you want to live a great life, discomfort is part of the table stakes.

- Are you willing to choose growth over comfort?
- In what areas of life right now are you allowing yourself to just be comfortable when you know that choosing discomfort would lead you toward the life you want?

Do a heart check.

- Do you really want the life you say that you want?
- Who would you need to become in order to live this life?

Identify and articulate your greatest fears.

- Write out a list. Determine if you want your fears to guide your life or if you'd rather have your courage guide your life.
- Bonus Points: Learn the Work of Byron Katie (www.thework.com). Hire a coach from Novus Global to help you question your fears through a process of inquiry. This will help you alleviate your fears.

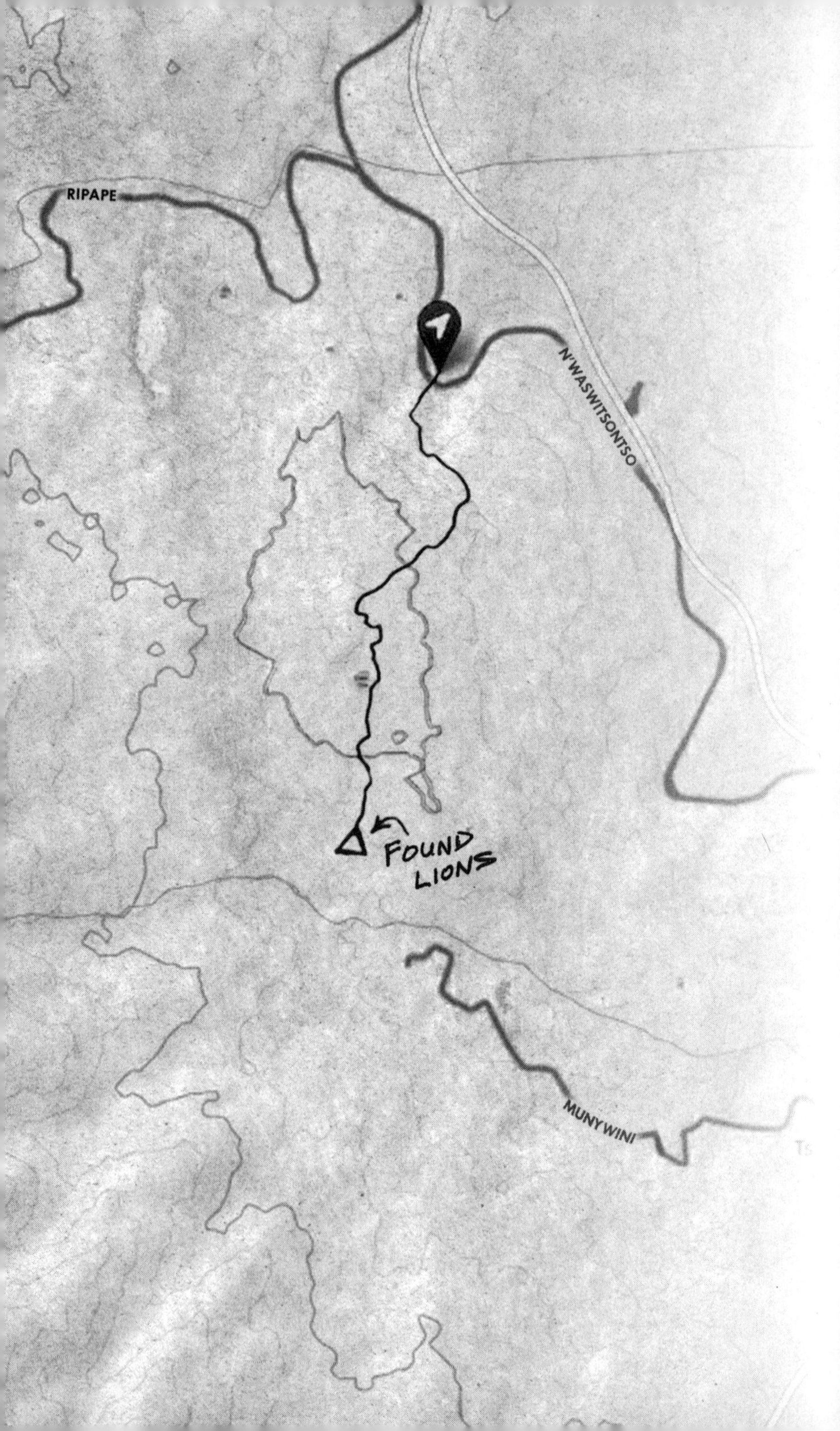
RIPAPE
N'WASWITSONTSO
FOUND
LIONS
MUNYWINI

CHAPTER 4

BORROW SOMEONE'S COURAGE

Most of these men don't believe the same way you do, but they believe so much in how much you believe.

CAPTAIN GLOVER, *HACKSAW RIDGE*[7]

"ARE . . . are they *surrounding* us?"

My fingertips pressed into Renias's arm. I'd instinctively grabbed him at the elbow when the reality of the situation dawned on me.

We'd been tracking a pride of lions that seemed to be hunting buffalo. We knew there had been a lot of activity close to our camp, so we left camp on foot that morning, leaving the Land Rover behind. We came across some fresh tracks only about five hundred yards from where I'd been sleeping. The tracks revealed the pride likely consisted of a male, at least two females, and one or two cubs. I was excited. Tracks that fresh, especially if they were on a hunt, meant there was a good chance we'd see some lions that day.

We pushed through the brush slowly, all senses firing, every nerve ending on high alert, as though a pride of wild lions could be just beyond the next thicket. That's when I heard it: the unmistakable growl of a male lion warning something—either another animal or our little group of curious humans—to stay away. The sound rolled through the brush like thunder. Logically, I knew it was coming from dead ahead, but it still somehow felt like it was coming from every direction—like our whole party had been enveloped in this creature's growl. I felt it reverberate through my sternum as it passed over and through me. It was a mixture of adrenaline and terror, intoxicating and fully alive.

Based on the growl, we were sure the lion was only forty or fifty yards ahead, but we couldn't see anything through the brush. We pressed onward one silent step at a time, thinking each next step might reveal the creature at the end of the string we were following. We could sense him, but we couldn't see him. Plus, we'd gone much farther than the fifty yards we'd anticipated. One mile ticked by, then two. I couldn't imagine the size and majesty of this male, to have a growl that traveled easily through dense terrain for several miles in every direction.

Finally, we spotted the pride about a hundred yards ahead. They were feasting on a fresh buffalo kill. They either hadn't sensed us yet or weren't overly concerned with us, so we kept closing the distance. Then, a rustling to our right got our attention. A female had apparently finished eating early and wandered away from the pack, making her way off to our right. Keeping an eye on her, we kept moving forward. Soon after, maybe seventy yards from the pride in front of us, we spotted another female break off from the pride and start heading back toward us to our left.

I could feel my muscles freezing up. We had a lioness to our left, a lioness to our right, and a pride directly in front of us. Trying to be as quiet as possible, I reached out and grabbed Renias's arm.

"Are they surrounding us?" I asked, trying to mask my rising fear.

"No," Renias replied softly. "The two on our sides don't know we're here. And even if they did, remember, they want nothing to do with us."

He patted my hand, which I hadn't even noticed was still attached to his elbow, and I felt a wave of confidence flow out of his body and into mine through that physical connection. The rising terror in me came to an abrupt halt as my mentor filled me with the confidence and reassurance of his decades of experience.

"Shall we go closer, David?" he asked, as I loosened my grip on his arm.

"Absolutely," I said with a smile. "Lead the way."

I'll never forget that day in the wild, and not because of the incredible view we got of the pride of lions later that morning. What will always stand out in my memory is the way I instinctively reached out for Renias's support. When I didn't know what to do, I knew I could depend on his experience. When I didn't know how to be brave, I knew I could depend on his strength. At times in tracking and in life, we face unnerving situations that make us feel like we're teetering on the brink of death and despair. We find ourselves at the end of our knowledge, at the end of our experience, at the end of what we think we can bear, and at the end of our courage. It is in those moments when our very survival can depend on the connection we have to the people around us. That day in the wilderness, I didn't have enough courage to get to the end of the string. But fortunately, Renias had plenty to share. Renias's courage made me braver.

I've come to see that this kind of courage is rarely something we generate on our own. More often, it's something we borrow until we're strong enough to carry it ourselves.

I've watched this same dynamic play out far from the wilderness—in locker rooms, boardrooms, and quiet conversations with people who appear strong on the outside but are privately running out of resolve. In my work alongside my colleagues at Novus Global, I've learned that the most meaningful growth doesn't happen by pushing a person harder. It happens when someone is willing to stand with them long enough for courage to return.

Sometimes in life, when we feel stuck, we just need to get around someone who has followed similar tracks and made it through, and then learn to draft off their fortitude.

SUPPORTED BY CENTRAL PARK

I love New York.

There is something about New York City that I've never seen or felt anywhere else on earth. It's like the city itself is alive—almost as if you can feel it cheering you on, celebrating your victories, and picking you up when you stumble.

In March 2021, I needed NYC's courage and vitality more than I ever had before.

The brisk spring air filled my lungs as I ran through Central Park, my favorite place in the world to run.

The noises of the city played a symphony for me—the birds, the children, the conversations of passersby, the street bands, the traffic, the sirens, and the car horns. Over the years, I'd run hundreds of miles in Central Park while training for marathons and Ironman races. It was always a place of serenity for me. I could just show up, run, and get lost in the beauty of the park and the people-watching, logging mile after mile, barely realizing how long I'd been running.

The park was a relief that day. I felt like I'd been dying a slow, merciless death in the four months since Lisa had told me she wanted a divorce. Running was one of my few escapes from the daily torture my life had become, and running *here* provided an extra level of support and comfort. Every time my foot hit the pavement, I felt the spirit of New York City supporting me. Its power shot up through my feet and filled my body and soul with a jolt of encouragement and strength, as if all nine million New Yorkers were running with me.

I was in town to do something I'd been working toward for several years: deliver my first TEDx Talk. This had been a huge professional goal of mine for nearly a decade—to have the opportunity to give a TEDx Talk on a topic I was deeply passionate about and to be recognized as a thought leader in this space. I'd always envisioned it being a highlight of my life. But through some fantastic act of cosmic irony I could not understand, this dream was coming true at the same time all my other dreams were falling apart. Somehow, my highest professional high coincided with my lowest personal low.

My TEDx Talk had originally been scheduled for a year earlier, in March 2020, but it got pushed an entire year due to the pandemic. If I'd been able to do the talk as originally scheduled, it probably would have lived up to all my expectations. Lisa would have been there to support me and share the experience with me. I wouldn't have felt like my world was crumbling down around me. I would have been capable of feeling real satisfaction at crossing a monumental goal off my professional bucket list. But a lot had happened between March 2020 and March 2021, and I knew there was no way this trip to New York could live up to the expectations I'd had the year before.

I still managed to drum up some excitement about finally being able to deliver this talk, but I was also feeling a great deal of despair, sadness, and disillusionment with everything happening in my life. The result: I just wanted to get through it. I wanted it to be over and done with—and I'm not just talking about my TEDx Talk. I wanted to be done with this whole season of my life. You've probably been there before, sitting in such a harsh reality that you wish you could just fast-forward a few months or years and skip all the pain life has thrown at you.

This wasn't how I'd always imagined feeling the day before my first TEDx Talk. I figured it would be the pinnacle of my career, but instead, I felt like a complete fraud. My whole talk, which I had been working on for literal years by that point, was all about how to weather brutal storms in life by making peace with, and even befriending, your inner critic. I had developed this talk because I thought I had "figured out" how to navigate challenging seasons in life and considered myself an expert on the subject. But that was before the storm I'd been living in for the past three months rolled in and blew my life apart. No wonder I was feeling so disconcerted. The very essence of my talk, which was intimately tied to my career and my whole identity, left me feeling fake.

My inner critic was beating the hell out of me as I ran through Central Park.

You're going to fail.

You're going to forget what you're supposed to say.

You're going to start crying on stage.

Why would anyone care what you have to say? Your own wife won't even listen to you.

Who the hell are you to tell people how to get through difficult times? You're barely hanging on!

Still plodding along through the park, doing my best to stay alert enough to dodge other people, dogs, and lampposts, I tried to remember why I'd even picked this particular topic for my talk. For most of my life, I had believed the voices in my head were only there to torment me, and it felt pretty on point that day. I believed my inner critic was my arch nemesis and that difficult circumstances were a sign of God's dissatisfaction with me. If I were a "good person," God would give me good things; if I were a "bad person," God would be upset with me and let bad things happen to me. Bad times were *only* bad; nothing good could come of them, and they certainly couldn't teach me anything. So, when I went through a difficult season, I could only grit my teeth and bear it, praying I'd get through it and get back on God's good side as quickly as possible.

This view of God and life was completely black and white. It was nice and tidy, and it reflected much of what I'd been taught about God growing up.

After years of reflection, coaching, therapy, and self-work, I thought I'd overcome this way of thinking. I thought I'd learned how to lean into the hard times and welcome my inner critic, engaging in dialogues with him and receiving his helpful criticism while discarding the rest. The work I'd done on resetting my view of these things had inspired my TEDx Talk. But then, my wife left me, forcing me to wrestle with feelings of failure and despair on an entirely new level. It was as though God had said, "I know you thought you had this all figured out, but you've only scratched the surface. To *really* get to the bottom of how to weather the storms of life, we're going to have to go *deep*."

So, here we are, I thought as I moved off to the side of the running path and came to a stop. I checked the running app on my watch—8.25 miles. Central Park had lent me its strength once again.

"IT'S NOT SUPPOSED TO BE LIKE THIS"

I had arrived in New York City four days before my TEDx Talk to settle in and spend some time exploring the city with my parents, sister, and niece. They'd made the trip so they could support me and attend the talk. None of them had ever been to NYC before, so it was a blast showing them around. We saw the One World Trade Center, went to Rockefeller Center, strolled through Central Park, and did all the typical "first time in New York" tourist things. But as fun as it was to see the sights and be their tour guide, it was difficult for me to stay present and fully enjoy the time with my family, given all the thoughts racing through my head.

Early in the morning, late at night, and in between all the activities and restaurants, I practiced my talk in my hotel room. I set up my laptop, recorded myself speaking, rewatched the recording, analyzed everything, and practiced again, over and over. I must've gone through it at least thirty times in the few days we'd been in New York. But my inner critic was relentless, especially at night when I tried to get some sleep in my hotel room. Lying in the darkness, I kept freaking myself out by imagining myself stepping on stage and totally blanking right off the bat. So, I spent the nights leading up to the event lying in bed and reciting the first ninety seconds of my talk. I figured if I could start off strong, the rest would flow smoothly.

I was putting so much pressure on myself, practically sweating with anxiety as I lay there trying desperately to shut off my brain. Just as I had so many times in the past three months, I found myself wishing I could jump ahead in time, skipping this agonizing time in my life. I felt utterly consumed with thoughts that felt too big for me to handle. *If I can just get through this TEDx Talk,* I thought, *I can finally let myself relax.*

I woke up the day of my talk and thought, *Today is the day. I'm finally giving this talk that I've been working on for so long.* I was proud of myself. I had prepared, and I was ready . . . but I was also exhausted and incredibly emotional.

I felt like I was on the brink of tears most of that morning. I waited to see if the feeling would pass before I had to leave my hotel room, but it didn't. So, I accepted it: I was ready *and* I was emotional. I was proud of myself *and* I was broken inside. I got up, left my room, and caught a taxi to the TEDx event.

Showtime.

TAKING THE STAGE

The TEDx event still had some rules from the pandemic in place, so I was only allowed to invite five people to attend as my guests. My five guests, plus two people from the TEDx team, brought my audience to a grand total of seven people. It felt strange to give the presentation of my life to an auditorium full of empty seats and only seven attendees, but it was also weirdly in line with all the other failed expectations I'd always had about this moment.

Fifteen minutes before I was scheduled to hit the stage, my family had taken their seats, but a friend I'd invited hadn't shown up yet. I checked my phone to see if he'd texted just as a new message lit up my screen. It was Lisa.

"Hey, I imagine you are already done with your talk, and I wanted to say congratulations."

It was a nice gesture . . . but it was also the worst possible thing I could have seen fifteen minutes before taking the stage. After my emotional morning in the hotel room, I'd managed to pull myself together and arrive at the venue with slightly nervous but surprisingly calm, ready-to-go energy. I had been excited, maybe even a little happy, but that message from Lisa completely threw me off.

I'd been teetering at the tip of an emotional cliff all morning, and her text sent me over the edge. It wasn't just mourning her absence, either. I was surprised by how much raw anger I felt in that moment. It came on me hard and fast, as though three months of pent-up rage I'd done my best to contain exploded out of its cage in a flash.

I couldn't get over the fact that she couldn't even be bothered to get the time right. Rather than messaging me right *after* my talk, she texted immediately *before*. Rationally, I know it was a simple time-zone calculation error. I know I should have been grateful that she was thinking of me on my big day. But reason had left the building. At that moment, I was operating on pure emotion, and I saw her caring message as the most *un*caring thing she could have done. Even though we weren't together anymore—it had been four months since she'd asked for a divorce—we'd been best friends for over a decade before that. She had been right there with me through the entire genesis of this TEDx Talk and the personal growth journey that had motivated it. She knew how important this was to me. I really thought she would have been more mindful about the details, even though she wasn't there.

A dam burst inside of me, and I started weeping uncontrollably. It was loud and dramatic. My eyes became red and puffy. Snot poured out of my nose. I felt completely broken as the realization struck: *I have less than fifteen minutes before I'm supposed to step onto that stage in what is supposed to be one of the proudest moments of my life—which will also be filmed and put on YouTube for the whole world to see. Get it together, man.*

I forced myself to choke down the big wave of emotion. I took a quick walk backstage, found a bathroom, blew my nose, splashed cold water on my face, and took some deep breaths.

A TEDx staffer spotted me as I stepped out of the bathroom.

"Are you okay?" she asked with a concerned look on her face. "You go on in five."

"I'm okay," I replied, trying to will away my flushed face and bloodshot eyes. I think I was hoping to reassure myself more than her.

Minutes later, I walked out from behind the curtain and took my place on the famous red circle. I was finally here. But it felt like everything had been working against me delivering this short speech. I wasn't certain I was going to make it through. I figured there was a decent chance I was about to become an internet sensation, with millions of eager viewers searching YouTube for "TED Talk Crying Guy."

Then, in the eternity between taking my place on the stage and getting the green light from the stagehand to start my presentation, right as I was teetering on the edge of tears again, I locked onto my parents' faces in the tiny crowd. They were smiling. I was sure they were praying for me. Their pride and excitement beamed as brightly as any spotlight bearing down on me from the rafters. They believed in me. Despite the hellish nightmare my life had been for the past several months, despite all the times they'd seen me break down in tears, despite all the emotional ledges they'd had to talk me down from . . . they believed in me. They knew I could do it. They knew I had an important message for the people who would hear my talk. They knew I would make them proud. They knew I could make *myself* proud.

Just like that, something in me shifted. I stood straighter. I breathed easier. My hands stopped shaking. I became fully present in the moment—in *this* moment, the moment I'd been waiting on and working toward for so long. It was time, and my wonderful parents in the front row knew that I was ready. In the precious few seconds before my talk began, as our eyes communicated more than words ever could, they lent me their courage.

When I was empty, they lent me their strength. And in that moment, their strength and belief in me made all the difference.

The stagehand gave me the signal. I launched into my first line, which, ironically, was, "Most of us humans are incredibly hard on ourselves. We put this immense pressure on ourselves to perform and get everything right. . . ."

I was doing it.

I got through the first ninety seconds, which I'd imagined would be my make-or-break window. Was my voice as pure and steady as I'd hoped it'd be in those first few minutes? No. In fact, I choked up a time or two, even pausing for a brief moment to find my words. By the five-minute mark, though, I was locked in. I caught my speaking flow, and the muscle memory I'd developed from countless hours of preparation and repetition took over. In the blink of an eye, my fifteen minutes were up. I said thank you, and then I stood silently in place for several seconds, just as the stagehand had instructed me, to give the video editors a clean fade-out point.

The TEDx crew broke the silence by letting me know it was "safe" to exit the stage, but I just kept standing there. It was like my feet were glued in place. As the spotlights faded and the crew started resetting for the next presentation, I realized I was feeling something new, something I wasn't expecting. Standing alone on that stage, with my talk now behind me, I felt . . . vulnerable. Exposed. Defenseless. And I didn't know why.

Then it hit me.

For the last four months, I had allowed the TEDx Talk to distract me from my divorce, from actually dealing with everything I was going through. I think somehow, in that moment on the stage, my body knew what was coming. Now that it was over, this big event could no longer be a distraction for me. The shield between me and the reality that my marriage was over was gone. I was now fully exposed to the onslaught of emotions, grief, and darkness that lay ahead of me, things I couldn't avoid if I were truly going to heal. I've seen this pattern repeat itself over and over with highly aspirational people, especially athletes and leaders. The summit is reached, the applause fades, and the unaddressed pain finally speaks.

My mind raced as I realized I had just crossed the threshold into a new phase of my trauma recovery. After standing there for what felt like an awkwardly long time (but was really just a few seconds), I walked over to the edge of the stage, sat down with my feet hanging off the platform, and resumed the weeping I'd pulled myself out of just a half hour earlier, before my talk began.

After giving me a much-needed moment to myself, my parents made their way up and joined me on the stage. They each put a hand on my back and sat with me as I wept. No words were offered, and none were needed. They simply held me with their presence, lending me their strength for the journey I still had ahead of me.

At times, the only way through difficult days is to feel our way through; to let go of our need to rationalize or intellectualize or make sense of something, to get out of our heads and into our hearts and honor ourselves by simply letting ourselves feel it all, all the way through. Only then can we begin to find our way back to the tracks we might've thought we'd lost forever.

TRACKER MANUAL

Step 4: Borrow Someone's Courage

- When you're going after the life you long for, a healthy community is essential. How are you cultivating community for yourself and others?
- When was the last time you sent a message to someone simply to check on them? Perhaps you could send a message right now to someone in your world, either to check on them or to simply remind them that they are loved.
- In what ways have you allowed yourself to borrow strength from others in difficult seasons of life? If you are in a difficult season right now, who could you reach out to and simply ask for help?

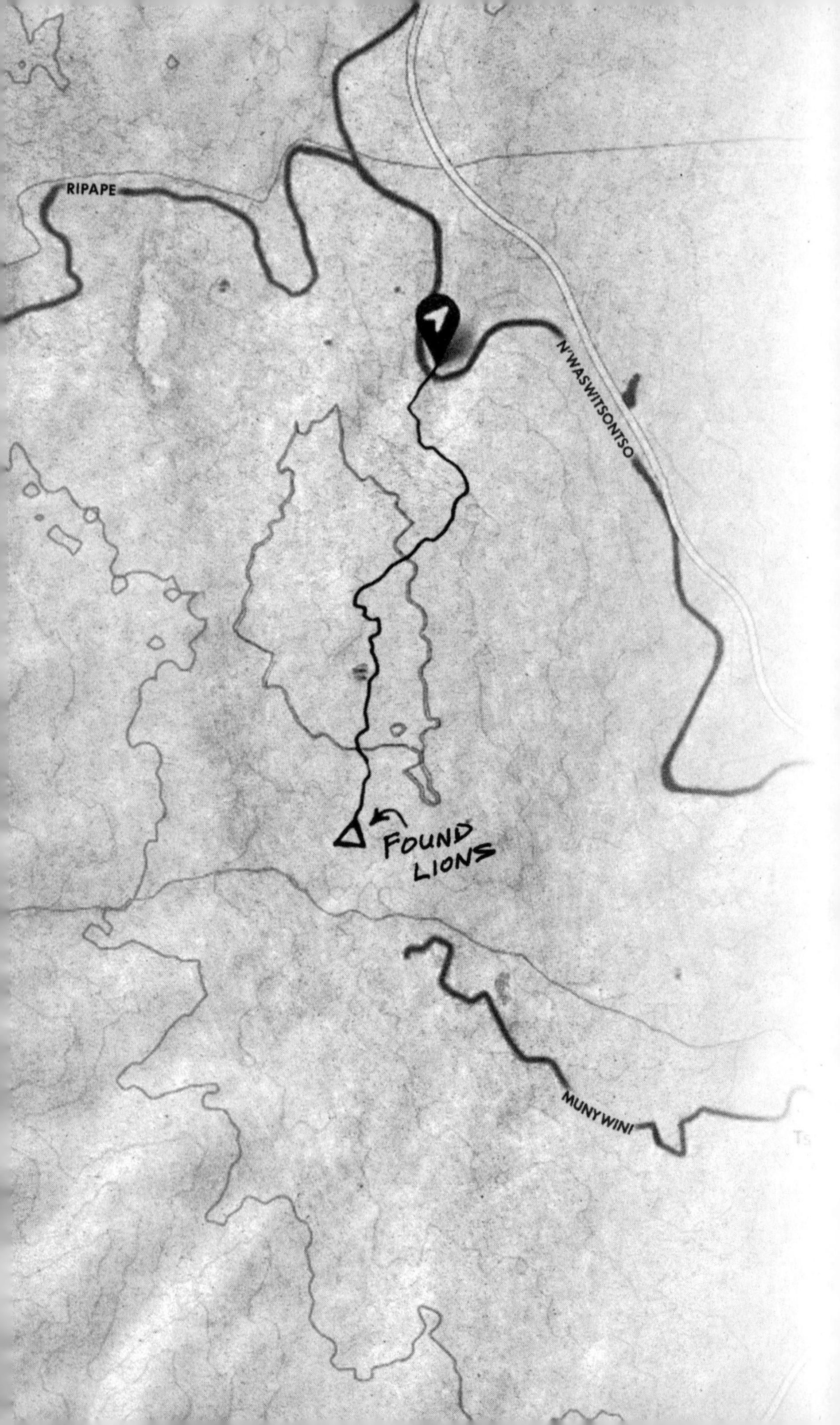
RIPAPE
N'WASWITSONTSO
FOUND LIONS
MUNYWINI

CHAPTER 5

TRUST THE EXPERIENCE

Be patient toward all that is unsolved in your heart and try to love the questions themselves.

RAINER MARIA RILKE, *LETTERS TO A YOUNG POET*[8]

ONE OF THE most frustrating parts of tracking lions and other creatures in the wild is . . . well . . . *not finding them*. Many times, I've been hours into a tracking expedition with nothing to show for it.

We might find a first track early in the day, which is always exciting. Maybe we stumble across a paw print under a shady tree, or spot a patch of dirt that's recently been an impromptu wrestling ring for two playful cubs.

"Awesome!" we'll say. "Let's follow this string and see what's waiting for us at the other end."

Then, for the next six hours, we will slowly make our way through the wilderness, creeping along riverbanks and scrutinizing every bush, looking for the next track on the string. We'll find several "next tracks," building our anticipation for the big reveal when we finally find the lions. Our imagination will run wild thinking about the different scenarios. *Will we actually see the cubs, or will we be charged by an overprotective lioness? Could we stumble upon a whole pride?*

But then, by late afternoon, it will become apparent that there's not enough daylight left to finish following this particular string. In order to make it back to our campsite before dark, a nonnegotiable when tracking in the wild, we'll have to throw the white flag and give up our search.

It is a unique feeling of disappointment, excitedly tracking in one direction, going deeper and deeper into the wild for several hours, but then having to turn around and head back to camp. It's easy to feel like the entire day was a waste, as though spotting a lion were the *only thing* that would have made the day rewarding. No other payoffs. No other rewards. No other accomplishments. It's lion or nothing, succeed or fail, win or lose.

As with many things in my life, I've had to learn how to grow beyond such limited, black-and-white thinking.

I've discovered that some of my richest experiences in the wild have been the days I've tracked for hours but never found the lion I was following. Those are the days when I've learned to look beyond the prize I *thought* I was chasing and broaden my appreciation for the entire adventure. Because sometimes the journey itself (and who you become in the process) is the treasure you *really* needed to find.

RIDING THE PENDULUM

I should have called a therapist right after the TEDx Talk breakdown. But I didn't.

With distance, and therapy, we can begin to see ourselves more clearly. Sometimes we're just too close. We lose the trail and need to step back and gain some distance to find it again, or we need to take a deliberate pause to catch our breath, clear our eyes, and regain some perspective.

Looking back, I can see I had a default pattern in my nervous system that wasn't serving me. Maybe you've already noticed it. When my buddy said Lisa didn't seem to like me anymore, I spiraled. Then I convinced myself I was okay, until I found the text messages. I crashed again, then told myself I could fix it. I tried to win her back. But she left anyway, and I fell apart, fumbling through the motions of separating our lives. A few months later, I told myself I was fine again. I started poking around on some dating apps and focused my time and attention on preparing for the TEDx Talk. When that was over, I broke down completely. I wasn't okay. I was wrecked mentally and emotionally. My body knew it, but I hadn't been listening. I was riding a life-sized pendulum.

I had this illusion of control, thinking I could power through the hard times and control the outcome I wanted through sheer force of will. I'd operated like this for a long, long time. As a kid, I chased affirmation and strived to be *enough*. Because we moved so often, I kept people at arm's length to avoid the pain of saying goodbye. And, as I've said, I had big feelings I didn't know how to handle. The world seemed to say, "Shh. Be quiet. Don't cry. Don't get angry." I didn't have the tools to process the emotions and self-regulate, so I learned to perform instead.

In adulthood, that same striving became a strategy for survival. I tried harder, pushed more, at work, in my marriage, in my exercise. If I just worked hard enough, I believed, I could keep it all together.

When life was stable, that worked, on the surface. But when everything fell apart, I found myself swinging wildly between feeling in control and being a total mess. The pendulum swung back and forth, back and forth, throwing me from one extreme to the other, with no middle ground. And I could never see the pattern at the time.

So, characteristically, I told myself I was fine after my TEDx Talk breakdown. But I wasn't. And the pendulum was about to swing way up toward "I'm good," just before taking a hard swing back, sending me lower than I'd ever been before.

NO TIME TO WASTE!

After a tough breakup, there's always that one friend who tells you to get back out there, play the field, and "get back on that horse." I had that friend, too.

At the time, I was riding the high end of my pendulum swing. I was telling myself, *I'm fine. I've got this. I'm in control.* I wanted so badly to believe it that I was admittedly a bit delusional about my emotional state. But jumping back into the dating scene seemed perfectly reasonable at the time. I mean, I was ready to move on and leave all the divorce wreckage behind. I loved being in a committed relationship, and I knew I wanted to get married again.

While I was in New York for the TEDx Talk, I connected on Instagram with a gorgeous woman from Texas. *This is good*, I told myself. *This is what healing looks like.*

Her name was Heidi. Over the next few weeks, we texted and FaceTimed, and the more I got to know her, the more amazing she seemed—thoughtful, grounded, funny, beautiful. She ran her own marketing agency. We had natural chemistry right from the start. Suddenly, my world looked brighter because she was in it. I could barely believe my life was unfolding this spectacularly just four months after my divorce!

I felt like a teenager again. My heart rate sped up when she texted. I couldn't stop thinking about her. One look at her face made all my problems melt away. It had been a long time since I had felt that way, and it felt good. After a month, we decided it was time to meet in person, so I planned a trip to visit her in Austin, Texas.

Just before the trip, I was in Phoenix catching up with my friend James. He's the kind of friend who isn't scared to ask the hard questions, the one who cuts through all the BS and shines a big spotlight on the things that need some attention.

I told him about Heidi. "She's incredible. I never thought I'd meet someone like this so soon after Lisa. Maybe this is how it was supposed to unfold. Maybe Lisa and I had to end so I could find the person I'm supposed to be with."

James listened patiently, nodding as I gushed about my new dream girl.

"I know it sounds crazy to talk about marrying Heidi, and I'm not saying I know she's *the one.* I just really feel a strong connection with her. I know there's something to this."

I concluded with a line that should have been a red flag for me: "I know that, in the divorce recovery world, they'd recommend I wait at least two and a half years to date again after such a long marriage, but I genuinely feel ready right now."

James smiled and said with sincerity, "It's good to see you happy, man." Then he paused, as his smile melted into a caring but serious expression. "But . . . you and Lisa were together a long time, more than *ten years*. And it's only been four months since the divorce. If the experts recommend waiting a couple of years, what makes you think you're different, that you could really be ready to date again so soon?"

It was a totally fair and appropriate question, and having the courage to ask it shows how good a friend he is.

How I answered him, though, shows how much I was fooling myself.

"Well, I've been doing some therapy," I replied. "Plus, I've been coaching for most of the past decade. I think I'm more equipped than most people to handle it."

I cringe just typing that.

That was like saying a physical therapist can heal from a broken leg ten times faster than anyone else, just because he's spent ten years coaching other people through their recovery. But a broken bone is still a broken bone, and a divorce is still a divorce. Healing takes time, but I wasn't ready to admit that yet. I was still high on the "I'm in control of my life" side of the pendulum. I wholeheartedly believed I was ready to not only date Heidi but be in a serious relationship with her, and I would not let anyone talk me out of it. I was 100 percent certain that I was meant to follow this string, and I believed this trail could potentially lead to a new relationship, a new marriage, and a whole new life.

FALLING HARD AND FAST

Just four months after my divorce, and only four weeks after first connecting with Heidi, I flew to Austin to meet her in person.

I've always been a hopeless romantic. In fact, when I was a kid, I was sure I'd marry my first girlfriend, in third grade. I loved being married. I loved doing life with my best friend. I loved being in love. I loved the idea of growing old with someone.

So, by the time I landed at the Austin airport, all my idealistic notions about Heidi were dialed up to eleven. I can't believe I'm admitting this, but as I headed through baggage claim to meet her at the curb, I recorded a video selfie and said, "Heidi, I just have this feeling we're going to get married. I'm filming this now, in the airport, as I walk up to meet you in person for the first time. One day, when I propose, we can look back on this and laugh."

Yep. I really did that. Of course, I also thought I was going to marry my third-grade girlfriend, so I have kind of a long history of being a hopeless romantic.

I stopped the video, slid my phone in my pocket, and walked out grinning. When she saw me, she jumped out of her car and ran over with a hug. It felt like one of those love-at-first-sight moments you see in movies—light, electric, and unforgettable.

The next two and a half days played out like the falling-in-love montage from a rom-com. When she picked me up, she brought little things she knew I liked, including fresh celery juice. (Don't judge me.) We got in her car, and I instinctively shook the bottle before taking a sip. Apparently, the cap was loose, because celery juice flew everywhere, covering both of us and the interior of her car. We looked at each other in mild shock and then burst out laughing.

That funny accident set the tone for the weekend, which was filled with fun, laughter, and budding romance. The first night, we walked around downtown Austin while waiting for a table for dinner, and it started to drizzle. I pulled out a disposable camera I'd brought to capture our weekend. She laughed, threw her arm around me, and we snapped a selfie in the rain.

I melted.

That closeness, that simple touch, hit me in a way I didn't expect. Lisa had never really been very affectionate, so this felt new and unfamiliar. I was on cloud nine.

Over the next few days, we went to yoga, ate BBQ, went running, watched reruns of *The Office*, and shared stories from our pasts and dreams about our futures. I loved the track we were following.

On our last day, we decided to go paddleboarding on Lady Bird Lake. It was a beautiful, sunny day in early summer, and I'd been having the time of my life with

Heidi. As we paddled through the lake, I steered the conversation toward *us*.

"I've had the most incredible time with you," I said. "It's been so good getting to know you better, and I'd love to know what you're thinking, because I really like you, and I would love to keep dating and see where this relationship might go."

She smiled back at me with the kindest eyes I've ever seen, then paused for a moment before gently replying, "David, I've had so much fun with you this weekend, too. I'm so glad you came out to visit. You are such an incredible guy, and exactly the type of guy I'd love to date."

I felt a wave of joy building in my heart. *After four agonizing months*, I thought, *my life is finally getting back on track!*

"But . . ." she continued.

Oh no. No no no no no no. Please, God, no.

"But I don't think you're ready to date yet."

I was stunned.

I couldn't believe she was hitting the brakes so soon, especially after how great our weekend had been.

I was devastated she didn't want to keep exploring the connection we clearly had. I tried not to show it, but I'm sure my face gave something away. I stayed quiet, still paddling, as she continued.

"I like you too, and I've had a great time with you. But it just seems like you still need some time to heal from your divorce," she said cautiously. "I don't know how long it takes to heal from something like this, but I think we should give it a little more time and space."

I was gutted. I wanted so badly for this to turn into something long-term. As we paddled back to the shore, I could feel the emotion rise in my throat, but I couldn't let her see it. That would only prove to her that I wasn't ready.

After leaving the lake, we went out for our last dinner of the weekend. We only had a few more hours together, but I was falling apart inside. I was angry. Heartbroken. Frustrated with myself and my situation. Irritated that I apparently hadn't come across as "healed" and "easygoing" as I'd wanted to show her. I thought about stepping away for a quick walk around the block to clear my head, but I didn't want to give her more evidence that she was right. So, I stuffed down the thought and did my best to put on a happy face.

After dinner, she dropped me off at my Airbnb, and we said our goodbyes. We agreed to give it a few days and check back in with each other later in the week. My flight home was early the next morning, so I went inside, packed my bag, took a shower, and then lay on the bed staring up at the ceiling fan for hours until I fell asleep.

That night lives in my memory as the most sobering moment of this whole experience. The one that peeled back my pride and laid me bare. It didn't matter how badly I wanted to be with Heidi; I couldn't force it to happen. I couldn't *will* myself into being ready for a relationship. And I had just realized how much work was ahead of me before I could be ready.

Strangely, it wasn't the breakup with Lisa that brought me to my knees. It was this. This gentle, honest insight from someone I barely knew. That's what cracked me open. I was beginning to see that all the *efforting*, all the analyzing and pushing and "powering through," wasn't going to cut it anymore. Sometimes it is moments like this that show us deeper wisdom about ourselves.

Lying there, praying for sleep to come, I began processing a deeper truth: I was nowhere near living the wild, uncaged life I claimed to want. Not even close. And worse, I was starting to realize that to live that kind of life, I'd have to risk everything. I'd have to be willing to go all the way to my breaking point and beyond, because a wild life is not an easy life. Lions might be the kings of the jungle, but nothing's guaranteed out there. They still have to hunt. They can still go hungry. One wrong move and they could get gored, trampled, or killed.

That was such a humbling realization, that even lions have to fight for every step of survival. Risk is baked into the wild. No safety net. No sure things. That terrified me, because I couldn't see a track to follow. There was no indication of where I was supposed to go or what I was supposed to do with all my pain. I knew I needed to heal, but I didn't know if I actually could. And even if I *could* heal . . . I was struggling to figure out the first step.

BACK TO REALITY

It's hard to describe what I felt when I arrived home the next day. I was experiencing emotional whiplash. I'd spent the past two and a half days in a state of pure bliss, having lost myself in a fantasy about starting a new life with this wonderful woman and truly believing I was ready to pursue a meaningful relationship. But then, reality tore through that dream like a wild animal, bringing me back to my senses and finally—*finally* forcing me to realize what my parents, my friend James, and Heidi had all been trying so gently to tell me: *I was not okay.* Not at all. Not by a long shot.

I knew I had been experiencing depression and brokenness over the past several months, but this felt different. This time, my situation felt overwhelming. Up to this point, I'd thought it was just a matter of time. Yes, it was hard, but I thought I just needed to wait it out and I'd get better. I even wished I could fall into a coma for a few months so I could skip all the heartache and wake up with some distance and healing. But now, I was beginning to wonder if I'd *ever* feel better. I worried that this is what my life would be like from now on, that this emotional wreck of a man was who I'd be for the rest of my life.

I needed help. A lot of help. And I needed it *right now*.

Within hours of arriving home, I hopped on a Zoom call with my therapist. I gave him a quick update. Then he simply asked me how I was doing, and my grief was unleashed again. It wasn't my first time in therapy, yet I felt awkward, even slightly embarrassed, to openly express what I was feeling in front of my therapist. Allowing him to witness my grief was new and strange. But I felt so broken and lost that I physically couldn't overthink it or hold it back.

During that session, my therapist asked me to grab a piece of paper and a pen and to draw what I was feeling. I'm no artist, but I did my best to sketch how

I felt. When I was done, he asked me to explain my drawing to him. In a weirdly flat, emotionless tone of voice, I said, "I drew a stick figure of myself lying at the bottom of the ocean, alone and running out of air."

"David," he said gently, "do you realize how *heavy* this is?"

Honestly, at that moment, I didn't. I looked back down at my drawing, then back up to my therapist's face on my laptop screen, then back at my paper. My brain was in a daze, like I was trying to figure out some advanced calculus equation. My body, mind, and emotions were all completely disconnected.

Trying to bring me back to my senses, my therapist asked, "What do you *feel* when you think about what you drew?"

I took a couple of deep breaths as I felt a huge onslaught of emotional waves approaching in the distance. With each breath, they got closer and closer. The first wave hit me, then the second, and the third, each one taking me further out to sea, as if forces outside my body were trying to bring my drawing to life right then and there.

I attempted to fight them, but there was no letting up. The waves kept coming, stronger and stronger, and

I kept getting pulled further out. All I could do was surrender to them.

My therapist did his best to guide me through this emotional tsunami. He explained that when we go through painful times in life, we can develop a kind of thick outer shell to conceal the pain and lock it away. It's a defense mechanism to show ourselves and the world that we're okay. Over time, and especially after multiple tragedies, the shell can become so thick that we start mistaking it for our true, authentic self. That may appear to work fine for a while . . . until we experience one too many tragic events and the shell begins to crack. Once it's weakened, the whole thing starts to crumble, which can be completely destabilizing. We feel like our whole world is falling apart, *because it is*. We let this thick shell envelop everything we think we know about ourselves and the world, so when it breaks, all the pain we've buried for months, years, or decades explodes back out to the surface. We're confronted by every trauma and heartbreak we've ignored, forgotten, buried, or simply haven't processed all the way through. And we experience it all at once.

"David, you will get through this," he said. "The deeper the darkness, the greater the insight on the other side. But no matter the depths you have to go, you can do this."

That day, fresh off my "highest of highs and lowest of lows" weekend with Heidi, three truths became crystal clear:

1. No matter how hard I'd tried to hide it, from others and from myself, I was in much, much worse shape than I'd ever imagined.
2. My usual method of figuring things out on my own and fighting my way through my struggles alone wasn't going to work this time. I needed *professional* help.
3. I had to get over my reluctance to lean on other people for support. If I ever hoped to get better, I would have to learn how to let others hold and support me.

That's when I decided to take my recovery seriously, when I committed to doing the work, the excruciatingly hard work, that would be required to face whatever pain lurked behind the emotional shell I'd just cracked open.

I was genuinely afraid of what I'd find, but I knew addressing it was the only way to finally break out of the cage I'd been living in for nearly forty years. I longed to live a wild, full, and free life, and I knew that could never happen as long as I kept myself locked in my little cage of ignored pain and neglected emotions. As hard as I knew it would be, everything in me demanded that I get up, find the tracks, and follow the string to find my true self and free him from his cage.

TRACKING AN INVISIBLE RHINOCEROS

Tracking my life through that rough season reminds me of the time I "wasted" three days tracking a rhinoceros. We started the trip tracking lions like usual, but early in the safari, we found the unmistakable tracks of a rhino.

"What do you think?" the guide asked our group. "You want to ignore these fresh rhino tracks and keep looking for a lion, or do you want to follow these and see if we can find the big guy who made them?"

Our small group of trackers didn't hesitate.

"Rhino! Definitely the rhino!"

The first day, we followed the string from the first tracks to the next, feeling like we were hot on the heels of a creature I'd always wanted to spot while walking in the wild. The tracks were so fresh that we knew he was nearby, but he seemed to stay a couple of steps ahead of us all through that first day.

When we got back to camp, we discussed what we wanted to do the next day: give up on the rhino chase and try to find some lions, or get back to work trying to track down this elusive, horn-headed force of nature. We decided that we'd come too far to give up now, so we'd keep trying to find the rhino.

The second day went much like the first. We'd find fresh tracks and follow the string to the next set of tracks. And then do that again. And again. But still, no rhino. I started to wonder if we were chasing an enormous ghost.

The next day was our last chance. We'd already spent two whole days of this safari tracking this thing, but we'd come up empty. Not only had we not found the rhino, but we also hadn't spotted any lions, leopards, or other wild animals that I thought would have made this trip worth it.

If we don't find this thing today, I thought, *this whole trip will have been a total waste. But man, if we do find him, I'll be so happy. It will be such a cool experience, and this will have been one of my best trips yet!*

As we went through that third day, tracking what I'd come to believe was an invisible rhino, I became increasingly aware of how much I was putting my happiness in the hands of some external event that may or may not happen. Why would my personal sense of happiness and satisfaction depend on whether I saw a sneaky rhino hiding behind the next bush? I was walking through gorgeous terrain that most people never see. The jungle was teeming with life, and I was right there in the middle of it. Forget about finding a rhino in the wild; I was in the wild myself! That week, on that trip, I was living wild and free in untamed lands. *Me*, not some rhinoceros. Why couldn't I be happy and content about finding myself in the wild?

So, I decided to shift my perspective. I was able to focus on the joy and excitement of the present moment, the moment I was living *right then*, instead of pinning all my hopes for happiness on some achievement that may or may not happen. I already had everything I needed to be happy, which turned out to be a good thing, because we never did find that rhino.

That safari holds a special place in my memory because it was the trip when I discovered that tracking isn't just about finding the animal; it's about who you are becoming in the process. That's true in lion tracking *and* in life.

A STRING, NOT A STRAIGHT LINE

People too often fall into a "straight line" way of thinking. A leads directly to B, B leads directly to C, and so on. That's how I approached tracking the rhino, and, though it's hard to admit, that's how I approached tracking my life in the months after my divorce. I pinned my hopes for happiness on getting married again as quickly as possible. It made so much sense:

1. I am happier married than I am single.
2. I need a partner to be married.
3. I meet this wonderful woman just a few months after my divorce.
4. I start a relationship with her.
5. We get married.
6. I'm happy again.

Problem solved, right?

Apparently . . . not so much.

I'm so grateful that Heidi had the wisdom to hit the brakes when and how she did. It would have been so easy to jump right into a new relationship, maybe even a new marriage, with her, pinning all my hopes for happiness on her instead of addressing all the damage I'd been burying within myself for so many years.

My tracks were leading me into a season of intense therapy and trauma recovery, which I knew would expose all the painful little pieces of myself that I didn't want to face. I'd fooled myself into thinking that all those hurts were behind me, and my "straight line" mindset wanted me to move forward, not backward. It dawned on me much later, though, that life tracking—like lion tracking—isn't about following a straight line; it's about following a *string*. And a string usually doesn't go in a straight line. A string goes forward, back, up, and down. It folds. It loops. It has twists and turns. Sometimes, it becomes such a knotted mess that you have to slowly and patiently untangle it a fraction of an inch at a time.

I was terrified of where this string was leading me, but by that point, I was so lost and broken that I had no choice but to trust that these tracks were leading me somewhere important—somewhere I really didn't want to go, but somewhere I realized I had to go if I ever wanted to get to the wild, untamed life I'd always dreamed of.

TRACKER MANUAL

Step 5: Trust the Experience

- Happiness isn't found "out there." In what ways have you pinned your future happiness on some external goal? What is the danger of looking for your joy outside of yourself?
- Let go of expectations. Life is not about what is happening to you; it is about who you are becoming in the process. What practices could you implement to remind yourself of who you are becoming?
- Be willing to ask for help from friends, family, mentors, therapists, coaches, and any other supportive presence in your life. Who specifically could you ask for help in your current season of life?
- Trust that progress is happening. Where is life inviting you to trust and let go right now?

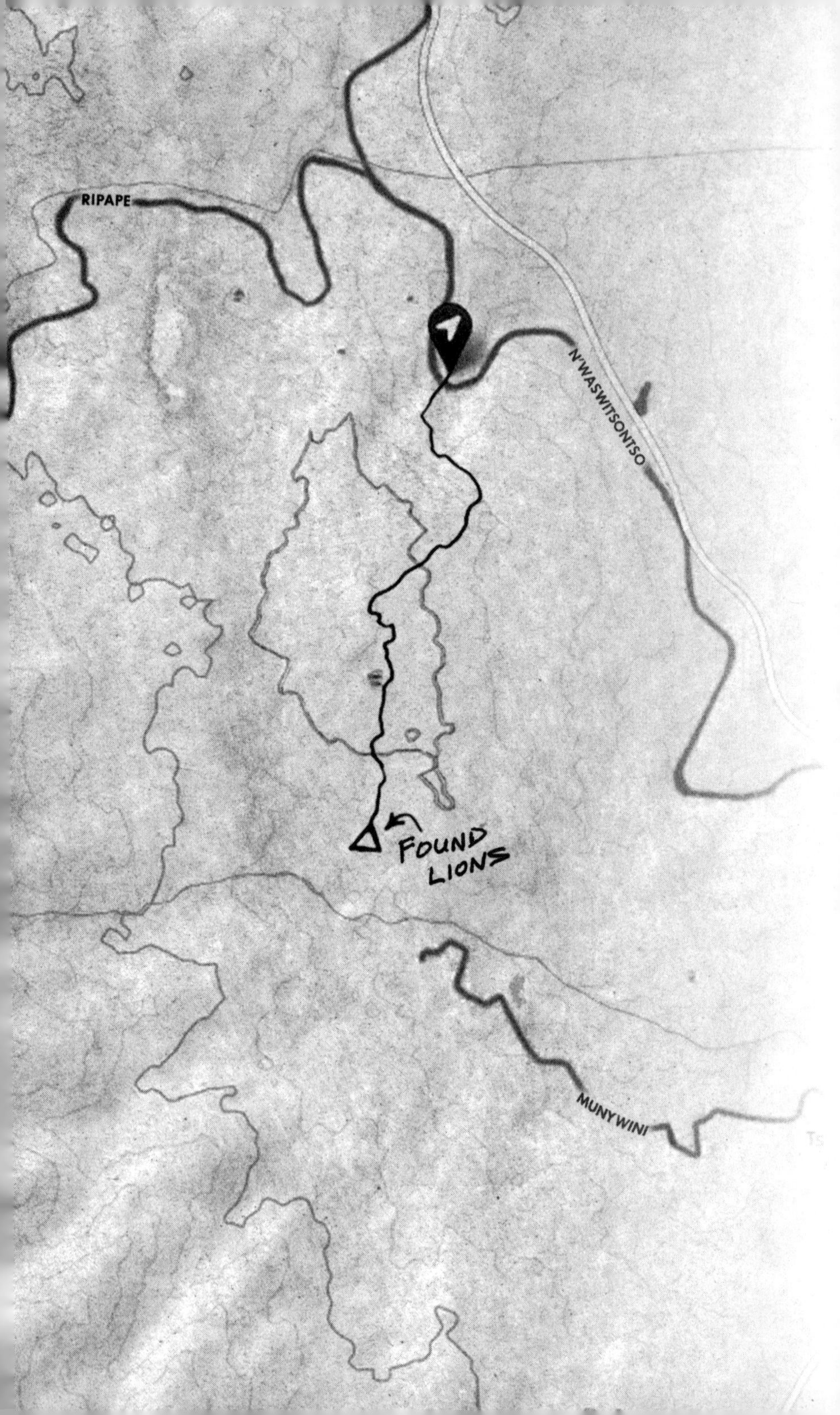
RIPAPE
N'WASWITSONTSO
FOUND LIONS
MUNYWINI

CHAPTER 6

PAY ATTENTION

The hardest tracks to follow aren't in the dirt—they're the ones inside us.

ANONYMOUS

"DAVID! LOOK AT this!"

My friend Renias, whom I first mentioned in chapter 3, is one of the best lion trackers in the world. He's always my first choice when I need to hire a tracker to take me and my clients on an expedition to see African wildlife in their natural, untamed, and uncaged environment. One of my favorite things about Renias is that he really *gets* how exciting it is to track lions, rhinos, and other magnificent creatures through the jungle. He never takes it for granted and, at least on our trips together, he never misses an opportunity to teach fellow explorers how to become better trackers. The way Renias teaches me to track lions often reminds me of how we coach people to track the fully alive version of themselves so they can live aligned and authentic lives.

On one of our early trips together, I was taking the lead for a while, with Renias following close behind me. When he called out to me, I realized I must have missed something important.

I backtracked to where he was standing, scanned the ground around us, and frankly had no idea what had gotten him so excited.

"Uh . . . look at *what*, exactly?"

"There! There!" he said, with a mix of excitement and amusement in his voice. "Look there! Don't you see it?"

"No, I don't see what you're seeing!" I cried. "Renias, tell me what I'm missing!"

He crouched down and pointed at several clumps of blond hair scattered along the tracks we'd been following that morning. They'd been practically invisible to me when he'd first pointed them out, but as I looked closer, I could see them everywhere.

"Tell me a story, David. What might have happened here?"

I had spent enough time with Renias to know that was one of his favorite questions. I've heard him ask it dozens of times. It's his go-to method of teaching novice trackers how to visualize what they might find at the end of the string.

"Well," I began, "these hairs definitely look like clumps from a male lion's mane."

"Good," he replied. "Now, why did this lion suddenly lose some of his mane right here?"

I scrutinized every centimeter of dirt at my feet, looking for clues. Taking two steps forward, I spotted something unmistakable: a claw that had been forcefully torn from a lion's paw. Renias smiled, encouraging me to go further.

I lifted my head a bit and scanned the area. My eyes focused on a nearby tree that looked like something heavy had scraped against it—hard. Looking closer, I saw what appeared to be a smear of blood on the tree trunk.

As the pieces started to form a picture in my mind, Renias brought it all together for me.

"Two lions were fighting here," he explained, "and it was a vicious fight. One or both pulled some of the other's hair out, and one slashed the other so forcefully that it tore his claw off. One of them either pushed the other into that tree ahead, or pounced and flung himself into the tree in the heat of battle. Either the impact with the tree or a slashing claw drew blood, leaving that smear."

While investigating the tree, I also spotted one set of prints leaving the scene. But the paw prints looked odd to me. Renias answered my question before I spoke it.

"The lion was injured badly. See the drag marks mixed in with the prints? He was dragging his left front leg as he retreated. And see there? He was dripping blood, too. Fortunately for him, the victor didn't pursue him."

"Is it safe for us to keep tracking him?" I asked, unsure what the poor guy's rough morning meant for our expedition.

"Yes," Renias replied. "But we must be very careful. An injured lion can be incredibly aggressive. His defenses will be on high alert. We definitely want to see him before he sees us."

We pressed on for a short while until, about sixty meters ahead of us, we spotted a weary-looking male lion resting. He was lying in the grass, swiveling his head back and forth as he scanned the area for any more would-be attackers. I could see matted blood on his left side, and he occasionally stopped scanning the area long enough to lick his front left paw.

It became apparent that the scene had played out just as Renias described. The experienced tracker knew that every track told a story, and he was a master at reading them.

In lion tracking and in life tracking, the ability to pay attention to the story the tracks are telling you is crucial. With experience, you can get a clear picture of what's waiting for you at the other end of the string.

This insight can be especially helpful when what you expect to find scares the hell out of you. That's where I was in May 2021.

THE STORY MY TRACKS WERE TELLING

May 2021 was a very difficult month for me. Ever since Lisa had asked for a divorce five months earlier, I'd gone through wild pendulum swings. One day, I'd think my life was over (or I wished it was). The next day, I'd be projecting some weird optimism, trying to convince others (like Heidi) that I was handling everything just fine. I guess I was really trying to convince myself more than anyone. But by May, after Heidi had helped me face the reality that I was very much *not* okay, the pendulum had swung further to the "my life is crap" side than it had ever gone.

I was facing depression. Deep, overwhelming, inescapable depression. I thought about the picture I'd drawn for my therapist that showed me at the bottom of the ocean and running out of air. I'd felt like that many days over the past five months, but now, *every day* felt like that. And it was getting worse. I was floundering. I'd been trying to swim back to the surface this whole time, but nothing I did was getting me there—not moving back to Denver near my family, not my TEDx Talk, not Heidi, not *anything*. The agony felt like it would never end, and I didn't know what to do.

The only two things I was certain of were:

1. If I wanted to have any kind of life moving forward, I had no choice but to follow this track.
2. I was scared to death to follow this string because I didn't know where it would take me . . . and I wasn't sure if I had the strength and courage to survive it.

It was like staring into a black hole, knowing the only way to escape it was to go *through* it. I knew I needed help, but I didn't know who to ask or what type of help would be best. I'd been an executive coach with Novus Global for a decade, helping high-performing executives and athletes improve their mental game and develop skills to reach goals they never imagined were possible. But this—this deep inner work of the soul, facing my greatest fears and the shame attached to them—this was something entirely different, something I wasn't prepared for.

As much as I just wanted to sit alone on my couch with my depression, I had a busy month planned with three back-to-back trips: first to Guatemala for a friend's wedding, then to visit my dying grandmother in Minnesota with my family, and then to Sedona, Arizona, for a short vacation with friends. Since my job allowed me to work from anywhere, travel had become an enjoyable part of my life over the years. I usually loved it. And, of course, it was probably a good thing that I didn't have the option to sit home alone and cry for the whole month. But honestly, it was hard to be excited about any of these trips, especially since I knew this would likely be my last visit with my grandmother.

I made it to Guatemala for my friend's wedding, and then went straight to Minnesota to meet up with my parents at my grandmother's house. She was in the hospital in the end stages of her battle with lymphoma, and my beloved Grandpa Don had already passed, so my parents and I stayed at their house alone. I'd been coming to this house since I was a little kid. It was the same house I rode my bike to after that long family drive, which will always be one of my favorite childhood memories. I stayed in the same room my brother and sister and I had always shared growing up. It looked exactly the same, still rocking the wood-paneled walls and the orange shag carpet from the '70s. It even smelled the same, with its trademark aroma of a house that's been well lived in. I could almost smell Grandma's cinnamon rolls, which she made for us every time we visited.

I loved that house. I loved my grandma. And I knew in my heart that I'd made this trip to say goodbye to her.

Because of the pandemic restrictions, we were only allowed to visit her once that week, so I planned the few days I was there around that visit. I took work meetings from the shag-carpet bedroom and went on several runs during the day, and at night, the extended family—me, Mom, Dad, aunts, uncles, and cousins—sat in my grandparents' living room swapping stories and laughing as we relived precious memories. I did my best to join in, but even as I sat there surrounded by people who loved me deeply, I felt completely alone. No one in my extended family had ever been through a divorce or experienced any kind of deep, inner-healing journey. I'd never heard anyone in my family even mention going to therapy. I'd grown up thinking therapy was reserved for people who were . . . well . . . *off their rocker*. My family had always acted like anything short of clinical insanity was just a simple matter of prayer, grit, and hard work. No matter how much I wanted or needed to engage with my family about what I was going through, I didn't know how to even begin explaining it to them. So, mostly I sat there and laughed along with their stories while I continued falling apart inside.

On the day of our scheduled hospital visit, we all piled into my uncle's SUV and drove mostly in silence to the hospital. As excited as I was to see my grandma for the first time in a long while, I was dreading the inevitable goodbye. I felt like 2021 was my year of goodbyes—to my wife, to my marriage, to my dreams of the future, to my home of fifteen years, and now, to my beautiful grandmother.

I was getting pretty tired of saying goodbye to people, places, and things I loved.

The hospital's pandemic protocols only allowed us to go in one at a time, for fifteen minutes each. When it was my turn, I walked into her room and offered a hushed, "Hi, Grandma."

"Hi, David," she said softly with a small, sweet smile. She was clearly unwell, but she looked better than I'd imagined, given how serious her condition was. I asked her how she was feeling and, without missing a beat, she said, "Well, you know, I've been better. But I sure am glad to see you."

We spent our fifteen minutes chatting as she brushed her hair. We laughed, held hands, and took a few selfies. It was good to see that, despite the lymphoma, she was still the same wonderful grandma I'd always loved.

When our time was up, I hugged her tightly and fought back my tears as I said, "I love you so much. Thank you for being such a great grandma." I kissed her forehead and walked toward the door. As I opened it, I looked back and said, "Love you, Grandma. You're the best."

"I love you, David. I will always be with you."

I stepped back into the sterile, fluorescent-lit hallway. Nurses walked briskly about. Doctors stood reviewing paperwork. Everyone there was just going about their normal day. But it *wasn't* a normal day. Didn't all these people—didn't the whole world—realize that I'd just said goodbye forever to one of the most important people in my life? Didn't anyone care that I was losing yet another piece of my heart?

I made my way down the ridiculously long hallway and down the elevator to where my family was waiting. I was still holding my tears, but seeing them all there waiting for their turn to go up to say their goodbyes opened the emotional floodgates behind my eyes.

My uncle came up, put a hand on my shoulder, and said, "Aw, come on now. Don't do that. Don't do that." I know he meant well, but my uncle was revealing what I later came to recognize as a deep-rooted pattern of emotional disconnection that I'd been raised in my whole life. My parents' generation had never really learned to fully "feel their feelings" and be present with them. I have a lot of compassion for them in this area now, but that day, all I felt was my family shutting me down.

I thought, *Are you serious? Grandma—your own mother—is dying, and we can't even all be with her at the same time. Why can't we recognize that this is an excruciatingly sad situation and just cry together?*

I know they were each feeling the pain and grief in their own way, even if they couldn't express it. I wanted the freedom to grieve together as a family, but that was something my parents, aunts, and uncles couldn't provide.

I see clearly now that we all process pain differently, but as I stood there, I felt so angry and broken inside. So, I stepped away to be alone with my emotions, which had become my default position. I went outside and walked around that muggy Fargo hospital parking lot, allowing the waves of emotions to roll over me . . . alone.

A DIFFERENT KIND OF ANIMAL TRACK

One night during my trip to Minnesota, after my family had all gone to bed, I sat on my grandparents' sofa and searched online for some fun things to do in Sedona, Arizona, where I was heading a few days later. I wasn't really in the mood for "fun things," but I knew I needed to force myself to find something that might spark some joy in me. I've always loved the outdoors, and that part of the country is an outdoor adventurer's dream. As I sat there scrolling, though, nothing jumped out at me. I was apathetic at best in the face of a world of exciting choices.

Then, amidst the sea of options, something unexpected caught my eye: *equine therapy*. This therapeutic practice involves guided interaction with horses to help process pain and grief. I'd done it once, years ago, and hadn't thought about it since. But something about this place stood out. I clicked through the website, read about the therapist, Michelle, and her horses, and even scrolled through her Instagram. For the first time in a long while, I let myself consider, *Maybe this could help me.* It was just a flicker—a glimmer of light in a dark stretch of days.

I flew back home the same day I said goodbye to my grandma. The grief I felt over losing her, piled onto the world of grief I was already living in, solidified my need for real help in dealing with everything. I was home just long enough to do laundry and repack for Sedona, but I couldn't stop thinking about equine therapy.

I went back and forth—talking myself into it and back out of it—until I finally texted Michelle, the therapist, to see if she had any openings the following week, and thankfully she did. So, I booked it.

Michelle followed up to schedule a short intro call before the session.

When she called, her voice was warm and kind—steady in that way people get after life has softened their edges and sharpened their wisdom.

"Hi David. It's Michelle," she said. Her tone immediately put me at ease. "Thanks for booking a session with me and the horses. I like to connect with new clients beforehand to get a little sense of what's going on."

"Well, I'm happy to fill you in on my crazy life right now," I said with a nervous laugh.

"Great," she replied. "Tell me what's happening in your world."

Something about her presence, even over the phone, felt safe. I didn't hold back.

"I'm thirty-eight, and I'm going through a divorce after ten years of marriage," I said. "And honestly

. . . I'm in the darkest season of my life. I don't even know where to start to get better. But I know I need to do *something*."

I paused, steadied myself, and continued, "I've done equine therapy before. I hadn't really thought of doing it again until I saw your site, but I haven't *stopped* thinking about it since then. I keep coming back to it. I think being around horses might help me right now." I exhaled. "So . . . that's kind of where I'm at."

Michelle didn't flinch. "That's a lot, David," she said, her voice full of grace. "Thanks for sharing. I'm glad you found me and the horses. They're amazing. I think you'll love them."

She explained how the first session would go and started wrapping up the call. "Any other questions before we hang up?"

I hesitated. "I think this all sounds great," I said slowly. Then, as if I needed permission to believe healing was still possible, I added, "Do you think this could actually help me?"

Michelle's reply was calm, steady, and certain. "Yes, I really do," she said. Then, after a pause, she continued, "I've been through a divorce too. I know those dark days. You *can* work through this. Healing *is* possible."

I let out a deep breath. "Okay, Michelle. I'll see you soon."

"I look forward to it, David," she said.

THE GROUNDEDNESS OF HORSES

My friends and I had a full schedule of amazing outdoor adventures that started the moment my plane landed. We went hiking, rode ATVs, and spent as much time outside as possible. For days, I flip-flopped on whether to keep my equine therapy appointment—right up to when it was time for me to leave. At the very last second, something deep down within me welled up and said, *Just go!* So, I forced myself out of my "analysis paralysis" and hopped in the car.

As I drove to Michelle's ranch, I realized how much I was craving the opportunity to be somewhere where I could break down for a little while and just let it all go. Being around a therapist—and especially around therapy animals—felt much safer. There was no need to put on a brave face in front of a horse, and he wouldn't judge me if I started weeping uncontrollably. It's not that the average person would judge me if I broke down in front of them; the issue was that my own fear about the *possibility* of someone judging me would always hold me back from being fully vulnerable around them. But with horses, I thought maybe, just maybe, I could feel fully free to be fully *me*.

The ranch sat on a relatively flat patch of land surrounded by the gorgeous Red Rock mountains. Tall saguaro and prickly pear cacti were scattered across the landscape. Michelle's farmhouse stood off to the right, and the horse corral and stable were just off the patio, as if she intentionally wanted to be as close to her horses as possible. A couple of horses rested in the shade of some tall trees around their pen, while a dozen or so turkeys and chickens wandered around minding their own business.

Michelle, with her wide-brimmed hat, T-shirt, jeans, and authentically scuffed-up boots, spotted me and walked over to greet me.

She had this energy about her that was both grounding and welcoming. I'd been there all of three minutes, and I instantly felt safe. The peace of this place wrapped around me. I took a deep breath and let my guard down one more notch. This place wasn't fancy or glamorous. It was simple. Uncomplicated. Exactly what I needed.

As we walked into the horse pen, I immediately felt drawn to one of the horses. "That's Cody," Michelle offered. He stood strong and serene and greeted me with a nod of his head and soft eyes, almost as if to say, "I see you. You're welcome to be yourself here. You can let down your guard." I walked over and placed my hands on Cody's calm, towering body, and as I did so, involuntary tears began to roll down my cheeks.

I was just beginning my journey toward healing, and I hadn't had a clue about where to start. But in that moment, I could almost hear Cody saying, "Right here, David. You can start healing *right here, right now.*"

So . . . I did.

This might have been the moment I really gave myself permission to heal, when my body and nervous system finally began to release, let down my defenses, and surrender to the process of healing.

I've come to understand equine therapy better, especially since I started tracking lions. Horses are prey animals, so they are by nature extremely perceptive. This acute sensitivity enables them to be attuned to the energy of the people and world around them. This discernment, combined with their strength and stature, makes them particularly capable of creating a safe, grounded, and even spiritual space for people to heal. Standing there with Cody that day, I felt deeply connected to something I can only describe as *divine*. It was as if God was using nature to break through my defenses and allow the healing process to begin—even if it was just the very first micro-step in the right direction.

THE UNDENIABLE TRACKS OF DEPRESSION

As Renias taught me, every track tells a story. A paw print is never *just* a paw print; it's a snapshot of a moment in time and a small piece of a much bigger narrative. Being able to read those tracks—to see the whole story all at once rather than just one small piece at a time—tells us not just where we've been but, more importantly, where we're going.

In May 2021, it became undeniably clear to me that my tracks revealed pure, devastating, suffocating depression. At that point in my life, I could not see the big picture. I could not see the whole story, and frankly, I had no idea how or even *if* this chapter of my life would end. When you're that deep in depression, you can't see clearly. You can't think clearly. You can't reason your way out of it. Finding the next safe step to take feels impossible.

In the first few weeks after I returned home from Sedona, I did my best to snap back into my routines, but everything I was doing—working with clients, exercising, spending time with friends—felt like I was simply going through the motions. None of it had any meaning for me. I couldn't point to a single thing in my life that brought me joy. In fact, I don't think there was a single thing that could have distracted me from how depressed I felt. I felt so much pain and anguish every waking moment of my life. That probably explains why I took so many naps throughout the day: sleep was my only escape.

Thinking back on those days now is terrifying to me. I'm not even sure how I made it through each day. I had to plan my whole day around my depression. I spaced out my work calls to ensure I'd have enough time between them to take a nap. A typical workday that year looked like this:

- Pull myself out of bed through sheer willpower.
- Take an ice-cold shower to shock my system and trigger a much-needed dopamine hit to my brain.
- Have one or two coaching calls with clients.
- Take a nap.
- Take another cold shower to wake back up and increase dopamine.

- Have another coaching call.
- Nap.
- Take another cold shower to wake back up and increase dopamine.
- Call.
- Nap.
- Meditate for an hour or two (another place of respite). Or sometimes watch sports, *Yellowstone*, or *Ted Lasso*.

I'm honestly not sure how I was able to stay present with my coaching clients. Somehow, I kept my business going during this season, but it wasn't easy.

I was seeing my therapist once a week, staying in touch with Michelle, and checking all the boxes I thought I was supposed to, but it all felt like drops in a giant bucket. I was working as hard as I could to stay motivated and believe that better days were ahead, but it became clear that what I was doing was not going to get me there. I had to do more.

With that realization, the unhealthy "just work harder" part of my brain perked up and convinced me that what I really needed was a rock-solid, intensive plan of attack to essentially get this healing journey over with. So, I pieced together a makeshift five-week therapy intensive to put my divorce behind me once and for all. My plan included back-to-back blocks consisting of two weeks of equine therapy and breathwork with Michelle on a second trip to Sedona; followed by a week focusing on somatic bodywork, acupuncture, and Chinese medicinal practices; followed by a week of 24/7 residential therapy at a clinic in Northern California that specialized in an intense program I had heard was like ten years of therapy rolled up into seven days; and capped off with another week on Michelle's ranch before I joined some friends on a trip to Colorado. I figured I'd throw all my stuff in my 4Runner and live on the road for five weeks, staying at and working out of Airbnbs while I finally got my head on straight.

I'll hit the high points of how all that went in the next chapter. Needless to say, though, I know now that I wasn't following Renias's instructions with these tracks at this point. Rather than paying attention to the story my tracks were telling me and following the string to see where they led, I was trying to write the story myself. I was trying to force my version of healing and my timeline on a process that wasn't fully mine to control.

And that proved . . . frustrating.

TRACKER MANUAL

Step 6: Pay Attention

- Notice the details. If you were to slow down and pay attention, what details might you see about your life? What things could you be grateful for in this season of life?
- Imagine the story. What story would the tracks of your life tell in this season? Is that aligned with the story you want your life to tell? If not, what changes could you make to realign?
- Envision the future. Where would you like the tracks of your life to be leading? What are you dreaming about? What call would you hear if you listened? What do you sense you must do even though there may be no rational reason to?

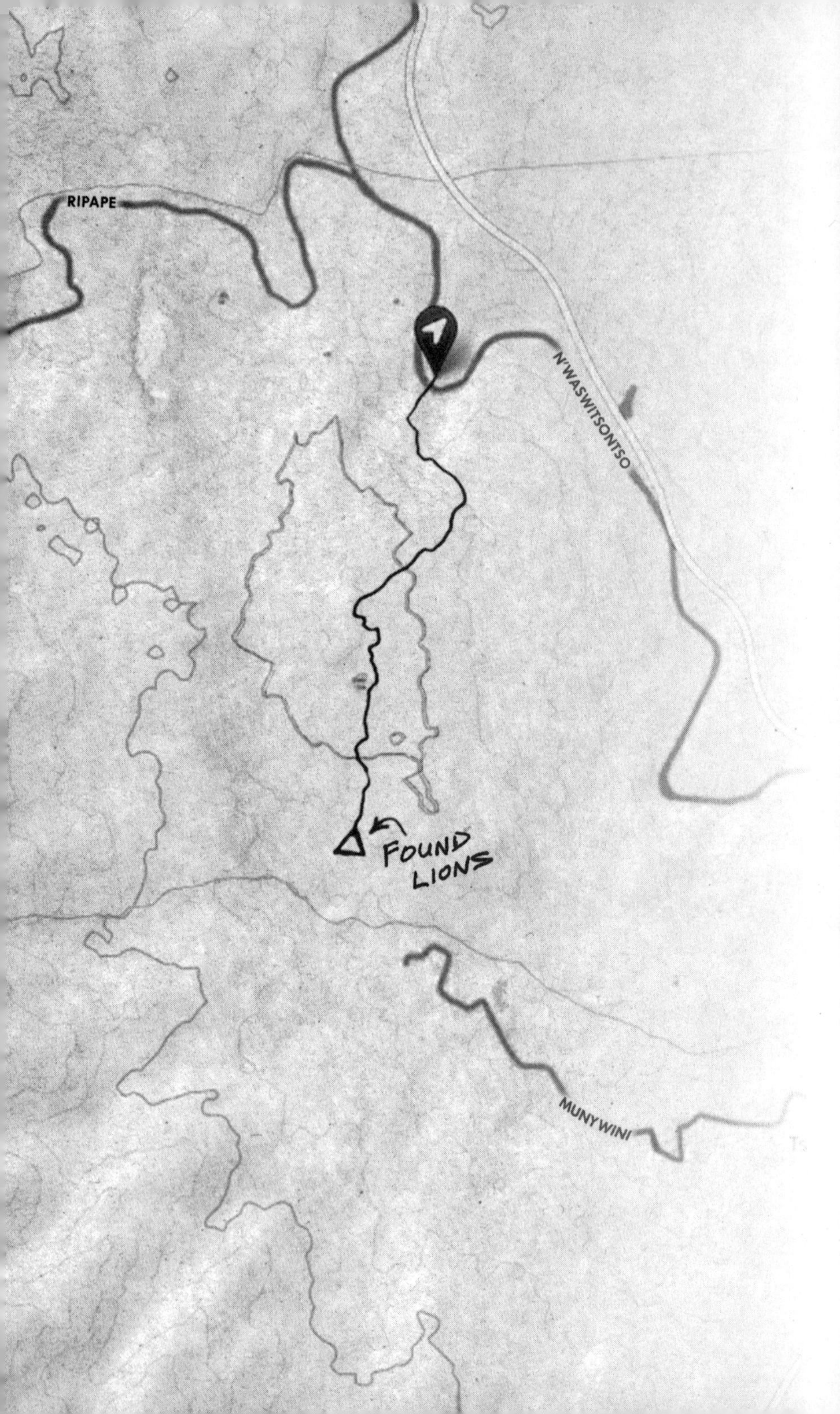
RIPAPE
N'WASWITSONTSO
FOUND LIONS
MUNYWINI

CHAPTER 7

RESIST THE URGE TO RUSH

Time won't heal what you don't make time to face.

CHRIS FERREIRAS[9]

OUT IN THE civilized world, or the "concrete jungle," we're taught early on to hurry up. We have to rush all the time—to learn to walk, to learn to talk, to catch the bus, to get to class, to finish school, to apply for jobs, to get to work, to start investing, to climb the corporate ladder, to get a raise, to find a partner, to have kids, to get *them* to school, and on and on it goes. We're rushing around from one thing to another in an endless cycle of frantic activity that too often leaves us overstressed, unfulfilled, and gasping for air.

I've seen the "hurry up" mentality dominate every area of my life—except one.

You want to know the one time when you absolutely, positively *never* want to rush?

When you're tracking lions in the wild.

Ever since Stretch stressed the importance of staying absolutely still when charged by a lion on my first tracking expedition, the guides I've worked with have taught the necessity of stillness in the middle of the most anxious, trying times imaginable. Resisting the urge to rush—especially when being charged—is literally a matter of life and death in the wild. You learn early and often that moving too quickly out there can get you into trouble without notice—in the case that you stumble upon a rhino or buffalo napping, or elephants eating, or lions feasting on a fresh kill.

That's not only true when being charged; sometimes, moving slowly and deliberately is the only way to find a first track . . . or rediscover a lost one.

EVERY TRACKER LOSES THE TRACK

I remember the first time I was the lead tracker on one of our group excursions. I had practiced a lot alongside Renias, and he decided it was time to see how I'd do taking the lead for a while. Everything went great for the first hour and a half. I'd found a clear first track early on, and I'd led the group along the string as I found a few successive tracks. But then . . . nothing. What had been a clear trail from A to B to C suddenly vanished. Not only could I not find the next track, but I had lost the string entirely. The confidence I'd felt all morning evaporated as I darted my head back and forth, unsure of where we were going, where we were, or where we'd come from.

I'd completely lost the track.

Irritated and, I'll admit, a bit embarrassed, my heart rate shot up. My breathing quickened. I was scurrying around like a frightened mouse. I'd run a few steps one way, then I'd turn and take off in a different direction, and then I'd jump back to where I'd started. The more I moved and the faster my movements became, the more lost I felt.

Renias stood quietly nearby, watching me flail around for a minute or two. Then, he walked up to me, put his hand on my shoulder, and gave me some of the best advice I've ever received.

"David," he said, "every tracker loses the track at some point. What separates a skilled tracker from an amateur is the ability to find it again once it is lost. And the only way to rediscover a lost track is to *slow down*."

Renias explained that the rush of adrenaline—the hurried breathing, the rapid pulse, and the frantic movements—all work against a tracker when the trail is lost. All those physical cues lie to us. They say: *People are waiting on you! You're letting everyone down! You look like a fool! You're wasting time! You're going to miss it!*

Mainly, these physical responses tell us that the thing we must do in those moments is *hurry up*. But that is the last thing we should do.

Everything in us wants to act here—to decide, fix, or push forward—because stillness can feel like giving up. But it isn't. Stillness is simply choosing not to outrun the moment before it has something to teach us. One of the things I've learned through my work at Novus Global is that the people who navigate these moments best aren't the ones who move fastest. They are the ones who create enough space to listen, often with a coach or therapist helping them hold the moment steady long enough for real clarity to arrive.

Renias used this opportunity to teach me what expert lion trackers do when they lose a track. "First," he said, "resist the urge to rush. Fight the impulse in your body that tells you to hurry. Close your eyes. Take a few slow, deliberate breaths. Come back to your senses. Understand that the only way to rediscover the track is to slow down."

Then, once I'd forced myself to slow down, Renias taught me the "expanding circles" method of rediscovering lost tracks. He said, "Starting right where you're standing right now, I want you to walk in a small, complete circle. Just seven or eight steps total. Take each step slowly, opening your eyes and all your senses to your surroundings."

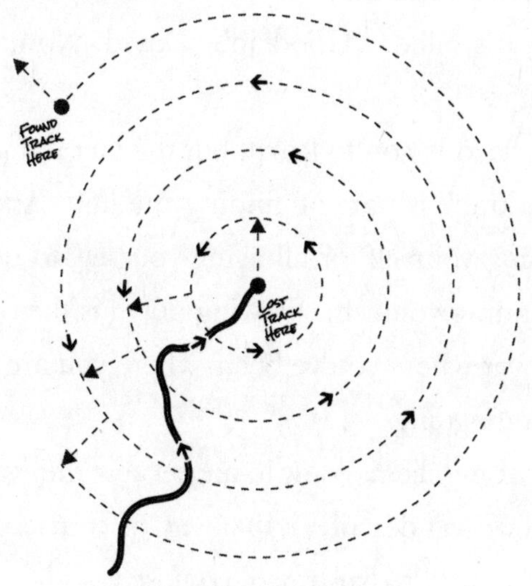

The Expanding Circle method of rediscovering lost tracks.

I did what I was told.

"It didn't work," I moaned. "I still don't see it."

"I know," Renias said. "That's okay. We're just getting started. Now, I want you to walk in a circle again. But this time, go a little farther. Make the circle a little bigger—maybe twenty steps total this time."

When I still didn't see the lost track, he had me try a few more times, expanding the circle a little more each time. Honestly, this was super frustrating for me. By the third circle, I was ready to start running laps around the jungle. But I did what my guide had taught me: I resisted the urge to rush. And eventually, I found the track.

Renias smiled. "Good job, David! Now, let's go find this lion!"

It's a hard lesson to learn, but the fact remains that losing the track is part of finding the lion. And oftentimes, losing yourself, or allowing yourself to be lost, is part of finding yourself. Slowing down is the only way to rediscover where you've been, where you are . . . and where you're going.

A lot of my clients come to me because they've lost the track. They don't describe it that way, of course. Instead, they say that they're frustrated, confused, and/or burned out. One executive I worked with described it this way: "The team is capable. The firm is moving. But our results are consistently falling short of what I know is possible, and I can't put my finger on why. I'm doing everything I can."

And he was, from his current perspective. He was stepping in to catch missed deadlines. Covering gaps. Rewriting work. Smoothing conflict. Picking up the load from others so the machine could keep running.

What he couldn't see was that the more he compensated, the more the system *depended* on him compensating. He had unknowingly trained the team to tolerate ambiguity, delay hard conversations, and rely on rescue. It wasn't that they didn't care; it was that the track had shifted and no one had stopped long enough to notice.

The turning point wasn't dramatic. In fact, a sudden change would have made things worse. Instead, this leader needed to slow down. The solution required a willingness to see what was actually happening instead of what he hoped was happening. As we traced the pattern, he realized how much he was tolerating: unclear ownership, vague agreements, and unspoken expectations. He hadn't lost his ability; he had lost the track.

From that place, the work became simple, but it was not easy. He started naming what was happening, having the conversations he'd avoided, and creating clear agreements that everyone could see and own. Slowly, the weight shifted—not because he worked harder, but because he stopped carrying what wasn't his.

He told me later, "I feel like I'm on the right track again. Things still don't go perfectly all the time, but at least now I can see when the track we're on changes, and now, I can change with it."

TRYING TO DICTATE THE SPEED OF HEALING

I began my intensive, five-week therapy plan on June 13, 2021, by driving twelve hours from Denver to Sedona. The first stretch of my healing plan would take place back on Michelle's ranch with Cody and the other horses I'd met a month earlier. I had booked an Airbnb for my stay and, since I'd be there a while, I made the place feel as much like home as possible. I unpacked my clothes into the dresser and closet, stocked the pantry, and set up a little home office for my work calls in between sessions with Michelle. By the end of the day, I was exhausted from the drive and busyness around the house. When I finally went to bed, though, a new emotion crept up on me, sneaking out of the shadows of a stranger's home and crawling into bed with me. It was fear. It dawned on me that this was the first time I'd been truly alone since the divorce. I'd been living near family since moving out of the condo I had shared with Lisa, and I had a close, tight group of friends and coworkers who had been by my side every day. But now, and for the next five weeks, I was on my own, unplugged from my support system. That terrified me.

Being alone wasn't the only thing I was scared of, either. I was afraid to face all the wild, raw emotions that were swirling around within me. I knew I was not okay, but I wasn't sure exactly *how* "not okay" I really was. I wanted so badly to get through these next five weeks and then be on my way, stepping boldly and joyfully into my new life, leaving my pain behind for good. I wanted my life back, and I wanted it *now*. But could I really get rid of the darkness and depression I had been drowning in for the past six months? Was it possible to do it, or at least get a big head start, in five weeks? Would a crash course in emotional wellness "work"?

I would find out soon enough.

BREATHING NEW LIFE INTO ME

I met Michelle on her front porch swing the next morning. We chatted for a bit before she explained the goal for that first week: breathwork.

"Breathwork," she explained, "is a form of therapy that uses particular guided breathing patterns and exercises, through both your nose and mouth, which help to calm the nervous system and allow the subconscious to release things that are holding you back. I've seen this practice radically transform many, many people's lives, and I think it can help you."

She explained that the full breathwork session would take about ninety minutes. In the first thirty minutes, we'd talk about my intention for the session. Then, we'd spend the bulk of the session on forty-five minutes of breathwork. During that time, I'd sit or lie down while Michelle guided me through a series of breathing cadences, each designed to unlock certain parts of my mind and help free thoughts and feelings that I'd kept hidden. She described this process as going *into* my breath, basically riding it into the entirety of my being—my mind, body, and emotions—and "meeting" an emotion or memory that was buried. Finally, we'd end with fifteen minutes of debriefing on what I'd experienced and trying to integrate it into my body.

"But go into this knowing breathwork doesn't give you what you *want*," she warned. "It gives you what you *need*. Do your best to remain open and trust it."

I felt a wave of anxiety right before we got started. *What is this going to be like? What is going to come up for me when I do this? What am I going to have to face that's buried in my subconscious?* But there was no turning back. I had given myself five weeks to get myself together, and the clock was ticking.

I stretched out on her sofa as we began. She instructed me to let my mind wander, to give myself permission to focus on whatever came up in that moment. That, she said, would be the *intention* we focused on for that session.

My mind immediately went in a million different directions. *Will this work? Did I lock the door at the Airbnb? What should I get for lunch?* I had to will myself back to the moment. *I'm here for healing. I want to move on from my anger and bitterness toward Lisa. Forgiveness—that's my intention. Let's go with that.*

I told Michelle I wanted to focus on forgiveness. We discussed it for a few minutes to help me connect more deeply to it, and then we began the breathwork cadence.

It felt so strange, using my breath as a tool to help me connect more deeply to myself and my inner world. As I began to get into the flow and rhythm of the breathing pattern, I found myself thinking less and less about the act of breathing and my physical body. I felt something shift as the breath started to take me to this inner place. It was almost as if my breath began to "breathe me," as weird as that might seem. I tried to focus on the intention of forgiving Lisa, but I found my mind going elsewhere. I resisted it at first, trying to keep forgiveness the focus, but it wasn't working. So, I just went where my breath led, trusting it would give me what I needed.

It struck me how wild it was that I was lying there doing this type of therapy, literally using my breath, something that was always with me and something I usually didn't even think about. And then this thought hit me: *God is breath*. For several years, I had been deconstructing and reconstructing the faith I'd grown up with, so this felt like a strange thought to come up. Yet, as I allowed the thoughts to flow without criticizing them, it was like all the dots connected.

My breath is always with me, whether I think about it or not. The Hebrew Scriptures describe the concept that God is breath, but I had never understood it. Now it was making sense. *God is with me. I can be in this struggle with God.* It's like I'm inhaling and exhaling God 24/7. He gave me this breath. He gave me this life and this ability to breathe. I'd never thought about it this way until that moment. God is breath. Breath is healing. Both are with me at all times.

Right then, Michelle began guiding me out of the breath cadence and back into my body. For the first time in a really long time, I felt the tiniest glimmer of hope as I opened my eyes.

FULL STEAM AHEAD

Those first two weeks of my healing journey in Sedona were packed. I maintained my full work schedule but squeezed in as many therapy sessions as I could. I was scheduled for various therapy modalities seven out of the fourteen days—five of those days were with Michelle for both equine therapy and breathwork, and I had triple sessions (three session blocks back-to-back) booked on two of those days. I also had three sessions with a somatic bodyworker, as well as an acupuncture appointment.

I was serious when I said I'd planned an *intense* five-week healing plan.

Despite all the self-work I was doing (or maybe *because* of it), it was becoming increasingly difficult to find the energy and right frame of mind to coach my clients. So, in between coaching calls and therapy sessions, I maintained my daily routine of cold showers and ice baths, naps, and meditation to help me show up well for work when it mattered most.

I also mixed in dirt bike rides on the many Sedona trails—something I had always loved. But this only made me realize how poorly I was doing emotionally. I felt almost nothing on my rides. I couldn't access any sense of vitality or vigor. I was doing a thrilling, dangerous, and generally badass activity against the backdrop of Sedona's stunning red rock landscape, but it was as if everything was muted, shadowed, and flat. I was essentially a robot riding around, stirring up dust, and making noise—a machine incapable of joy.

Occasionally, I'd have a flash of insight and hope during a therapy or breathwork session, and I'd think, *Maybe this is it! Maybe this is the breakthrough I've been waiting for!* But then, the warm light would fall back into shadow, like sunshine peeking through a crack in a cloud-filled sky, only to disappear moments later. The transition from darkness to light to deeper darkness left me wondering, *Am I so far gone that I can't even maintain more than ten seconds of peace?*

Those first two weeks of my plan were perhaps the hardest days I'd had in the past six months. It was an unsatisfying, exhausting, and, at least from my perspective at the time, completely ineffective experience.

Until my last day there.

MEETING LITTLE ME

On my last day with Michelle, I was lying on her sofa during a breathwork session. I was having a difficult time focusing on my intention for the session. Once again I was trying to force myself to stay focused on the intention of fully forgiving Lisa, but my breath kept pulling me toward something else. Something unexpected.

A clear image formed in my mind. I was in the backyard of the home my family lived in during our time in Grand Forks, North Dakota. I saw myself at eight years old, running and playing in the summer sun. "Little Me" was full of energy, jumping from one thing to the next: running around with a football, swinging on the swing set, and rolling around in the grass, laughing without a care in the world. I called Little Me over and got down on one knee so we could be face-to-face. Without hesitation, he ran over and hopped up on my knee.

I put my hand on his shoulder and said, "Little man, I need to tell you something important. When you get older, you're going to go through a divorce, and you're going to have a really, really hard time getting through it. There will even be moments when you're not sure you want to be alive anymore."

He shot me a confused look as the news sank in. He considered it for a moment before simply replying, "Okay. I got it."

But I didn't feel like he was *really* hearing me, so I pressed a bit more. "I just needed to come back in time to tell you about it, so that you'll know it's coming. Maybe that way, it won't be such a shock when it happens."

Little Me got right in my face and put his hand gently on my cheek.

"No," he said, "that's not why you're here."

"What do you mean?" I asked, with a mix of amusement and irritation. Who was this little kid to tell me why I was there?

With the gentlest yet most unflinching confidence imaginable, Little Me said, "You didn't come here to warn me about the divorce. You came here so that I could tell you that we're going to be okay."

Then, he reached up, put his arms around my neck, and gave me a hug.

With that, I started coming out of the breathwork visualization and back into the real world. I was lying on Michelle's couch, tears streaming down my face. I fought my return to reality; I just didn't want that moment to end. This was the most hope I had felt since before Lisa asked for a divorce.

As I tried to process what had just happened, I felt more waves of emotion approaching. As if she sensed it too, Michelle gently said, "As best as you can, just let it all in."

So, I did. I allowed the fullness of each wave to roll over me as I lay on the sofa weeping. When the final wave had passed, I let out a long, deep exhale.

I didn't yet know how to get there, and I still felt a lot of darkness, but I had to believe that Little Me was right. We could and we would make it through this.

YOU CAN'T GO HOME AGAIN

At the end of my two weeks in Sedona, I thanked Michelle, packed my bags, and hit the road. Next stop was Oakland, California—an eleven-hour drive, which gave me time to reflect on how things were going so far. I'd had a handful of experiences I considered helpful, but overall, I was still feeling disappointed with my progress. I'd allowed myself to believe this five-week intensive plan would "fix" me, and I'd hoped I'd feel the darkness starting to lift after the Sedona phase of my plan. I'd had little glimmers of hope like the interaction with Little Me, but given the state I was in, each one quickly faded, leaving me desperately reaching out for the *next* therapy session or the *next* breakthrough.

I still have three weeks to go, I reminded myself as the miles ticked by. *I just have to stay focused and do the next thing on the list.*

That "next thing" was a weeklong therapy intensive using a process people had described as essentially being ten years of therapy packed into seven days. I don't think I realized it at the time, but I was putting an enormous amount of pressure on the process—and on myself. Based on what others had told me, I had fallen into a belief that if this couldn't "fix" me, nothing could. That is an impossible standard for any therapy modality to live up to.

I put everything I had into my healing that week, following the Hoffman Process to the letter. But at the end of seven days, despite a few meaningful realizations throughout the week, the needle really hadn't moved much on my mental health meter. My high expectations had become my undoing. Rather than leading me into healing, it had caused me to feel even more hopeless and even more like a failure than I had at the start of my five-week healing plan. I probably would have given up at that point if I hadn't already made commitments and appointments back in Sedona for phase three of my five-week plan. So, I packed my bags and loaded my car again, and I made the eleven-hour drive back to Arizona.

A little piece of me, deep down, hoped there was still time for a miracle before my five weeks were up . . . but most of me doubted it.

BACK TO THE RANCH

I had one week left in my five-week therapy intensive, and so far, it was kind of a bust. Ahead of me were four more breathwork sessions with Michelle, two equine therapy sessions with her horses, and a few more somatic bodywork and acupuncture appointments. With Oakland in my rearview mirror, I drove down I-40 pleading with God to give me a breakthrough before the week was out. The pain of my depression was excruciating. I honestly wasn't sure how much longer I would be able to take it. This five-week adventure was supposed to be all about me racing down the string of tracks toward healing—my dream destination. Instead, I felt like I had lost the track altogether and had been running in circles, trying frantically to find it again.

The circle was kind of literal, as I ended my therapy intensive right back where I started: Michelle's breathwork couch. That big, comfy sofa had become a haven for me, a symbol of support to my body and mind, despite the pain and struggles I faced while lying there. In perhaps a small sign of at least a tiny bit of progress, I noticed it felt a little easier for me to dial into my intention this time. Again, I chose to focus on forgiving Lisa.

Inhale. Exhale. Forgiveness.

Inhale. Exhale. Forgiveness.

Inhale. Exhale. Forgiveness.

Michelle guided me into the breathing cadence. For the first fifteen minutes or so, lying there with my eyes closed, I focused on my breathing and my intention. Then, just as I'd experienced before, I began to drop into this . . . *other space* . . . as I let go of my conscious efforts to control my thoughts and let the breath take me wherever it wanted. I found myself in a deep, almost trance-like state of peace while lying there, breathing in cadence. This time, though, my mind stayed mostly blank. I had no visions or visualizations of any kind. My mind was quiet. Still. Almost peaceful, if such a state were even possible for me at that point. That's where my mind stayed for almost the entire forty-five minutes of breathwork.

Then, without warning, my entire body aggressively jerked upright in a state of utter panic. I sat straight up, eyes open wide; one hand flew instinctively to my chest while the other clung to the back of the couch for support. I was desperately gasping for air, as though my body was convinced I was trapped underwater. As I shook, wildly trying to find my breath, I saw myself again at the bottom of the ocean—alone, losing air, and desperate.

I had no idea what had happened or why I'd been jerked so suddenly out of a place of relative ease. Michelle helped provide some context for what had happened. She explained that when someone comes out of breathwork like this, it carries an indication of being *reborn*. My gasping for breath was, in a way, me taking my first breath in this new life. That gave me some hope that I actually was on a path toward healing, even if I couldn't see it yet.

Maybe something helpful and important *had* come out of these five difficult weeks, after all. But whatever it was, it still hadn't connected to my conscious mind.

WHAT NOW?

With that, my five-week sprint to recovery came to an end . . . leaving me arguably more depressed than I'd been five weeks earlier. It was different now, however. It wasn't just that I didn't know *how* to get better; it was that I no longer knew if I ever *could* get better. If the most effective therapy and recovery practices I could find didn't even make a dent in my depression, then what, if anything, ever could?

I'd planned to cap off my travels with a few days in Telluride, Colorado, with some friends. I was surrounded by people I loved and some of the most gorgeous scenery in the world. I sat on a gondola staring at endless shades of green, orange, and yellow leaves practically glowing across the Rocky Mountains in the summer sun. It was magnificent . . . and meaningless. I felt like a ghost haunting a cabin full of living, vibrant, fully alive people.

I went through the motions for those two days in Telluride, mainly trying not to spoil my friends' good time. But I didn't want to be there, and I was glad when it was time to go. I loaded up my 4Runner one last time and headed home. As I drove the winding mountain roads back home, two thoughts played on an endless loop for the entire six-hour drive: *How did my five-week recovery master plan seem to fail so miserably?* and *What the hell am I going to do now?*

So, why *did* my aggressive, rock-solid, surefire healing plan go absolutely nowhere? In retrospect, I view it through the lens of lion tracking. Remember how we started the chapter with me learning how to be a lead tracker? I think often about what Renias said to me then and how much it applies to life. "Every tracker loses the track at some point. What separates a skilled tracker from an amateur is the ability to find it again once it is lost. And the only way to rediscover a lost track is to slow down."

At that time in my life, I had lost the track. I was stumbling around blindly, grasping at anything I thought might take me where I believed I wanted to go. Rather than calming myself and going in slow, careful concentric circles to rediscover the lost track, I was darting around in different directions, desperately hoping to find a string to follow.

That's not to say any of the therapy methodologies I tried—equine therapy, breathwork, somatic bodywork, acupuncture, or the weeklong intensive process—were *bad* or *useless*. They each had some key benefits that contributed to my eventual healing. No, the problem wasn't the tools I tried; the real problem was the expectation I set for myself. I had given myself an arbitrary deadline to become "okay." That deadline wasn't based on what I needed or where the tracks were trying to take me; it was based purely on when I *wanted* to be okay. I tried to rush the healing process, to force it to fit my schedule and my demands. By rushing, by running around in a blind flurry of activity rather than taking one slow, methodical, reflective step at a time, I just became more lost. Rather than pushing my grief out of the way, I pushed myself further into despair. And I felt certain that things were going to get even worse before they started getting better.

TRACKER MANUAL

Step 7: Resist the Urge to Rush

- Understand why you might be rushing. What are you hoping to gain by rushing? Is it working?
- Develop your patience. What is one area of your life where you could benefit from slowing down? What might it practically look like for you to slow down?
- Don't be afraid to lose the track—it might be a way of life redirecting you to find a new track. Where might you be hesitating right now out of fear of doing the wrong thing? What would be a small step in fully going for it?

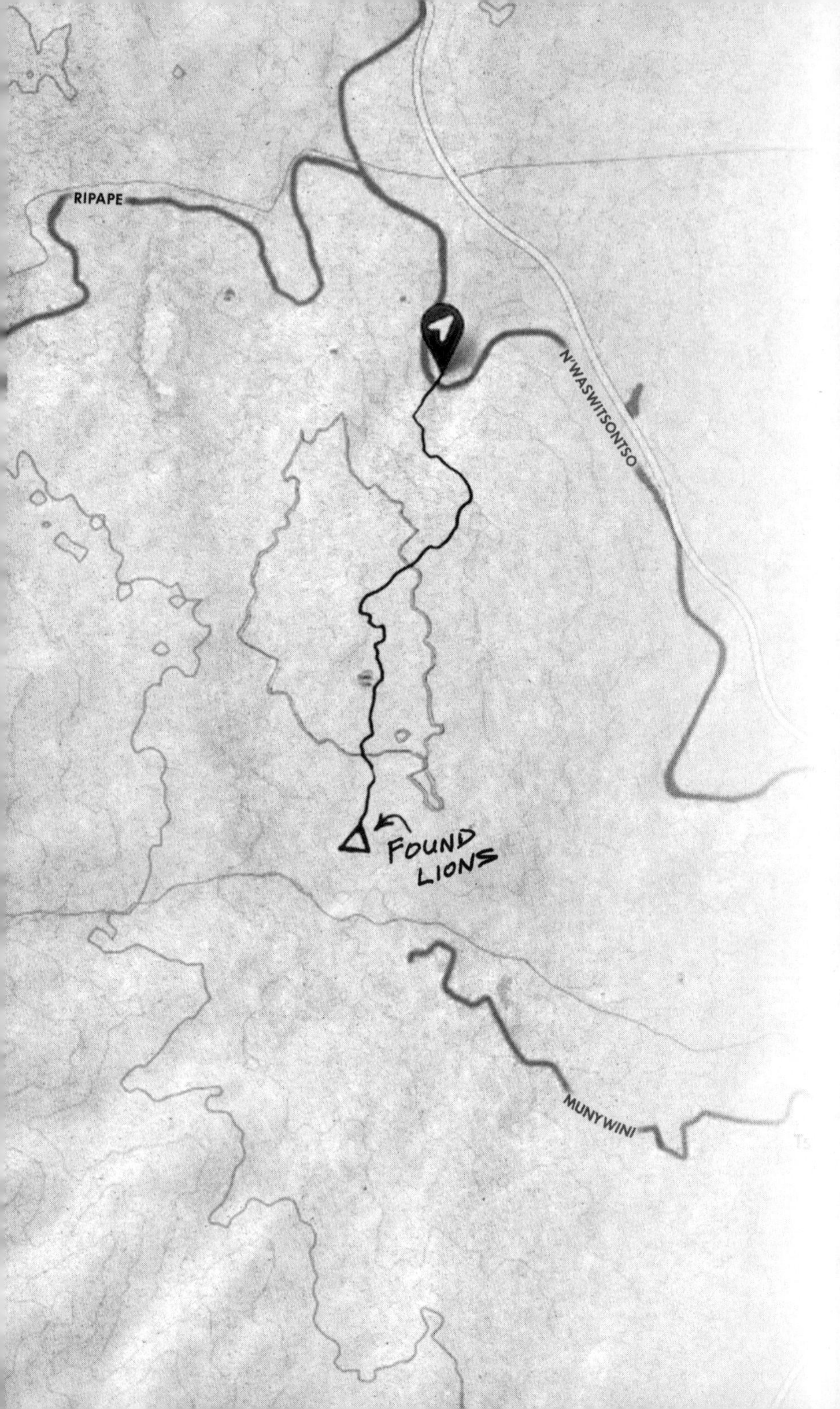
RIPAPE
N'WASWITSONTSO
FOUND LIONS
MUNYWINI

CHAPTER 8

EXPECT PAIN

Your new life will cost you your old one.

BRIANNA WIEST[10]

I WANT TO be up front about what this chapter is and who it's for. This chapter is a little different from the others for a few reasons. First, there aren't any cool and exciting stories about tracking lions in the wild. This one is laser-focused on me dealing with some issues that millions of men struggle with . . . but nobody wants to talk about. Second, I'm going to risk oversharing a bit in this chapter—not to be shocking or edgy, but because there's no way to have this discussion without risking some discomfort. And third, this is the part of my journey that I really don't want to talk about. I can't tell you how many times I've gone back and forth in my head about whether to include this. But I think this issue is important enough and, I'm afraid, *common* enough, that it's worth being vulnerable about.

What does that mean for you? Mainly, it means I've tried to keep the details of these issues just within this one chapter. So, if you skip it and jump ahead to the next chapter, it won't hurt your overall experience of this book. But if you're a man who has been so affected by emotional and/or sexual trauma that it has literally turned your own body against you, making your experience ten times worse in the process—or if you have a loved one with similar experiences who you're trying to better understand—then read on.

THINGS I'D RATHER NOT SHARE

A quick recap: Lisa told me she wanted a divorce in December 2020. I did my TEDx Talk in March 2021, around the same time I connected with Heidi on Instagram. In May, I spent an almost-perfect weekend with Heidi in Austin and admittedly allowed myself to fall for her way too hard, way too fast. When she hit the brakes on what I had hoped would be a new relationship, it felt like my heart broke all over again. Then, in June, I started on my five-week intensive healing plan, which also didn't work out the way I'd hoped. Clearly, there was a lot going on in my life—externally *and* internally.

Something else happened in May 2021, between the weekend with Heidi and my five-week therapy intensive, that I haven't mentioned yet. I stumbled upon some tracks that led me right into a thicket—a dense, nearly impenetrable bramble of thorny shrubs, vines, and trees. Speaking as an active, healthy adult man, it was the scariest, darkest place I could have imagined.

That May, in the middle of everything else that was going on, the sexual part of me disappeared. I don't say that lightly, and I don't just mean I wasn't "in the mood." I mean that whole part of my being—any sense of passion, vitality, vigor, and physical stamina—was gone. It felt like I woke up one morning and discovered half of what made me *me* had died overnight. Everything in me that I'd ever associated with masculinity was missing. My body felt like an empty shell. I didn't recognize it. There was no energy, no desire, no zest for life, no arousal, no sexual ideation. And it wasn't only that I didn't feel these things emotionally; the effects showed up in my physical body, as well, leaving me struggling with impotence for the first time in my life. It was as though I'd been shot through the heart, but instead of bleeding out, I'd been drained of all my testosterone and vitality.

I wasn't sure what was happening. Initially, I viewed it as purely a physical condition completely disconnected from the emotional trauma I'd been going through for the previous six months. I approached it medically and scoured the internet to find out what could cause such a sudden and complete loss of sex drive and vitality. My searching led me to several posts on Reddit and other community discussion sites—specifically to the many posts by men who had taken a hair-loss drug called finasteride and had subsequently experienced devastating sexual side effects that sounded very similar to mine.

I'd been taking finasteride preventatively for nine months at that point. My doctor had prescribed it for me when I'd expressed some concerns about some mild hair loss in my late thirties. I did some light research online before starting it and saw there was a *chance* of sexual side effects, but I didn't pay much attention to that warning. I mean, every medication comes with a laundry list of potential side effects, right? I started taking it in September 2020, and I hadn't had a single negative side effect at all. I'd forgotten all about the warnings. But then, when my sex drive vanished in May 2021 and so many websites pointed to finasteride as the cause, I became convinced I'd brought this problem on myself.

I read dozens of online posts from guys who had suffered severe, and seemingly permanent, sexual dysfunction after taking finasteride. *Great*, I thought, *I have irreversibly wrecked my hormones and nuked my sex drive with this stupid hair-loss drug.* My concern quickly grew into full-blown panic, which led me to more horror stories online, which in turn led me into even greater panic. Some of the guys online said they'd been impotent for years after taking the drug, and they'd given up hope of ever feeling "normal" again.

Days turned into weeks, weeks turned into months, and any hope I had that my "condition" would get better after stopping the medication faded into sorrow and desperation.

Now, you may be reading this thinking, *Uh, David . . . I can think of some other things that might have caused this response in your body. You kind of had some difficult times that year. Did you even consider the possibility that this was a physical response to your emotional trauma?*

The thought crossed my mind, but for some reason, it was easier to believe that the medication had caused it. It was almost as if my mind had completely turned on me. Maybe blaming the finasteride was a better option for me than having to admit that my divorce had greatly affected one more part of my life and my identity. But let's face it: the unrelenting grief and depression of the previous six months could certainly have caused the symptoms I was having.

In the years since then, I've learned how the body tries to protect itself during times of intense trauma. First and foremost, when experiencing physical or emotional trauma, the body prioritizes bodily functions that are needed for survival. It's almost like the brain says, "Okay, we're in trouble. We've got to keep the heart pumping and the lungs breathing, so we're going to start shutting down anything we don't need to survive." Because sex isn't strictly needed for survival, the brain can take that system offline and redirect that energy elsewhere.

I still don't know if my issues were all caused by the drug, or by the trauma from the divorce and all the grief I was processing; perhaps it was a combination of the two. With the benefit of time and healing, it seems most likely that this was one way my body was trying to adapt and defend itself from the devastating effects of emotional trauma, but I just could not accept that at the time. I was utterly convinced that I had brought this on myself, that I'd allowed my concerns over a little hair loss to steal whatever dignity and masculinity I had left after the divorce and rob me of any hope for a fulfilling sex life in the future. The regret I felt for taking the medicine compounded the fear and panic I was experiencing about the symptoms, which only took me further down into the depths of darkness and despair. I'd never experienced anything like it, and I became increasingly aware of how little I wanted to wake up each morning.

If this is what the rest of my life is going to be like, I thought, *I don't want it.*

Looking back, I think a big part of why this affected me so much is that it forced me to take a good, hard look at something I had tried to bury emotionally for decades. It was bringing to the surface some longstanding and long-neglected wounds I had never addressed or even really ever talked about: the emotional trauma I experienced as a result of the painful sexual challenges I experienced throughout many of my relationships.

Many people my age grew up in faith communities that advocated for abstinence until marriage. This set of beliefs developed within Evangelical Christianity in the 1990s and became known as "Christian purity culture." It was a strange time to be a teenager in the church. Pastors, youth pastors, Christian camps, Christian weekend retreats, Christian music, and Christian books became fixated on the dangers of sex before marriage.

I heard the central message dozens of times in one form or another. If you're around my age and have a similar background, this might sound familiar. It went something like this: You should not have sex until you're married. If you do, it's a sin and something to be deeply ashamed of and might send you to hell to be tortured forever. You have to ask for God's forgiveness and promise not to do it again. Even though God will forgive you, though, your virginity is still gone forever, which means you've stolen something precious from your future spouse. Oh, and you've probably ruined your future sex life in marriage, too. Sucks to be you.

I doubt this was the intended outcome, but the big takeaway for teenagers like me at the time was that sex is something shameful and bad. When you're sixteen, it's hard to think about anything *except* sex, but then you keep hearing people you respect say that sex will ruin your life, your relationship with God, and your hopes for an awesome future marriage. It really screws with your head at that age . . . and for years afterward.

The payoff, purity culture promised, was that your sex life would be a million times better once you got married. At that point, sex would stop being something to be ashamed of and suddenly turn into the most beautiful and exciting part of your life. Once you got married, you could "rejoice with your spouse" and have tons of fantastic sex whenever you wanted!

In the twenty-five years since then, I've experienced a lot more of what life has to offer than I knew as a teenager. I've been in relationships. I've been married. I've been single. I've talked with a lot of adults my age who grew up with similar church backgrounds. And if there's one thing I've learned about purity culture, it's that having "tons of fantastic sex whenever you want once you are married" is rarely, if ever, the case. I've heard of a few couples who claim to have experienced amazing sex right from the start of their marriage after following the purity culture framework, but I've never personally met any.

Based on what I've experienced and what I've heard from others who grew up like I did, the painful reality is that most of the couples who followed this path in their faith and romantic relationship had a *lot* of trouble "flipping the switch" in their minds about sex, and the result was years of difficulty connecting with their spouse physically. Many of these couples, sadly, never experienced anything close to a healthy, mutually fulfilling sex life. That makes sense to me now. We were taught during the most sexually charged years of our lives to ignore and/or feel ashamed of what our bodies were screaming for, to not only shove all that passion and excitement down but to flat-out be ashamed of it. How are people expected to hear that message for years and years and then immediately feel fully free sexually as soon as they say "I do"?

Let me be clear here that even after everything I've been through, I still believe sex is a sacred thing and should be treated as such. But the unfortunate result of this faith-based phenomenon was that millions of young people around the world, including me, grew up with shame-filled, unrealistic expectations and beliefs about their own bodies and about sex.

Now, this chapter isn't focused on the unintended consequences of Christian purity culture on people. However, I think that context is important in understanding what was happening to me in the aftermath of my divorce. I was hammered with the purity culture message as a teen, and it messed with my head. I'll admit that I had sex a few times while still in high school, and the result was *years* of deeply felt guilt and shame. I felt like an absolute failure, like I couldn't control myself even though I knew what the "right" thing to do was. I faced serious challenges connecting with my partners in nearly all of my future relationships and eventually found myself almost forty years old but still extremely inexperienced sexually.

Through all of that, though, I had a strong sex drive and vitality. It was part of me, and while I wished I'd had a more fulfilling sex life, I enjoyed that part of me. This is hard to admit, but even in the anguish of divorce, I took some slim solace that maybe, just maybe, the divorce would open the door to me having a whole new lease on life, including my sex life. As broken as I was by the divorce, I was actually excited for the opportunity to finally develop a healthy, mature sex life, to finally embrace this part of my identity after a lifetime of feeling ashamed of it.

The thought of finding a new life partner and getting the chance for an entirely different and deeply connected sex life was one of the things giving me some hope. Sure, a big part of that was being excited about having sex. I'm human! But it went so much further than that. I deeply wanted to get married again and have a family. I loved being married. I loved having a partner to do life with. I wanted to be a dad. I wanted to be a grandpa. I didn't want to be a single, lonely old uncle who faded into the background of everyone else's lives. But with my sex drive shutting down and the very real fear of the permanence of it, all of those hopes began to disappear, giving way to absolutely debilitating fears, imagining what my life would look like if this *were* irreversible.

My mind attacked me. I was convinced I'd done this to myself, and the self-hatred made everything worse. I was 99 percent certain it was permanent, and I was mentally spiraling out of control. I couldn't find my way out of the negativity and anger. I was sure that I'd never have sex again. I'd never date or get married again. I'd never live out my dream of becoming a father or a grandfather. I'd waste away and lose all sense of purpose. And the worst part of it all was that I truly believed I couldn't do anything about it. I was enveloped in a cloud of depression, anger, and rage. Blaming myself. Blaming the drug company. Blaming purity culture. It went on and on. My mind was so fixated on the belief that this was permanent that I kept spinning deeper and darker inside of myself. There was no hope or light anywhere to be found.

There were many moments when I was convinced that this was the end of me. The happy David who wanted to change the world, be in love, and be a great father, husband, and family man was gone. What was left was this bitter person who drifted ever deeper into resentment, anger, and resignation. I only saw myself as a helpless victim—someone with no agency, no choices, and no options. And there I sat, miserable and hopeless, as this new reality settled in on top of the hell my life had already become.

Being assaulted on so many different fronts felt like being out in the wild, all alone, and suddenly finding myself surrounded by several lions, coming at me from all sides. I was trapped, and escape felt impossible. I was ready to lie down and die. Literally.

Because I promised you this would be a mostly self-contained chapter, I'll go ahead and tell you that, even though it seemed impossible at the time, I did recover from all this physical torment. After a long and difficult few years of therapy and healing, my sex drive and vitality returned to normal. But it was a long, hard, desperate journey filled with terrifying days when I thought my body, mind, and spirit were all broken beyond repair.

Michelle, however, gave me a different perspective early in this part of my journey.

At one point in the early days of experiencing the sex drive shutdown, after a breathwork and equine therapy session, I told Michelle about this struggle I was having with my body. She looked at me and, in her incredibly empathetic way, said, "David, this is going to be a portal to your deeper healing. God knows you need to go deeper into yourself than you would have if something like this wasn't pulling you under."

I had no idea what she meant, yet it felt like one of those deeply profound moments that I needed to store away and remember.

With some time, healing, and reflection, I think I have a better sense now of what Michelle meant. As much as we might wish it weren't so, the things that make us better and wiser, and certainly the things that make us stronger, are the experiences we never *want* to go through. These are the tragic and unforeseen left turns, the times when life surprises us with something we can only see as *all bad* in the moment. But then, sometime later, after we've had time to process the situation and, when needed, recover from the emotional blow, we can look back and say, "No, that wasn't all bad. That experience revealed *this* about me. It showed me I was a lot stronger than I thought I was, that I can bear a lot more pain and pressure than I ever imagined. It showed me that *this* person isn't who I thought they were or that *this* relationship was limiting me in ways I couldn't see."

Philosopher Peter Crone describes it like this: "Life will present you with people and circumstances to reveal where you are not yet free."[11] That is, many of the challenges we face show us which parts of our lives are still trapped in cages, and those painful experiences become, in Michelle's words, "portals" for us to escape these cages and move on in freedom.

Most of the time, when something "bad" happens to us, we ask, "Why do bad things happen to good people?" But the better question is, "How can I see everything that's happening, whether I like it or not, as a catalyst for my freedom?" With that mindset, I move beyond the idea that I can succeed *in spite of* an obstacle and embrace the conviction that I can succeed *because of* the obstacle.

Yes, it still hurt.

Yes, my divorce felt like it was going to kill me.

Yes, my struggles in my body with sexual dysfunction and loss of masculine vitality felt devastating at the time.

I would not have chosen any of those things for myself.

But the reality is, I am a much better man today than I was before God walked me down this path. I'm stronger, more experienced, more empathetic, and more grateful for my physical health than I ever was before all this happened. I'm also much freer, because all these experiences revealed to me the walls of the cage I never would have seen otherwise.

I'd eventually come to learn that the only way to face lions coming at you from multiple directions is to surrender and let go. Sometimes you've got to let the lions inside of you take you down and destroy the parts of you that helped and sustained you but that now must die so something new can spring to life.

Sometimes, surrender is the way through.

Sometimes, you have to let yourself die, metaphorically speaking, in order to find yourself.

TRACKER MANUAL

Step 8: Expect Pain

- Anticipate some agony. What things do you want for your life so badly that you are willing to go through some pain to grow and achieve them?
- Express it and feel it. What practices would support you in really being present and feeling the fullness of life?
- Push through the resistance by welcoming it. What is something you are resisting right now that is inviting you to surrender and let go?

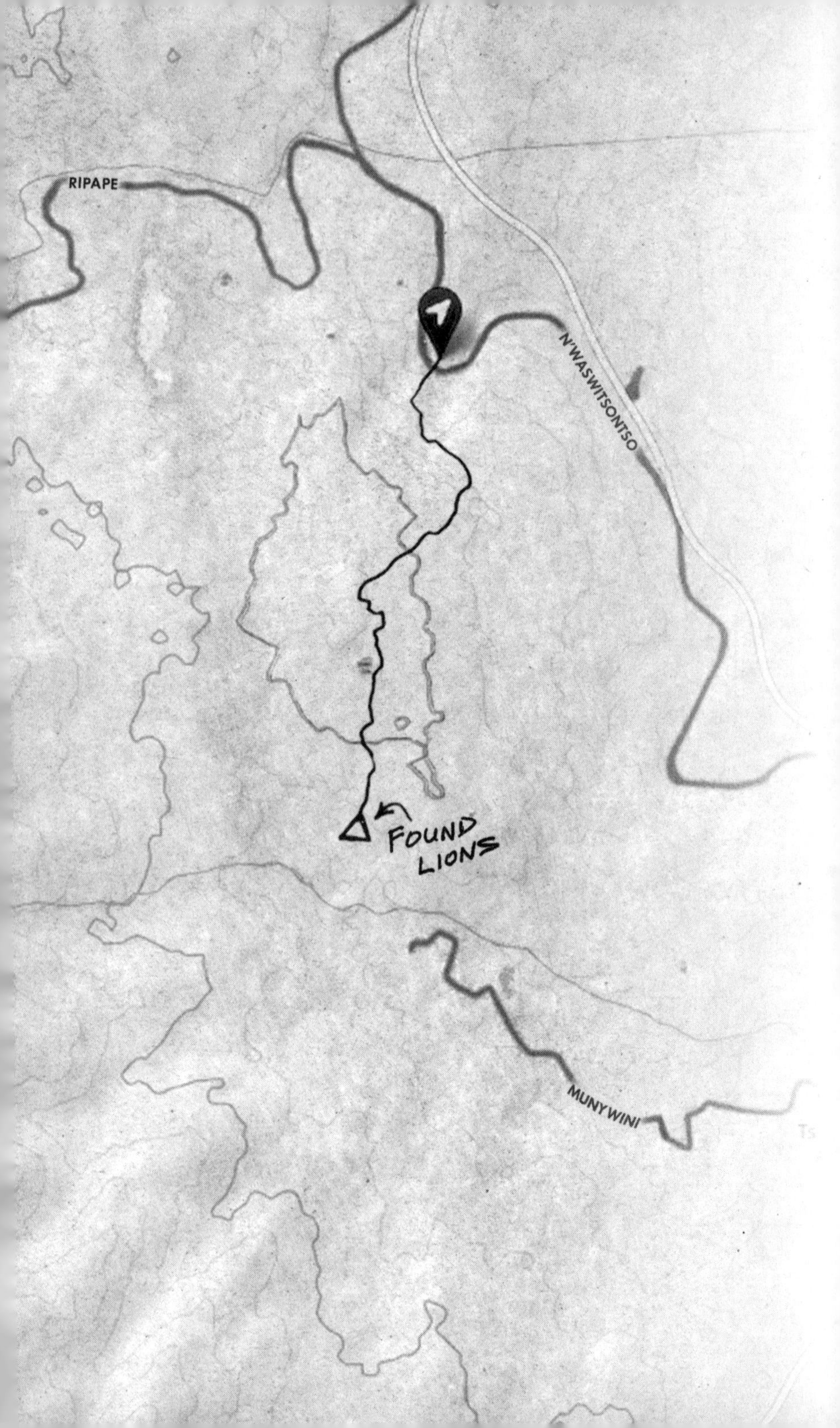
RIPAPE
N'WASWITSONTSO
FOUND
LIONS
MUNYWINI

CHAPTER 9

BE OPEN TO WHAT YOU FIND

There is some strange intimacy between grief and aliveness, some sacred exchange between what seems unbearable and what is most exquisitely alive. Through this, I have come to have a lasting faith in grief.

FRANCIS WELLER[12]

IN THE BUSH, as in life, the most significant and beautiful experiences can be the ones we never even know to look for. The moments when nature's magnificence and wonder catch us completely off guard. The times when we allow ourselves to sit still—even just for a moment—and let God or nature show us what it wants us to see rather than what we think we're looking for.

AN ELEPHANT POOL PARTY

One evening, at the end of a long day of tracking through the African wild, our group decided to cap off our adventure with a drink while perched on a large rock overlooking two small ponds. Animals often enjoyed a lazy drink from the ponds at the end of the day, and we hoped a few would join us for a "sundowner."

I'd spent enough time in the wild to know to keep my expectations reasonable. Sometimes, you see nothing. Sometimes, you see a lion or a small pride or maybe a stray rhino. High expectations are the quickest path to disappointment when tracking, so I was content to simply enjoy my drink beneath a breathtaking sunset.

Little did I know nature was feeling like showing off a bit that evening.

Not long after we took a seat on the rock overlooking the ponds, a large herd of about fifty elephants—mainly mothers and their young—wandered down to the farther pond, which was about seventy-five meters away. It was amazing. I'd never seen so many at one time before.

Then, as the elephants enjoyed their drink, a hippo that had been swimming in the second pond shot out of the water like a cannonball. He positioned himself on the sand between the two ponds, as though he was telling the pack of pesky pachyderms to back off.

Maybe in response to the implied challenge, or maybe just feeling confident in their numbers, the elephants decided they wanted to move from the pond they were in to the one closer to us—the one the hippo was defending.

Faced with an overwhelming army of encroaching elephants, the hippo quickly decided his claim to the pond wasn't worth getting trampled, and he retreated back beneath the water, with only his snout visible above the surface.

The happy herd of elephants had a late-afternoon pool party that evening, drinking and splashing and firing mighty blasts of water at each other from their trunks. I sat mesmerized on the rocks just above them, taking it all in for about thirty minutes. Even in such large numbers, each individual elephant radiated strength and presence. I couldn't help but wonder what it would be like to get even closer, to actually sit side by side with such an enormous creature. Would it even notice me?

Watching the elephants play was one of the purest, most delightful moments of my life. It was absolutely breathtaking—and a great reminder that sometimes, we just need to slow down, stop trying to control everything, and let life show us what real peace and beauty look like.

LOSING MY TRACKS

I was so sure that my five weeks of intensive therapy were going to "fix" me. I'd been so careful and intentional about plotting a course, about mapping each stop on my healing journey, I had felt confident it would take me where I wanted to go. It didn't. Looking back, of course, I can see that I wasn't really *following* the tracks of my life; I was trying to draw my own map. I wasn't tracking a lion; I was trying to outrun it. And I was scared of what I'd find if I ever actually faced it.

Coming out of those weeks of nonstop therapy and travel, I was wrecked physically, mentally, and emotionally. My plan had failed, and now I didn't know what to do. It was like a gust of wind had erased whatever scant tracks I'd thought I could see, leaving me lost and alone in the wild. For the first time, I was beginning to believe the whole idea of healing wasn't worth the effort. Deep within, I felt this might just be it for me. This depression would either be the only existence I'd ever know from here on out . . . or I simply wouldn't make it much longer.

Suicidal ideation was becoming more and more a part of my everyday condition. To be clear, I never considered actively taking my life, but I'd gotten increasingly comfortable with the idea of suddenly dying in my sleep or in some other way. Sometimes, it went beyond mere comfort, and I found myself wishing God would just swoop in and take me out of this overwhelming darkness in a flash. The thought of blinking my eyes and suddenly finding myself on the other side of heaven wasn't scary to me. It was comforting. It was . . . preferable.

How the hell am I worse off now, after all this therapy, than I was eight months ago, when Lisa ended our marriage? I went to bed every night with that thought banging around in my head. I felt like I was sprinting on a hamster wheel of fear, failure, anxiety, anger, and depression. I was running for my life, but I wasn't making any progress. In fact, every step was taking me further away from where I wanted to go.

It was time for me to stop running, stay still, and let the lion find me.

OVER THE RIVER AND THROUGH THE WOODS

"I *(inhale)* am *(exhale)* here *(inhale)* now *(exhale)* in *(inhale)* this *(exhale)*."

I repeated that phrase a million times as I lay in the back seat of my father's F-150 for the entire fourteen-hour drive to my grandparents' house. My grandmother had passed away shortly after my visit with her in her hospital room. I hadn't attended the funeral with my parents, because I had already said my final goodbye to her and because I honestly didn't think I could handle another emotional blow like that. When Mom and Dad asked me if I wanted to go with them to clean out her house a couple of months later, before they sold it, I agreed. I didn't feel up to it, but my grandparents' home had been the source of so much joy for me throughout my entire life, and I knew I'd regret not seeing it one last time. Besides, as much as I didn't want to be around other people, I knew I needed to be.

I had told my folks that I would only go if they and everyone else understood I wasn't feeling very social. I didn't want to talk much, and I wanted to have a place to retreat to whenever I needed to. They'd offered me my grandparents' bedroom, which was at the end of a long ranch home, offering more privacy than the orange shag-carpeted room I'd always stayed in before.

That had been a purely practical decision, and I hadn't thought much of it since my parents suggested it. I was distracted by the endless stream of debilitating narratives and intrusive thoughts that swirled through my mind day and night. I couldn't concentrate hard enough, pray passionately enough, or yell loudly enough to drive them out. It was as though my own mind had turned against me, and I was powerless to take back control. So, for hours on end, day in and day out, I did the only thing I could think of: infinite rounds of the breathing cadence I'd learned from Michelle.

"I *(inhale)* am *(exhale)* here *(inhale)* now *(exhale)* in *(inhale)* this *(exhale)*."

It was weird walking into my grandma and grandpa's bedroom and seeing it completely empty for the first time. It had always been exactly the same for as long as I could remember, but now, all their half-century-old furnishings were gone. The permanent impressions in the 1970s shag carpet were the only reminders of where their bed and dresser had stood for my entire life. This was their room. And now, they were gone.

Sitting on the floor to fill my air mattress, I felt a flash of peace being back in this house and especially in this room. It's like I could still feel their presence, their life, their love. It was comforting. But that feeling of peace came with a sense that staying here was going to stir something deep within me that I did not want to face.

I was right.

One afternoon during that trip, I took a short walk around the neighborhood to clear my head and get some fresh air. Walking past the same houses I flew by on my bicycle decades earlier, I was caught off guard by a sudden, powerful wave of emotion. I had gotten used to crying a lot during that season of my life, but it was usually in the context of a therapy session or in response to something like an old picture, a message from Lisa, or some other reminder of the life I'd lost. This time, though, I was just out for a walk on a nice day. I didn't know why this was happening.

I made it back to my grandparents' house and slipped into their bedroom to be alone. My baseline was sadness in those days, but this experience was different somehow. Heavier. Darker. My throat constricted. My chest was in a vise grip. I curled up in a tight ball on the floor, clutching my knees to my chest. For some reason, I felt compelled to text my parents and ask them to come sit with me. This was odd, because I always wanted to be alone during moments like this. But this time, something in me knew I'd need extra support for what was coming.

My parents entered a few minutes later. Without a word, they walked over to me, sat down on the floor on each side of me, and wrapped their arms around me just as a tsunami of tears crashed over me more violently than ever before. I was completely at the storm's mercy, unable to control where my thoughts went or even guide my emotions through this.

I had no choice but to let God show me whatever He thought I needed to see.

My first clear thought was, *This is for my grandma.* I had been so consumed with everything else that I hadn't given myself the space or permission to grieve the fact that she was gone. A carousel of memories played in my mind. Sitting at the kitchen table, licking cinnamon roll icing off my fingers while she asked me silly questions. Watching a Minnesota Twins game late into the night, followed by *The Tonight Show with Jay Leno*, and laughing together until she fell asleep in her rocking chair. Shoveling her driveway after a big snowstorm, and then looking up to see her waving me inside to warm up with a cup of hot cocoa topped with mini marshmallows.

Eventually, the memories of my grandmother faded and were replaced with scenes from my marriage.

That's when the second realization hit me: *This is about my divorce.*

It felt like everything painful about my divorce hit me full force all at once. This second set of waves pounded and tossed me around in the torment of knowing that the life I'd known and loved—my predictable little "7 out of 10" life—was gone. Forever. And now, here I was, thirty-eight years old, single, no kids, and alone, trying to figure out where I would live next and having no clear trajectory for where I was going or what I was doing.

That onslaught batted me around for a while until the mental kaleidoscope of images from my marriage faded and gave way to . . . nothing. I felt like I was *supposed* to be seeing pictures glide by, but all I saw was darkness.

This is for my future, I realized. Staring into that darkness, the third and heaviest set of waves crashed over me. In the absence of clear pictures, my greatest fears for my life ahead ran wild. I would never recover from this depression. I would never be married again. I would never again feel the loving touch of a woman. I would never be a father or a grandfather. I would never regain any sense of vitality or vigor. I would never feel genuine excitement, anticipation, or joy again.

Thinking back to that experience, I now know why the Ghost of Christmas Future was so terrifying for Ebenezer Scrooge in Charles Dickens's *A Christmas Carol.* My future was unknown and unknowable, and in that lack of certainty, all I could envision were the things I feared the most. Those "Ghosts of David's Future" tormented me. It was as though I felt the next fifty years' worth of fears all at once, concentrated into one blast of sheer torture and terror. I thought for a moment that I might never even make it off my grandparents' bedroom floor.

I hated myself for being "that guy"—the lonely and depressed son, brother, uncle, friend, and colleague. I wanted to be anywhere but here, feeling this agony that reached through my flesh, deep down into my soul. But I couldn't escape. It found me, and like a passenger on a boat being capsized by a massive swell out at sea, I had no choice but to surrender to the waves. I couldn't force them back down, and I knew intuitively that I shouldn't push them aside, no matter how much I wanted to. Part of me—maybe even the wild, untamed lion part of me that was hiding in the bushes of my soul—knew I *had* to feel this. I *had* to experience it, to open myself up to it. I had to plant my feet, stand my ground, and face the charging lion.

Eventually, the episode subsided. My breathing slowed. The tears mostly dried up. I became aware again of my surroundings and that I wasn't alone. Sensing the change in the atmosphere, my parents unfurled from their positions on the floor next to me and left me alone to collect myself.

How long have we been in here? I thought as the door closed behind them. I checked the clock on my phone: 5:23 p.m. I unlocked my phone and checked the time stamp on the text message I'd sent them, asking them to come sit with me: 3:23 p.m.

Two hours. They sat with me for two hours, holding me through this storm, lending me their strength.

But it wasn't only my parents who had held me. I realized why my most intense attack of panic and sorrow yet had hit me then and there: it was because my Grandma Verona and Grandpa Don were sitting there, holding me too. There, in the same house where they'd held me and loved me countless times throughout my life. I had feared that staying in their room would bring up new pain, and it certainly had. What I hadn't counted on was that being there would also give me their strength and support.

I heard a gentle whisper in my spirit: "This is exactly where you were supposed to be right now. This is where you were meant to really sit with your sadness and feel it all the way through." It was as though several generations of our family had surrounded me that afternoon, giving me the courage to go deeper into my pain and finally start tracking my grief.

Exhausted, I lay back down on the floor. Using a posture Michelle had taught me, I put one hand on my chest and the other on my belly, and allowed my breathing to bring me back home into my body.

"I *(inhale)* am *(exhale)* here *(inhale)* now *(exhale)* in *(inhale)* this *(exhale)*."

Although I was not expecting the raw intensity of this experience, and obviously still had a long way to go in my recovery, what happened that afternoon released something within me. It was a moment when I'd let go of my efforts to control the journey, to push the string instead of following it, to control the destination instead of finding it. Somehow, while I could not yet see exactly how and why, I knew this experience mattered. It was the first time I'd felt like I'd made a positive step in the right direction. And frankly, it felt damn good to simply let go and allow myself to be lost for a little while.

TRACKER MANUAL

Step 9: Be Open to What You Find

- Take it all in. What practices do you have that allow you to slow down and take life in?
- Pause and receive. What are you grateful for?
- Let the wave fully break. After you allow a full wave of emotion to hit you, how do you feel after you resurface?

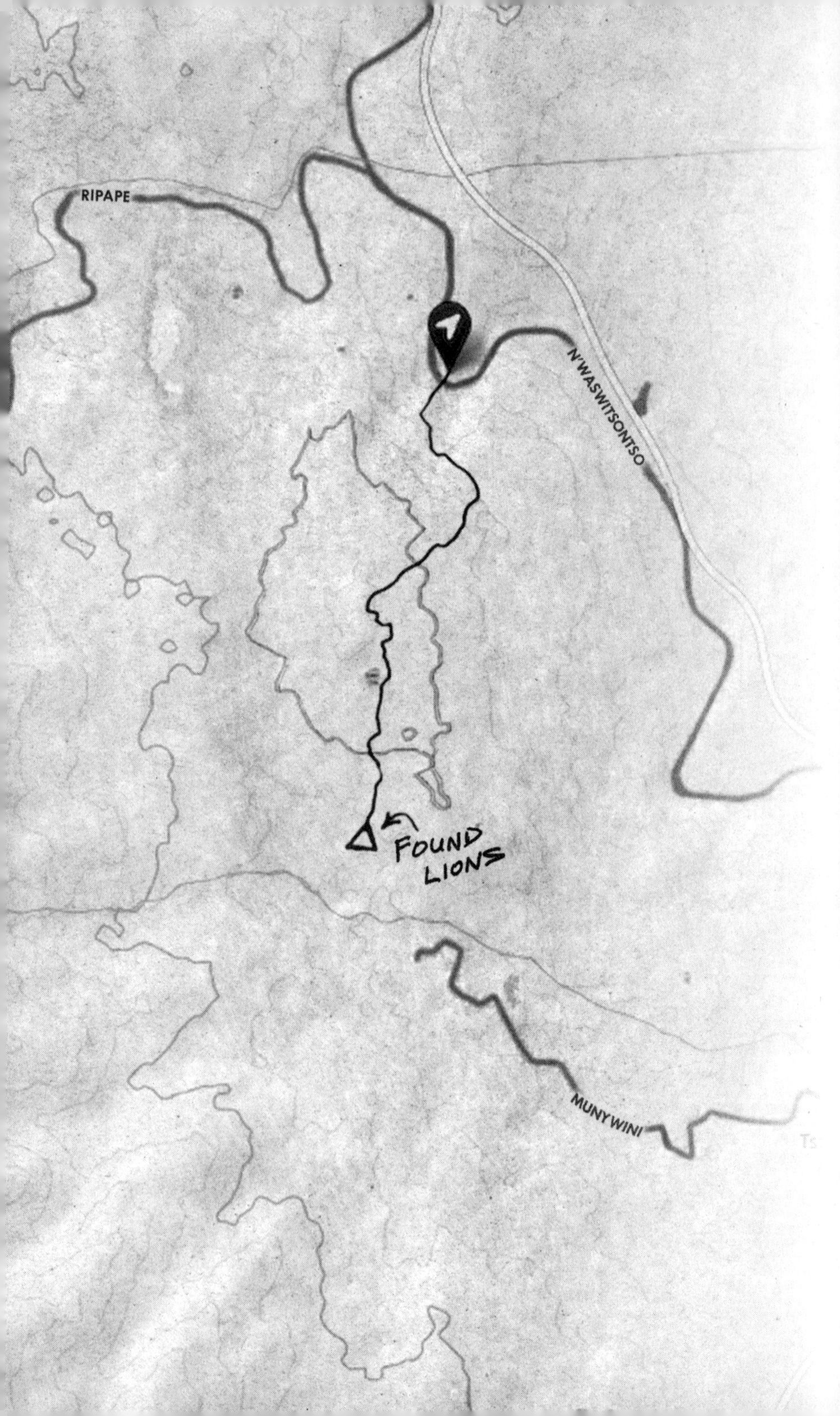
RIPAPE
N'WASWITSONTSO
FOUND LIONS
MUNYWINI

CHAPTER 10

MEET THE CHALLENGE HEAD-ON

Those who undertake the full journey into their grief come back carrying medicine for the world.

FRANCIS WELLER[13]

THE WHOLE DATING app thing is weird.

When Lisa and I first got together, there weren't a lot of dating apps out there. Online dating had been around since at least the early 2000s, but Lisa and I had met the old-fashioned way, and then I'd been married throughout the 2010s, when "app culture" really took off. So, as soon as my divorce was finalized, I had several people encouraging me to "get on the apps" to meet people. I went on a few dates and met some nice women, but nothing really clicked for me at first. I did, however, match with a woman named Emma in the spring of 2021. She seemed great, but she was in Lincoln, Nebraska, and I was in Denver. Plus, I was traveling a ton for work at the time, so we never got a chance to meet up. We exchanged a few messages every now and then, but the timing and distance never made her seem like a real possibility. But then, in September 2021, about a month after my intense emotional experience at my grandparents' house, Emma messaged me that she was going to be in Denver for several days, and she asked if I wanted to grab dinner while she was in town.

I tried to keep my expectations low. I was still new to the dating apps, but my friends who were more experienced had all warned me that most of these dates turned out to be complete flops. Worst case, though, I'd have an awkward dinner with a beautiful woman. So, why not?

When I arrived at her friend's house, where she was staying while she was in town, she burst out of the front door before I'd even made it to the porch. Walking toward me, she said, "Hi, David! It's so great to finally meet you in person!" in an alluring Portuguese accent. Her energy was incredible. She was beaming with kindness and warmth, which made her hug feel that much sweeter when she finally reached me. And her smile . . . my God. I threw all my low expectations out the window. Game on.

We made our way to the restaurant and opted for a table outside where we could soak in the ambiance of café lights, casual passersby, and a gorgeous autumn evening downtown with the changing leaves of the red maples sprinkling pops of color down the street. Right from the get-go, Emma was so easy to talk to. It all seemed too perfect, idyllic even. My mind was spinning with thoughts like, *How am I on this date right now? My life is in shambles. I'm a disaster. This was supposed to be a random, mediocre date, but here I am sitting with this girl who seems absolutely amazing.*

Our conversation flowed like we were old friends as we got to know each other over a delicious fire-roasted pizza. Emma was fun, relatable, approachable, beautiful, and interesting. I couldn't believe she was even on the dating apps. *How is this girl even available?* I kept asking myself.

While we were chatting, two older ladies strolled past us in the restaurant. They smiled as they passed, and we could see them giggling and whispering to each other. Then, one of them suddenly turned around and scurried back to our table. She bent down and said, "I just had to come back and tell you that there is just this beautiful glow around you two. It's so obvious that you're in love!" Then she hurried off, leaving us sitting there in a slightly vulnerable, certainly amusing, and exhilarating moment.

Emma and I exchanged bewildered looks. The crazy thing was, the woman's comments didn't seem *that* strange. In fact, we felt it too. Was it possible we could feel something so strong between us this quickly? Had I really been plucked out of my misery and darkness and dropped into a new relationship made of pure light and joy? Just when it seemed the tracks were nowhere to be found, like I was wandering aimlessly in the wilderness, maybe the lions were closer than I ever could have imagined.

Leaving the restaurant, we passed by a wall emblazoned with neon letters that had obviously been set up as a photo backdrop for tourists and young lovers. Emma, acting as though she hadn't gotten a good look at it, asked, "Hey, what did that sign say?"

I turned around and read it out loud: "'I like where this is going.'"

"Me too," she replied with a flirty smirk, turning her back to me and strolling a few steps ahead, practically calling me to catch back up to her.

I don't know what is happening tonight, I thought, *but I am so into this*.

It was wonderful to feel so light, so alive again. I quickly caught up to her and took her hand. Our eyes found each other's, and the pain and grief I'd been drowning in vanished. Nothing else existed as I looked into her eyes. Time seemed to stand still as we stayed in the moment and let the unspoken chemistry we both clearly felt linger between us. Strolling down the city streets on a flawless Denver fall night, all I could think was, *This is a new track I want to follow.*

Two days later, I texted her and invited her to join me for a hike, and she immediately responded with an enthusiastic "Yes!"

Emma and I spent the day together trekking up Emerald Lake Trail. We talked the entire day, and I never felt a lull in the conversation. One topic flowed into the next effortlessly, and it felt really, really nice to have that kind of connection with someone. The whole day was filled with connection, laughs, and surprisingly deep conversation. To top it off, she was willing to do an impromptu cold plunge with me, jumping off a twenty-foot high ledge into the freezing cold mountain lake. I don't think I'd ever seen anyone look more beautiful than she did emerging from the frigid waters that day. It was one of the most—if not *the* most—fun, romantic dates I've ever had.

I fell hard and fast for Emma, and I couldn't help but wonder if maybe she was the answer to my prayers. Maybe meeting her would be the tipping point in my grief journey. Maybe the worst was over. Maybe Emma would be the catalyst for all the healing I'd been working and praying for all year. Or maybe I was fooling myself. How could I know? How could I trust any of this?

I tried my hardest to push the doubt and fear out of my mind and focus only on the positive. I had this amazing, kind, energetic, and gorgeous woman in my life. And she *wanted* me—she wanted to spend time with me, to talk to me, to share all the big and small parts of her life with me. Feeling truly wanted like that—not tolerated, but genuinely pursued and wanted—was intoxicating. It felt like a cold drink of water in the desert. It made me realize how long it had been since I'd felt that . . . if I ever had at all.

Emma and I lived in different cities, but we fell into a serious, committed relationship almost immediately. How could we not? It was like destiny itself was bringing us together. A month into the relationship, we made plans to rent a place in San Diego for an extended working vacation. We both had the flexibility to work from anywhere, so we met in San Diego and spent five weeks working next to each other during the day and taking in the sights of Southern California every night and weekend. She spent Thanksgiving and Christmas with me and my family in Denver, and I traveled to meet her family in early December for her birthday. Everyone accepted us as a couple, and it seemed like the writing was on the wall for us.

I was so thrilled about where this string was leading me, and I couldn't wait to get there.

WHOLEHEARTED (UN)CERTAINTY

Right when we met, Emma had told me she had a three-month trip out of the country planned that she was excited about. She was set to leave right after Christmas, less than three months after we started dating. As we grew closer, she considered canceling her trip. She didn't want to risk interrupting the incredible momentum of our new relationship so soon. However, I wasn't comfortable with her making that kind of decision just because of me. I knew she'd been looking forward to this trip for a long time, and besides, it was just three months. It wasn't ideal, but it was manageable. We could still talk on the phone and FaceTime, so I figured it wouldn't be that different than what we did when she and I were each home in our respective cities. So, she left the country just before New Year's, and we settled into a new, longer-distance relationship for a while.

Despite the joys of this wonderful new relationship, this was such a confusing time for me. Every day, I was flipping back and forth between such strong competing emotions. One moment, I'd be dreaming of a "happily ever after" with Emma. The next, I'd feel like I was falling off a cliff into a pit of fear and shame. I was so disoriented all the time, moving left, right, forward, backward, upside-down, and inside-out all at once. I was strapped into an emotional rollercoaster that never ended, and now, I was taking this amazing woman along for the ride.

I truly loved Emma, but the death of my old life sat so heavily on my heart and mind. It was a pitch-black cloud that smothered every other thought and emotion. I hadn't kept all this a secret from Emma, though. I'd been honest with her about what was going on with me, and she'd been an angel about it all. She had reassured me several times that she wasn't afraid to walk through these difficulties with me—as long as we both remained completely honest with each other. That was a commitment

I took seriously—which led me to a devastating discussion in January 2022, not long after she'd left the country.

"I don't know how to explain it," I said, struggling to spit the words out. Emma's face was perfectly framed in the small, glowing screen of my iPhone. "I care about you so much, but I am really struggling inside. For reasons I cannot figure out or explain—even to myself—something is not settling for me. And the truth is, I cannot look you in the eyes and say I'm truly *all in* on us. It breaks my heart to say this, but I promised you I would always be honest with you about this."

By the time I got that much out, Emma and I both had tears streaming down our faces.

"David . . . I don't understand. I thought. . . ." Her words trailed off as she lowered her head, cradling her beautiful face in her hands. She was quiet for a moment before drawing a big breath and releasing a pained sigh. She looked up with resolve in her eyes and said the words I knew were coming.

"If you cannot tell me with wholehearted certainty that you're all in on this relationship, then I just can't do this."

There was nothing left to say. The relationship I had once thought would save me from my grief was over.

I didn't want to let her go. I desperately wanted every ounce of my being to align and feel "right" with her, but it just didn't. I was raging inside. Here was this gorgeous, kind woman who wanted to be with me, but for reasons I couldn't for the life of me figure out, I felt a disconnect. I hated myself for it. I hated that I couldn't make myself feel what I deeply wanted to feel. I hated that I couldn't get out of this hole that seemed to be pulling me down just when I sensed I was close to gripping the edge to pull myself out.

Isn't that what grief is like? Wanting so badly for something to be different than it is, for the person you lost to be by your side again, for the diagnosis to disappear, for the accident to have never happened? I'm convinced grief is the most agonizing of human emotions. It has no sense of time, hitting you hard when you aren't expecting it and staying quiet when you are. Sometimes, it fades into the background; other times, it storms to the surface. It gives no prolonged sense of peace. It may sit idly by for a day or a week, giving you a glimpse of what a rich, fully happy life could be like, but then it roars back to life, reminding you of how much you've lost.

This was me—drowning again in the grief I had tried to ignore. I just couldn't see it clearly yet.

THE SADNESS THAT IS CALLING YOU

That same month, with the trauma of my divorce now compounded by my feelings of guilt and loss over ending my relationship with Emma, I began seeing a new therapist, Syanna. By that point, I'd given up trying to control everything and had settled into a long-term, slow and mostly steady attitude about my healing journey. The persistent and overbearing grief, the suicidal ideation, a frightening crash in my sex drive (covered thoroughly in chapter 8), and a corresponding loss of vigor and vitality had driven me to find more help through different therapeutic modalities.

Syanna had been an absolute godsend and had introduced me to somatic therapy, nervous system therapy, internal family systems (IFS), and "parts work," which had begun to help me see some shifts and improvement in my body and mental state.

One day, about nine months into our counseling relationship, I showed up to our weekly session feeling a lot of sadness and frustration about how slowly the process was going.

"I'm so frustrated that I'm feeling this heaviness again," I said. "In the last few weeks, I've really noticed an improvement in the intensity of my sadness and grief, and I thought I was past this. It feels like I'm taking ten steps back."

She listened and nodded understandingly, then asked, "Why not just go and meet the sadness that is calling for you?"

My immediate reaction was confusion as I tried to wrap my brain around what she'd just said.

"Why would I want to go and meet my sadness?" I asked. "That sounds like a terrible idea."

"We dishonor our emotions when we avoid them," she explained. "They are there, showing up for a reason. The way we honor ourselves and work our way through emotions is by meeting them—by feeling them."

My face softened, and my eyes opened wider as I took in everything she was saying. She went on to describe how the way we experience emotions often resembles a bell curve: It can start small and subtle but then grow rapidly in strength and intensity. Amusement can grow into exuberance. Hesitation can grow into terror. Nervousness can grow into panic. Embarrassment can grow into shame. Annoyance can grow into rage. She said, "It is at this point—especially with unpleasant emotions like anger, sadness, shame, and grief—that most people jump off the bell curve by distracting themselves in some way, such as with drugs, alcohol, sex, social media, entertainment, or even busyness."

Syanna paused to study my reaction and could see that I was locked into what she was saying. I'd never heard anyone describe emotions like this before, but it was making perfect sense.

She continued, "But when we stay with the emotion as it intensifies, right up to the peak of the bell curve and down the other side, we allow the entire experience to pass through us like an ocean wave. And if we are willing to really *feel* that emotion all the way through, as it surges up to its peak and then gradually settles back down, we often experience a huge insight about ourselves and the whole experience."

I sat there speechless, processing what she'd just explained.

To use Syanna's analogy, I'd spent two years trying to outswim the wave when what I really needed to do was let it pick me up and carry me for a while as it passed over, around, and through me. It seemed so obvious, yet it pierced me to my core. It was one of those moments of clarity that you wait for in therapy: when the fog you've been wading through for months or years finally clears and you're able to see a reality you've been blind to for God knows how long.

I could so clearly see that all this time—since the moment Lisa told me she wanted a divorce—I had been doing everything I could to avoid my sadness, distract myself from it, or attempt to control it.

Even though I'd let the tears flow. And flow. And flow. And flow some more.

Even though I'd talked to therapists for hours on end.

Even though I'd moved my body and focused on my breath.

Even though I'd poured my heart out to a horse named Cody.

Even though I'd done what I thought were all the right things . . . I had never welcomed my sadness and grief. I'd never looked it in the eye and befriended it. I'd never just sat with it and given it the chance to tell me whatever it wanted to communicate.

Well . . . *almost* never.

My mind flashed to one year earlier, when I had sat on my grandparents' bedroom floor in the aftermath of an intense, two-hour emotional event I couldn't explain. I remembered feeling something after my parents left me sitting there that I never would have expected: relief. That was easily one of the most painful experiences of my life, but I could not deny that I felt a tremendous sense of calm and relief when it was over. Now, I had a way to describe it: That was probably the one time I had sat still and allowed a wave of grief to approach, rise, and fall without fighting against it. It was one of my first experiences of surrendering to the grief that rose up to meet me.

Maybe that was what this whole experience was trying to show me. Maybe that was where these tracks had been leading me. Maybe the lion I'd been looking for was waiting for me just on the other side of grief's bell curve.

Spoiler alert: It was.

TRACKER MANUAL

Step 10: Meet the Challenge Head-On

- What pain are you trying to outrun instead of meeting it head-on?
- Which emotion do you habitually avoid when it starts to rise?
- When have you allowed an emotion to fully rise and fall—and what happened on the other side?
- If grief is a track, not a dead end, where might it be leading you?

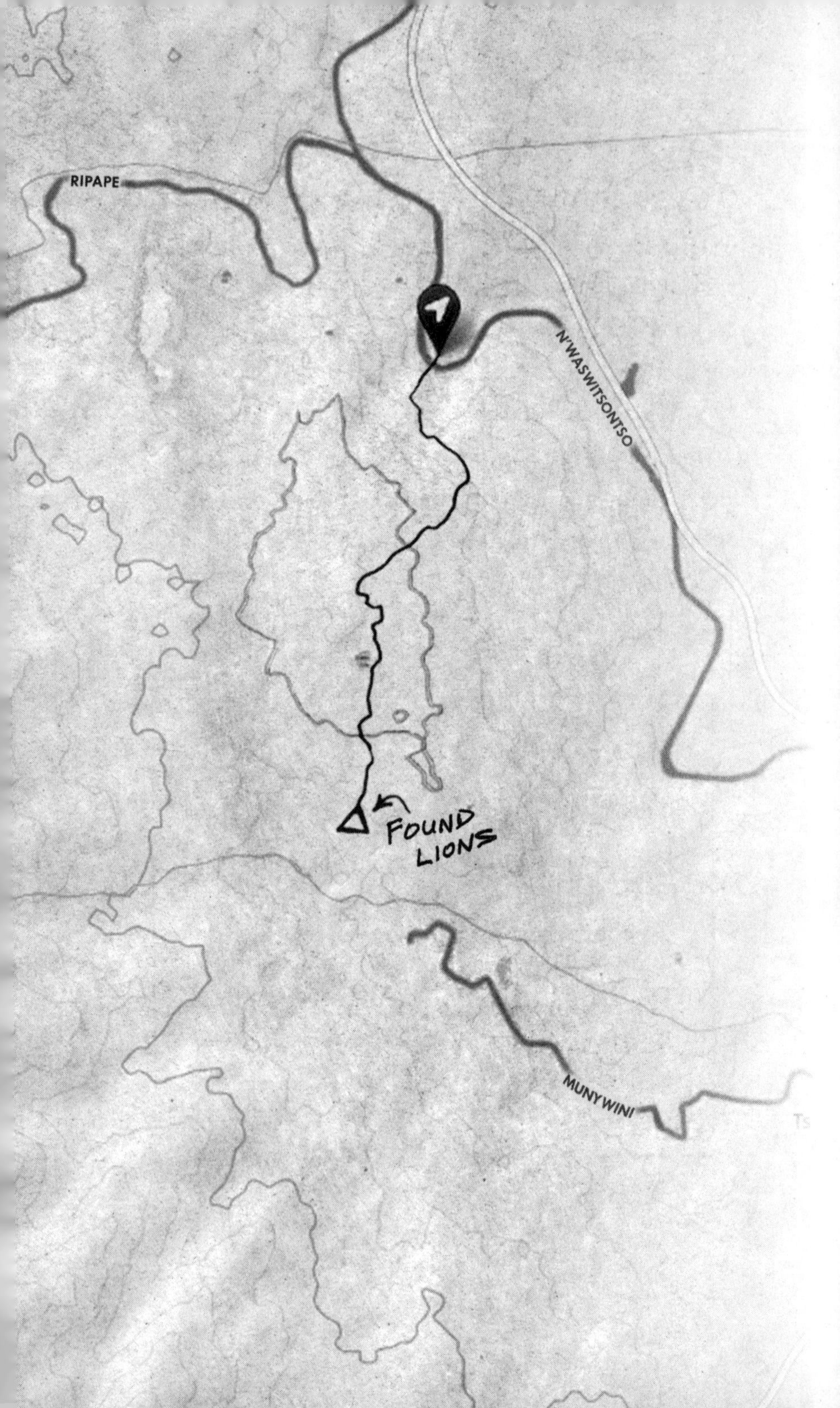

RIPAPE
N'WASWITSONTSO
FOUND
LIONS
MUNYWINI
Ts

CHAPTER 11

WELCOME IT IN

We must learn to read the subtle tracks of the body, the way it relaxes and opens when something feels right, the contraction and tightness when we are not where we are meant to be. . . . Bringing attention back to the landscape of the body allows you to find the trail of the wild self.

BOYD VARTY[14]

GREAT TRACKERS HAVE a saying: "Good tracks have an energy to them that you *feel* in your body."

When it comes to following the tracks of life, though, that doesn't mean the tracks make you feel *good*. In fact, the tracks of our lives can lead us through the darkest, scariest, and most painful places imaginable. But the best thing we can do in those times is also the hardest thing: Keep going.

One thing we work on with our clients at Novus Global is helping them see that life tracking isn't just about finding what makes you happy; it's about discovering and connecting with the most vibrant, fulfilled version of yourself. It's about learning how to attune to and follow what ignites a feeling of excitement and aliveness within your body, rather than chasing external results or pinning your hopes for happiness on "stuff" or other people. And it's about following those tracks—the string—wherever they lead.

As I recounted in the previous chapter, my therapist, Syanna, added a new dimension to my understanding of life tracking when she introduced me to the bell curve analogy. She made me realize that a big part of life tracking is learning to feel your feelings all the way through, including your sadness, anger, grief, and fear. That string is so difficult to follow, but it can lead to profound insights. In fact, the darkest parts of the trail can often lead you to the clearest vision of who you are.

ENERGIZED IN AFRICA

October 2022

A month after Syanna had challenged me to "go out and meet my sadness."

Fourteen months since someone had asked me at a Napa Valley networking event, "What is something you have wanted to do for a long time but haven't done yet?" The answer had popped into my head before the guy even finished asking the question: I wanted to go on a safari. I wanted to be with the lions in the wild.

And now, the time had finally come.

I stepped off the plane and took the biggest breath my lungs would allow. I held the life-giving African air in my lungs as long as I could before releasing a long, slow exhale.

Aaaaaah.

It had taken four different flights and thirty hours of travel time to get to Zimbabwe. I should have felt exhausted, but I wasn't. In fact, I would've felt just as invigorated stepping off that plane if it had taken twice as long to get here.

The ground here felt different beneath my feet. I felt wildness coming up from the earth, as if I were pulling the vibrancy and spirit of Africa right out of the soil and into my body. My nervous system was buzzing with this fresh infusion of almost supernatural energy and vitality.

Part of me couldn't believe I was actually here, that I'd actually gone through with it. If I'm honest, it had always felt like a *someday* kind of thing. You know what I'm talking about—the kind of idea that lives only in fantasy, the thing we love to daydream about, the thing we tell ourselves we'll do "when I can afford it" or "when the kids graduate" or "when I retire." But a conversation with a friend who lives in South Africa unexpectedly led me to take this fantasy off the shelf and finally make it a reality.

She told me she knew of someone who led safaris on foot and offered to put me in touch with him. The next thing I knew, I had specific dates, prices, and booking details staring at me from my email inbox. The closest word I can come up with to describe how I felt is *giddy*. I felt like a six-year-old whose parents had just told him they were on their way to Disneyland!

But then, the doubts and fears flooded my brain. Could I take the time off work? Was it wise to go so far from home by myself when I was still dealing with so much depression and anxiety?

You know how, oftentimes, once you make a big decision to go through with something—book the trip, sign up for the race, start the business—all sorts of things start popping up unexpectedly to throw a wrench in your plans? Well, my plans for my first safari got hit with a *huge* wrench. Professionally speaking, it was the wrench of a lifetime.

For my entire career, I had been working to break into the professional sports market—specifically the National Hockey League (NHL). I'd literally been knocking on that door for ten years. My good friend and colleague Dan Leffelaar had begun working with professional athletes and had built a new division at our firm called Novus Global Sport that was focused on coaching athletes on the mental side of the game. Within weeks after booking my trip, Dan had invited me to join him in leading a training with an NHL team. It was the biggest opportunity yet in my career, but I couldn't do it *and* the safari. I spent days agonizing over what to do. I had so much fear and scarcity-thinking creeping in, and I couldn't make up my mind. What if I made the wrong decision? What if I never got this opportunity again? I was stuck.

Then, one night while I was mulling it over, I suddenly saw myself at fifteen years old at the Henry Doorly Zoo in Omaha, Nebraska. I was standing in front of the lion enclosure, gazing into the eyes of a living, breathing lion for the first time in my life. Captivated by his presence. Baffled by how massive his head was. Unable to look away and break our intense eye contact.

With that flash from my past, I knew my answer. I needed to go be with the lions in the wild. The subtle tracks of my body were confirming it. I couldn't fully explain it, but it was almost as if the creature moving at the other end of the string—the one I'd been trying to find as I searched through the darkness of the last two years—was calling for me. It was like the energy of the lion had reached me from thousands of miles away, leaping time and dimensions to convince me to come find him.

I committed to the trip and felt a jolt of electricity surge through my veins. By the time I landed in Zimbabwe, that little jolt had grown into a full-scale lightning storm. The contrast between the excitement I felt about this trip and what I felt about literally everything else in my life was laughable. Back home, I'd still been struggling with suicidal ideation. But here, I felt more alive than I'd ever felt in my life. It's funny, life is never *all one thing*, is it? Even in the midst of our darkest struggles, we can get such blinding flashes of light and life.

That's how I found myself standing here now, on my way to Mana Pools National Park to fulfill a lifelong dream of tracking lions on foot in the wild.

Not one thing in the past two years—since my life had fallen apart—had felt this *right*. I was learning to listen to my nervous system and follow it even when it felt irrational. Syanna's advice about meeting my sadness rang in my ears as I looked across the African plains and thought, *What if that's why I'm here? What if whatever I'm supposed to find is out there right now, hiding in the bushes and waiting to be discovered?*

"YOU WANNA GO SEE SOME LIONS?"

As I mentioned in chapter 2, a guide from the safari company picked us up at the airstrip and loaded our small group of explorers into an old, open-air Land Rover for the twenty-five-minute drive to our camp. As we drove over the bumpy dirt roads, enjoying the afternoon sun, eyes peeled for wildlife, I noticed another safari vehicle coming toward us. The driver signaled to our driver to stop. They seemed to know each other. The other guy got out of his vehicle, walked toward us, and started chatting with our driver. I was immediately annoyed, and the frustration and irritation I thought I'd left behind at home jumped right back to the front of my mind.

Who is this guy? I thought. *Why is he stopping us? Enough chitchat. I'm here to be on safari. Let's get going so we can drop off our luggage and have the chance to still get out on a game drive. I'm here to see some lions!*

Just then, as my impatience was getting the best of me, the guy from the other vehicle looked back to where the other safari guests and I were sitting. With a smirk and a glimmer of excitement in his eye, this stranger leaned in close, like he had a secret to share with us.

"You wanna go see some lions?"

That's how I met Stretch, the master guide I introduced earlier in this book.

"Yes!" I screamed, answering for the group without checking with them first. "How far away are they? Are we going to walk or drive? Actually, I don't care. Let's just go!"

I had not been that excited about anything for as long as I could remember—and certainly not in the past couple of years. My inner child was tired of being trapped beneath a mountain of grown-up worries and was more than ready to take charge for a while. I was unabashedly excited, fully free to show up as authentically as I once did as a child. It felt so natural, so right, as if this version of me—the real me—had finally woken up and taken the steering wheel of my life.

We were literally minutes from the airport, and our adventure had already begun. All our luggage was still rattling around in the back of the Land Rover with us, we hadn't seen our camp, and we hadn't even signed our don't-sue-us-if-you-get-eaten-by-a-lion legal forms yet. This was happening so quickly, in fact, that I wondered if Stretch was just playing a joke on us.

We left our stuff in the Land Rover and followed Stretch on foot. He pointed out a herd of Cape buffalo in the distance, and I saw a majestic bateleur eagle fly overhead. This was a completely different world from the one I lived in. And yet . . . no lions. We'd gone maybe two miles into the jungle when my childlike enthusiasm began to fade just a bit. The impatience that comes from a life lived in our fast-paced, high-tech, instant-gratification culture crept in, and I began to give up on the idea of seeing the lions that day.

It's not a total loss, though, I reminded myself. Simply being here, standing in the bush in Africa, knowing there could be lions within a few hundred yards in any direction of where I was standing—the anticipation and thrill of it—that was an experience in itself for me.

And then, another thought hit me unexpectedly—a thought I never would have imagined having at that point in my life:

I like this version of me, the David who is present in the moment and believes in magic.

I smiled to myself as I felt my nervous system relax another notch.

We approached a slight hill, and Stretch motioned for us to come closer, as if he knew something special was nearby. Had his six-foot-seven vantage point revealed something to him that we hadn't noticed yet? *Is it a lion?* I wondered. And more importantly: *What do I do if it is a lion? We haven't even had our safety lesson yet!*

My heart pounded so intensely that I thought for sure Stretch could hear it.

Stretch whispered, "Stay close. Move slowly. Stay low."

I crept up the slope ahead and peered down the other side. There, under the shade of a baobab tree about thirty yards away, was a pride of five lions.

Oh my God! There they are! Right in front of me!

I was mesmerized, in absolute awe that shifted into slight terror once the pride spotted me. The male stood up to get a better look. He fixed his eyes on me and let out a low growl. I felt the rumble of his displeasure travel across the distance between us, almost as if it reverberated through the ground, up through the soles of my feet, and right into the center of my being. It held so much power, strength, and confidence. It was as though he knew a roar wasn't even necessary. He simply stood up and did what little he needed to do to tell us, "I see you."

His raw, primal energy hit me in waves. It was intoxicating.

"One of them got up," I whispered to Stretch, as if he needed my insight.

"I know," he replied. "Stay still and low. Don't turn your back. He's just checking you out. He's just a big cat, after all, and cats are curious."

Inhale.

Exhale.

I am here now in this.

As I knelt on the ground and soaked in the lions' energy, it struck me that it wasn't just the lions that I was taking in. I was allowing myself to "take in" the fullness of my joy and excitement of the moment.

My mind jumped back to that therapy session I'd had with Syanna a few weeks earlier, when she'd explained the bell curve of emotions. She'd said that the bell curve wasn't just for the unpleasant emotions; it was for all emotions.

I had to learn to welcome not just the anger, sadness, fear, disappointment, and shame—but the joy, contentment, love, excitement, and happiness too. Jumping off the curve and refusing to fully feel everything was the problem.

It was *my* problem. Crouched in the dirt overlooking a pride of wild lions, I realized that I'd forgotten how to let myself feel the goodness of life. In trying to survive the intensity of the "bad" emotions, I'd turned down my experience of *all* emotions. I'd tried to escape the valleys, and in doing so, I'd flattened my experience of . . . everything.

Inhale.

Exhale.

I am here now in this.

But this time, being "here now in this" meant raising the volume of my emotions. Staring at that pride of lions, I welcomed the joy in and let myself just feel it *all the way through.*

Having grown up feeling mostly disconnected from my body, it felt really nice to be present to what joy actually felt like—and to know that this might be part of how God speaks to us.

Not a bad way to spend the first few hours of my first tracking safari.

COMFORT IS A 13,000-POUND ELEPHANT

I woke up at 4:30 the next morning to the sound of hippos grunting right on the other side of my thin tent wall. You'd think a lifelong suburbanite like me would have been a little nervous, but I wasn't—at all. I lay in my bed, smiling to myself and thinking, *I'm here. I'm actually doing this. What could be better than having wild hippos serve as my alarm clock for a whole week?*

It was still dark, so I stayed in bed listening to the hippos and imagined they were inviting me to come hang out with them near the river—that they, like the rest of nature, were as happy to enjoy my company as I was theirs.

As the sun slowly lit up my tent and the sounds of the hippos moved further into the distance, I got ready for the first full day of my walking safari adventure. It was surreal that I had already seen a pride of lions within less than twenty-four hours of being here. I'd heard stories of people who, like me, had made this trip from across the globe and never once caught a glimpse of a lion. It wasn't lost on me how extraordinary this trip already was, and I wasn't even a full day in yet. Just thinking about the lions from the day before built my anticipation and excitement for what was in store for me today.

I unzipped my tent door and cautiously peeked my head out to look around for any animals that might have wandered into camp. Since the campsite was just a small area with tents and an eating area with a firepit with no fence around it, literally any wild animal—hippo, elephant, leopard, lion, mamba, hyena, or otherwise—could wander through, day or night. So I had to be alert at all times, even when we were "safe" at camp.

It looked clear, so I stepped out of the tent and looked around again, then took a few more steps, scanning the area around me and the nearby bushes to make sure it was safe. I didn't know a lot, but I knew that if I ever found myself between a hippo and the water (its safety zone), I was in big trouble. No hippos in sight, though. It was all clear.

As I walked through the sand that surrounded the campsite toward the deck that overlooked the Zambezi River, I noticed a huge, round crater in the sand where a hippo must have slept before trudging back into the river. *Who knows?* I thought. *Maybe that was the one that woke me up.* I then noticed what looked to be elephant tracks that led straight across the camp right between two of the tents, and I could just imagine the big lumbering fellow slowly wandering through, looking for foliage to snack on, unbeknownst to all of us as we slept peacefully in our tents.

The rest of the guests and I had our morning coffee and a light breakfast out on the deck, and then it was time to head out for the day's tracking.

The plan for each day was pretty simple: We'd start in the Land Rovers, looking for signs of lion tracks, elephants, rhinos, and other creatures in the wilderness. Once we'd found clear evidence of some activity, we'd get out and spend most of the daylight hours tracking on foot. Stretch welcomed us that first morning with what I'd come to learn was his typical morning greeting: "Okay, guys, let's get serious," while he grinned ear to ear. He clearly loved this job. It was his life. It was his joy and utter delight. I noticed the vigor with which he showed up each day, even after doing this for thirty years, and it gave me hope that maybe I'd find a way to have that type of fulfillment, awe, and enthusiasm in each of my own days—and that maybe the wonderment of this safari wouldn't wear off.

Mana Pools National Park spans nearly a thousand square miles and is known for incredible, close encounters with wild elephants and lions. On this particular day, we set out first to find some elephants. As we drove, Stretch taught us a bit about the elephants. I always loved listening to him speak, with a beautiful Zimbabwean accent that graced each word.

"Elephants in the wild can be incredibly dangerous if you don't know what you're doing and how to read their body language," he explained. "You never want to approach a female elephant, particularly one that has a young one nearby. They are extremely protective, and they will almost undoubtedly charge at you, even from long distances away. So, most often, we find the male elephants who tend to be off by themselves. The key is that you never want to walk directly at an elephant. We will go and sit down at a point along his presumed path and let him interact with us on his terms. That way, if the elephant comes closer, it indicates that he is comfortable with us being there and feels safe in our presence. He gets to dictate how close he gets to us."

Stretch went on to answer questions and share the expansive insider knowledge he had about elephants. I was enamored and awed by the breadth of what he knew and the stories he told of insanely close encounters with elephants on foot. I clung to each word, wanting to soak it in and make the absolute most of this entire experience.

Amazingly, Stretch knew the land and the elephants at Mana Pools so well that within just an hour of leaving camp, we were able to find a solo male elephant Stretch had named Boswell. We parked the Land Rover a good distance away from Boswell, got out of the vehicle, and followed Stretch's lead. We walked to a spot that lay in the direction the elephant was walking in as he moved from tree to tree, eating leaves and seed pods. Stretch directed us to sit down on a fallen tree and quietly, calmly watch Boswell, allowing him to approach us if he wanted to. My heart raced with excitement. *This is absolutely insane*, I thought. This elephant weighed thirteen thousand pounds and could crush me in a second with one wrong step or moment of displeasure. And here I was, waiting for him to come closer to me.

Adrenaline shot through my system, and I loved it.

I sat there taking quiet, deep breaths to slow my nervous system, hoping to exude a calm energy and presence. Boswell noticed us and slowly began to approach. It seemed like he was happy to see us. I got goosebumps. He kept an eye on us as he moved in our direction, stopping for a snack at each tree as he slowly sauntered closer.

I began to feel his presence once he got within thirty yards of us. His energy felt even heavier and more grounded than his thirteen-thousand-pound frame. He came closer and closer, stopping about ten yards from us for another snack. He reached his trunk up to grab some branches, ripped them from the tree, and then pulled them into his mouth to chew.

Stretch taught us how to watch Boswell's body language, explaining that we could tell how calm and relaxed he was by the way he was moving. My whole being was locked in. When a wild elephant is ten yards from where you're sitting on the ground, you don't dare look away for even a second! Every few moments, Boswell would take a peek at us. And then, when I felt like there was no way he could get any closer, he did. He was inching closer than I'd ever imagined in all my daydreams about this kind of safari—stopping so close to me that his trunk nearly hit my knee. I just sat there, looking up at him in awe and nearly shaking with nerves, knowing that if he took one more step, I'd become a permanent part of the Mana Pools National Park terrain.

Stretch whispered to us to stay calm, sit still, and just take it in. My nervous system began to calm as I looked up at Boswell and felt a connection with him. And almost as if it were an instinctive reaction, I said hi to him—not verbally, so as not to scare him, but with my body's energy and presence. I could have sworn he understood my greeting. There was this pause, this powerful sense that we were just two beings who'd wonderfully crossed paths on our journeys today, and I let it in.

I stared up at this massive wild animal—clearly seeing his long eyelashes, the sparse, coarse hairs on his head, and the texture of his skin—arguably feeling more alive and alert in my body than I have ever been in my life. A thought came to me, further solidifying what Syanna had taught me. For the last two years, I'd thought grief would take my life, that it was too big, too heavy. But what if my grief was more like Boswell? What if it wasn't the rampaging monster I thought it was? What if it simply wanted to slowly, calmly come beside me and just . . . sit with me?

Could I welcome my grief the way I'd just welcomed this enormous, semi-frightening, and magnificent creature? Could I look up at my grief and see its texture, scars, and tears without trying to run it off—or running away myself? Could I let it reveal something new to me about myself that I had never seen before?

What if, I thought, *my grief isn't out to get me? What if it's just been trying to teach me something all this time?*

Boswell interrupted my train of thought for a moment, swinging his trunk right in front of my face as he reached up to grab some more leaves. Feeling the *whoosh* of that mighty trunk swing inches from my nose, I became acutely aware of another layer to all of this: my powerlessness. I was entirely defenseless against this elephant. In the same way, I was powerless against the enormity of my grief and depression. I'd never try to kick, scream, and fight my way through this elephant, so what made me think I could force my way through my grief? The idea of me pressing my shoulder into Boswell's massive leg and shoving him out of the way was laughable, but wasn't that what I'd been trying to do with my pain? Wasn't that the whole goal of that five-week healing intensive I'd tried a year earlier? I hadn't wanted to sit with my grief back then; I'd wanted to kill it. But that was futile. All I could really do was sit there with my grief, "taking it in," as Stretch always told us to do with nature, and feel what I was feeling all the way through. Then, after my grief and I had shared a moment and I'd learned what it wanted to show me, it would slowly wander off, just like Boswell did several minutes later.

I inhaled deeply and let out a long, slow exhale, thanking Boswell the elephant for helping me find more healing.

LEARNING TO FACE THE LION

By the end of the first full day of our safari, I felt like I'd already gotten ten times my money's worth. Seeing the pride of lions the day I arrived, followed by my experience with Boswell the next day, was already more than I had hoped for. And it wasn't just the "cool factor" of being there in the wild with these creatures; it was the lessons they had taught me in our short time together. I could have gone home after that, feeling perfectly content with my first walking safari experience.

I never would have imagined the revelations I'd have missed, though. Because the fourth day of the safari literally (yes, *literally*) changed my life.

That was the day a wild, angry lion charged at me for the first time—when my life had flashed before my eyes in a heightened state of awareness that was unlike anything I'd ever experienced. I told this story in chapter 2, so I won't repeat it here. What I didn't tell you earlier, though, is the extent of the life-changing impact that experience had on me.

The reality of my finite existence hit me in full force that day. I realized, maybe for the first time, that I will not live forever. I'd always *known* that, of course. But this was the first time in my life when I really *felt* it—the reality that my physical life on this earth will one day come to an end. At that point, I'll have done everything I will ever do. And one thing became crystal clear during my few days in the wild: Until that time comes, I didn't want to just survive. I didn't want to live a trapped, domesticated, caged life. I wanted to *really live*. I wanted to *feel alive*. I wanted to live wild and free, far beyond the 1–10 life I described earlier in the book.

"The lions are afraid of your courage."

Those words echoed in my head all night as I lay in my tent.

"The lions are afraid of *your* courage."

I knew he was referring to standing my ground during the charge, but in light of everything I'd been wading through the last two years, there was so much more to it for me. I felt a whole new level of courage welling up from deep within me.

It became obvious to me that this trip wasn't just about fulfilling a lifelong dream. It was about learning how to truly live, about tracking my own lions and standing my ground against them. It was about welcoming the lions and going out to meet them face-to-face, whatever the circumstances—the good moments and the challenging ones—whether the lions in my life were relaxing under the shade of a tree or defending the kill of the day.

My tent was pitch black. I couldn't see anything—but I could hear *everything*. The birds, bugs, and creatures of the night singing, chirping, and chomping—some even just outside my tent. As I listened, I thought, *I wonder how often God speaks to us through His Creation just to help us heal?*

So many times since I'd arrived at Mana Pools, I had heard God whispering to me. During each of the encounters I'd had with lions, leopards, elephants, hippos, African wild dogs, and even a snake, I heard this gentle voice in my spirit: "Just let it in. . . . Let the healing in. . . . Don't rush it. . . . Nature is never in a rush. . . . Don't force it. . . . Just learn to feel it."

As hard as it was, I did just that: I let it in—all of it. All the pain. All the sadness. All the grief and loss for what was and what could have been. I welcomed it, just as Syanna had taught me, inviting it in so it could pass through me, do its work on me, and leave me changed by the experience.

It was no coincidence that I realized all of this here, in this place, at this time. This is where I was supposed to be. This is where my tracks had led me. There was no doubt that God had brought me here. I even wondered for a moment if He'd created Mana Pools and all its animals specifically for this trip, this moment, just to help me learn how to truly heal.

BACK TO (MY) LIFE, BACK TO (MY) REALITY

I spent my final night in Mana Pools staring into the campfire and reflecting on how fortunate—how *blessed*—I was to have spent the past six days immersed in pure wonder and discovery. I couldn't believe how this experience had far exceeded every expectation I'd had for the trip. As grateful as I was, though, I also felt a growing sense of loss. I was dreading getting back on the plane and flying far away from the magic of this place.

I didn't want to move on from the state of peace I had found.

I didn't want to go back to my reality.

Then, as the flames of the campfire danced and reached up toward heaven, a calm, reassuring thought came to me fully formed, as though Mana Pools itself was whispering encouragement to me before I left. *If God could create this amazing place and all these wondrous animals*, I thought, *maybe He can create beauty and wonder in my life again. Maybe I can find a way to trust life and rediscover joy, even in the most challenging circumstances. Maybe I'm not destined for a mediocre life after all. And maybe, just maybe, I don't have to leave this wild-for-a-week feeling here in Africa when I go home.*

There was peace and comfort in the thought—but not enough to wipe away the creeping sadness in the pit of my stomach at the thought of getting back to my "real" life at home. I had mentally and emotionally crammed my entire life inside a lockbox for the last six days, and now I had to unlock it. How would it feel to go home? What opportunities at work had I missed out on? How would things feel . . . with Emma?

Yes, Emma. The same Emma who'd appeared like a beam of light into my life just thirteen months earlier. The same Emma I'd quickly fallen into a serious relationship with. The same Emma whom I'd broken up with over FaceTime in January, ten months earlier. That breakup hadn't lasted.

When she returned home from her three-month trip out of the country, we reconnected and quickly fell into the same kind of amazing, comfortable, familiar, and loving relationship we'd established right after we met. But then, a couple of months later, we broke up again. And then, a few weeks later, we had gotten back together about a month before I went to Mana Pools. She was so supportive of my trip and excited for what I'd experience in Africa.

Yet, even though we were together when I was in Mana Pools, something still didn't seem to quite sit right for me, and I was really struggling with things. I felt like such a mess and unsure of what to do. She and I just had such a strong connection. It felt like the universe kept bringing us back together, despite how much my grief had tried to pull us apart. But if we were supposed to be together, why couldn't I get myself and my nervous system to relax into it and simply let it in?

Inhale.

Exhale.

I am here now in this.

TRACKER MANUAL

Step 11: Welcome It In

- Slow down. It is essential for connecting to the deeper parts of you. What could you do this week to intentionally slow down and just listen to God and life? Listen intently and ask: *What must I do, even though I have no rational reason to do it?* For example, it might have been considered irrational for me to want to go track lions, given they were ten thousand miles away from where I lived.
- Hone your skills. Who do you admire for the way they live life? How could you learn from those people?
- Learn the subtle tracks of the body. Attune to your nervous system. Go out for a walk or hike in nature without any distractions. Find a therapist or practitioner who can help guide you in better understanding yourself. Find books and podcasts to learn more about how your nervous system works so you can attune to it.

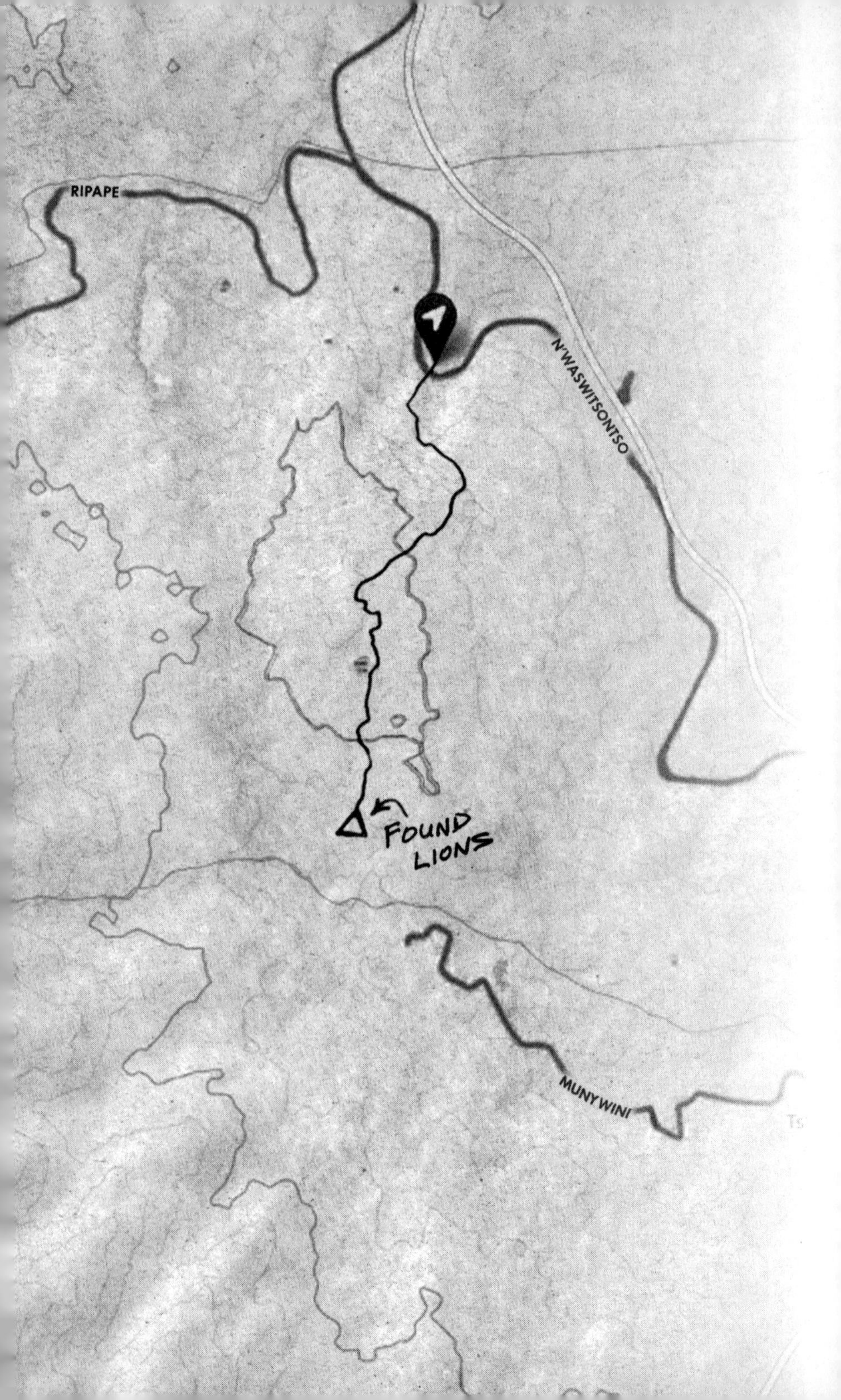
RIPAPE
N'WASWITSONTSO
FOUND LIONS
MUNYWINI

CHAPTER 12

DON'T RUN

The first reaction is one of fear. It's not that we fear the unknown. You cannot fear something that you do not know. Nobody is afraid of the unknown. What you really fear is the loss of the known. That's what you fear.

ANTHONY DE MELLO[15]

"DON'T RUN!" RENIAS commanded, his voice revealing a more forceful authority than I'd heard him use before. "Stay perfectly still."

I spotted the danger at the same time Renias did. It was hard to miss: an angry lioness charging at us from two hundred meters away.

We'd been looking for tracks near a dry riverbed, or *donga*, as the locals call it, when we first heard it—the unmistakable growl of a lion expressing her displeasure. We all stopped and immediately began scanning the area. I looked up and down the opposite side of the donga just as this queen of the jungle exploded out of the bushes at top speed.

A lioness can run up to twenty-two meters per second—that's nearly fifty miles per hour. That meant we had about eight seconds before she closed the gap between us.

It is unusual for a lioness to charge so aggressively. They usually keep their distance. She almost certainly had cubs hiding nearby and was taking quick action to protect them. But the same motherly instinct that sent her racing toward us could also be our saving grace—and Renias was counting on it.

She dropped into the dry riverbed from the opposite bank and disappeared, the raised edge on our side blocking our view. We couldn't see her anymore, but we could still hear her growls—nature's unmistakable way of saying, "Get out of here!"

"Do not move," Renias said again, as we all focused on the invisible growls nearby.

She could reappear at any moment. We were at a standoff.

This wild beauty must have paused to weigh her options. Although aggressive, a lioness with cubs will usually try to avoid altercations. She knows her top priority is taking care of her young, and she worries about what could happen to them if she doesn't make it back to them.

After about thirty seconds (which felt more like three minutes), the lioness sauntered back across to her side of the donga, lay down in the sand, and kept a watchful eye on us until we moved on.

This experience was one of many I've had while tracking when I had to make the conscious, willful decision to stand my ground—even when every fiber of my being was telling me to run.

BACK INTO MY CAGE

My final night at Mana Pools in October 2022 was rough. Part of me was grieving what I was leaving—I wasn't ready to leave the wilderness of Africa and all it had taught me—but another part of me was grieving the task I knew I was flying back home to.

Lying in my tent, blanketed in darkness and surrounded by sounds of life outside, I had this sense that I needed to break up with Emma for the final time. I did not want to. Everything in me wanted to feel fully and completely at home with her and build a life with her. And yet, after these last few days of experiencing true harmony and alignment in my body, mind, and soul, I knew something wasn't quite sitting right for whatever reason, even if I couldn't explain it. The subtle tracks of my body knew. As much as I wanted to feel complete in our relationship, and with her, I could not escape the fact that for some reason . . . I didn't.

I drifted off to sleep, smothered in a heavy blanket of fear and sadness.

Morning came, bringing with it the hardest part of the safari. It was time to go home. I took a final breath of the Mana Pools air, hopped into the back of the Land Rover, and began the long trek back to Colorado.

Later, pressed into my seat on the plane somewhere over the Atlantic Ocean, the turbulence of the flight matched the turbulence in my heart. I felt the absurd contradiction between how relaxed my nervous system had been sitting with Boswell the elephant and how anxious I was right then, on my way home to say goodbye—again—to someone I was so deeply in love with.

The anxiety began rooting in deeper as all the previous, ever-so-familiar fears bubbled up. *What happened to that sense of peace? What happened to that hope that maybe I could bring Mana Pools home with me? What happened to that belief that the wild "out there" could somehow stay with me and enable me to expand the wild inside of me? What happened to that lion energy that fueled me with so much courage?*

I had a layover in New York before the final leg of my trip back to Denver. Sitting at the gate, waiting for my flight, my head was a chaotic mess of fear and anxiety. I couldn't stop thinking about Emma—how much I didn't want to break up with her and how angry I was with myself for not "feeling right" with her. My depression and anxiety—which I had mostly put on pause during my trip—came roaring back to me.

I don't want to lose her, I kept thinking. *What the hell is wrong with me? She's incredible! Why can't I let myself have this?*

I felt like I was in a cruel lose-lose scenario with no good option. Whatever I decided, there would be pain, for me and for her. If I stayed, I'd carry the pain of staying in something that didn't feel right in the core of my being. But if we broke up, I'd have to bear the pain of letting her go, forever wondering if I had made the right decision and facing the gnawing fear that I'd never find the person I was supposed to be with. I felt pretty sure I would never find another woman with a light and energy quite like hers.

Needless to say, it was a difficult trip home.

Normally Emma would have picked me up from the airport when I got back to Denver, but she was out of town with her family. So I made plans for my mom to get me. I texted her when the plane landed and told her to meet me at the curb near baggage claim. I pulled my bags off the conveyor and stepped outside into the crisp autumn Sunday morning. I breathed in the fresh Denver air and began scanning for my parents' red Ford F-150. I looked all around, but I couldn't see it anywhere. And then, just as I went to call her, a white sedan pulled up right in front of me. Only it wasn't my parents' vehicle. It was Emma's.

"Surprise!" she exclaimed as she jumped out of the car and ran toward me. She fit perfectly into my arms and gave me the most amazing welcome-home hug and kiss.

It was perfect.

And agonizing.

Chaos raged through my body. This was a scene right out of a movie. It was the kind of reception you dream about getting from someone you love. And I *did* love her. How could I not? But I could not ignore the fact that some part of me was holding back, resisting this perfect love story and screaming at me that this wasn't right.

As I threw my bags into the trunk, she said she'd changed her plans to be able to surprise me at the airport. Sliding into the driver's seat of her car, my body and mind were so at odds with one another. *How is it possible that I feel I need to break up with this woman? She's everything I ever wanted and more. What the heck is wrong with me?*

Emma had been kinder, more supportive, and more gracious than I'd deserved over the past year of our relationship. She had already stuck with me through so much as my heart and mind wrestled through my trauma recovery. I was not going to put her through that again. If I broke up with her now, I knew it would be forever.

I had such a hard time trusting myself. How could I know if leaving her for good was the right call? What if this was just a divorce-trauma issue that needed more time to heal? What if I was just afraid? Maybe I just needed to do some more intensive therapy work around my fear.

She sat in the passenger seat, cheerfully telling me about the week she'd had with her family and peppering me with questions about my safari. I found myself looking at her so often that it's a miracle I didn't run the car off the road.

She is gorgeous, I thought. *And such a gentle soul. She is joy and sunshine rolled up into a person . . . and she loves me. She wants to be with me. What am I thinking, letting her go?*

But then, just as reason started winning the argument, I felt again an unmistakable sense that something wasn't right in my body and nervous system. I just could not make sense out of it.

By the time we got back to my place, I was prepared to tell God, my inner voice, and all these tracks to take a hike. I was just going to do what I wanted—hold on to Emma. I wanted to sweep her up and shut the rest of the world out for eternity. But after what I'd just experienced in Africa, I knew I couldn't run away. I couldn't ignore myself. It felt like ropes were tightening around my heart, and the harder I fought, the tighter they got.

I didn't know that joy and anger could coexist in my body at such high levels. Joy because of Emma. Anger because it felt like God was against me. Joy from the electricity that surged through me when we kissed. Anger that, for whatever reason, something inside me kept repelling this relationship. Then there it was again: that overwhelming sense that life was so painfully unrelenting.

I wasn't ready to make a decision or do anything with what was inside of me yet, so I did my best to ignore it and not let on to Emma what I was feeling. We spent the entire day together. Being with her felt like home—safety, calm, ease, and comfort. This is how I always envisioned it would feel when I found "my person." So, why did I still have resistance inside me? What was seemingly so messed up in me that I couldn't just rest and be at peace with her?

We went for a long walk with our dogs, caught up on (almost) everything that had happened in both our lives over the past week we'd been apart, cooked dinner, and cozied up on the couch at my place to watch a movie until we fell asleep. From the outside looking in, it was a normal Sunday that dreams are made of.

I'd hoped she hadn't caught on too much about how I was feeling, because I just wasn't ready to make a decision or talk to her about it yet. But I wasn't so sure I'd been successful in hiding my inner conflict. We had a very open, honest relationship, and I sensed she knew something was up.

We both had to work the next day, which was a decent distraction. That evening after work, we went for another walk around the park, and a thick emotional heaviness settled around us, like a huge gray storm cloud had rolled in and was about to pour down on us. That's when I knew she suspected there was something going on with me. The energy between us was off. I could feel it. She could feel it. At the same time, neither of us wanted to acknowledge it—as if ignoring it would make it go away and allow us to escape into our own little bubble of existence.

After walking in the park, we went back to her place and had dinner. It was hard for me to focus and to be fully present with her because I was so consumed with delaying the inevitable. After dinner, as we were cleaning up the kitchen, the undeniable sense of inevitability finally overtook me. I could not put it off another day. The time had come, whether I was ready or not.

And man, was I *not* ready.

I excused myself to the bathroom to collect myself. My heart pounded, and a thin layer of sweat covered my body. I leaned against the bathroom door and lifted my face upward, practically begging God to just fix me, to take these feelings away, to swoop in and stop me from what I was about to do.

Inhale.

Exhale.

I am here now in this.

Do not run.

My breath slowed my nervous system, and a conversation I'd had with one of my friends came to me. I'd been talking to her about how strange it was that I felt this almost supernatural draw to lions when she'd posed a question I couldn't answer.

"Have you ever asked yourself why certain things seem to draw in your curiosity and wonder so deeply, like the energy of lions?"

I stumbled and stammered a bit, trying to come up with an answer off the cuff, but nothing felt particularly insightful or genuine.

"Do you mind if I offer up a thought?" she asked. "I wonder if one of the reasons you're drawn to lions is because they exude such a powerful energy. The energy of a lion is to *not* run away from where they are. They have a grounded energy that exudes a gravitas—a connection to the earth and to the present moment. It is almost as if they simply trust life and what life is giving them."

I was stunned at what she'd said. I replayed it in my head several times, allowing it to sink in. It was another one of those moments of clarity that you wait for and long for—a little piece of wisdom and insight that takes five seconds to hear but a lifetime to integrate.

As I stood in that bathroom, I realized that this was one of those pivotal moments of integration, and I was currently exuding the exact opposite energy of a lion. I wanted nothing more than to run away from where

I was. I *hated* where I was. How could I *not* want to run away from this moment?

But then, a deeper truth came to me. I didn't just want to run away because I wanted to stay with Emma, although that was certainly a huge piece of it. Beyond that, though, I wanted to run away because I didn't trust life. I didn't trust that all of this was really *for me*.

Keeping your feet planted firmly in the face of fear requires a lot of trust, and lions have plenty of trust. A lion trusts itself. It trusts the way of things. It trusts its power, its pride, and nature. And I didn't. I was operating not on trust but on fear. Fear had shoved me around like a schoolyard bully for most of my life. But this bully hadn't stuffed me in a school locker; it had stuffed me in a nice, comfy, little cage—a cage that I had begun to outgrow for the first time in my life.

Unexpectedly, a montage from my childhood scrolled through my mind, with scene after scene of the times in my life when I'd wanted to run away. In third grade, when my "girlfriend," Rebecca (who I was sure I'd marry), dumped me. Fifth grade, when my girlfriend, Amber, broke up with me in front of the whole class during recess. Piled into a moving van with my family, driving away from one house after another and trying not to think about all the friends I was leaving behind. The moment my mom told me Grandpa Don had died. Waving goodbye to Grandma Verona at the hospital, knowing it was the last time I'd see her. It was all connected. I could see it so clearly.

I stood there, holding it all, feeling it all, and thinking, *How can I possibly let Emma go? After all I've been through—the divorce, the depression, the sexual trauma response in my body, and all the inner darkness I've been walking through. And now I'm supposed to let her go?*

Then, suddenly, everything fell into place. I knew what was happening—and why it had to happen.

I thought Emma was going to be my resolution. I thought she was going to be the silver lining to all the turmoil and sadness of my life these last few years. All this time, I had thought that the string I was following was leading me to "my person," the woman I was supposed to spend the rest of my life with. I thought all the therapy, all the trauma recovery, all the searching and tracking would lead me straight to her, and that then, this whole journey through hell would be worth it.

Then, like I'd just taken the red pill in *The Matrix*, the revelation went another layer deeper. It wasn't just about Emma. It was about fulfilling this dream I had of getting married and starting a family. It was about having a loving partner for life again. Someone to come home to. Someone to adventure with. Someone to build a life with. It was about the realization that, if I let Emma go now—really let her go for good this time—that would be the end of this illusion, this hope I'd been holding onto that she was my answer, my "fix."

But if this whole journey hasn't been about finding her, I thought, *what the hell have I been tracking all this time? If it isn't a happy life with Emma, what is it that's waiting for me at the end of this string?*

I did not know. The one thing I did know, however, was that it wasn't this. It wasn't her. It wasn't *us*.

It was time to face the truth I could not escape. I had to let her go.

Our eyes found each other as I walked back into the kitchen. The moment she saw my face, she knew something was wrong. We sat together on the couch and talked. We both cried. We knew this was the end of the road for us, but we weren't quite ready to let it all go. We held each other into the night, and I fell asleep, praying God would change how I felt by the time I woke up in the morning so I could tell her it was all okay and we could stay together.

The moment my eyes opened, the familiar pain of grief I'd been drowning in for the last two years met me like a violent set of waves thrashing me against the rocks.

In the deafening silence, I lay there motionless, pulled between the desire to stay and hold her forever and the urge to rush out the door as fast as I could to avoid the misery of what came next.

I finally found the strength to get out of bed. Emma got up, too. Neither of us said anything as I grabbed my bags. Our eyes found each other's. With tears in both our eyes, we hugged and said "I love you" for the last time. Then I walked out the door. With every step I took, I desperately hoped that something would shift in me. That it would suddenly click, I'd know she was "my person," and I could run back and tell her that we could stay together. But it didn't happen. I unlocked my truck and got in. Anger welled up inside me, and I slammed my hands on the steering wheel over and over, tears streaming down my face as I drove away.

"YOU HAVE TO LET YOURSELF COLLAPSE"

Over the next couple of days, it felt as if all the pain from the past few years had come to a head. I had desperately hoped the pain was behind me, but it was very clearly not. And now, I had nothing to hide behind. Not Emma.

Not a TEDx Talk. Not even another lion-tracking safari to look forward to. It was just me and this pain I'd try to run away from. The pain that seemed to be waiting for me at the end of the string I'd been tracking.

I've talked a lot in this book about the connection between what we feel in our bodies and our emotions. I've learned how important that connection is and how essential it is to honor what we feel, both in our hearts and in our bodies. But at this point in my journey, all I felt was numbness. It was like life had pressed the shutdown switch in my body, leaving me stuck in place, unable to move or feel.

About a week after the breakup, I met my brother Tim for an ice bath. I'd been doing them for a few years at this point. It started mainly as a way for me to wake myself up and score a dopamine hit to get through my days after my divorce, but I had come to enjoy the sensation of shocking my system and submitting to five minutes of intentional discomfort. I'd recently gotten my brother into cold plunging as well, so we suffered the frigid waters together every now and then.

It had been a helpful way for me to recenter myself during the dark days of my healing journey, kind of like how rebooting a computer can usually fix weird glitches and slowdowns. When I started, I aimed for three to five minutes in the water, which was usually somewhere between 32°F and 50°F. That's still where my brother was. By this point, though, I'd gotten to the point where I could stay in the ice water for much longer.

My brother had a large tub at his house, and we'd bought a hundred pounds of ice to get the water down to 38°F. Tim wanted to go first, so he got in and I coached him through how to breathe and stay present, one breath at a time. He hit the five-minute mark and was done. Now, it was my turn.

Most of the time, I'd get into the ice water with the intent to heal—my mindset on presence and surrender. Generally, once I was forty-five to sixty seconds in, the cold would send me into this almost cathartic space. It forced me to learn to focus on my breath in order to endure the frigid temperature. Cold plunging seemed to open pathways and channels in my psyche, emotions, and nervous system in ways few other modalities could, which is why I kept coming back to it. Yet every once in a while, I'd find myself using ice baths as a sort of punishment, as though I was trying to force the cold to speed up my healing and shock my system out of depression. These occasions were infrequent, but I noticed they happened most often when the rage inside me was all-consuming and seemingly unbearable.

On this day, my goal was ten minutes. That was certainly attainable for me and something I'd done many times. I still felt the cold, of course, but it wasn't quite as shocking as it was when I had first started taking ice baths regularly.

As soon as I hit the water on this day, though, I knew something was off. I inhaled deeply through my nose as I stepped in and sat down, immersing my body up to the top of my neck. I exhaled, letting the air out through my mouth as slowly as I could, even as my body screamed at me for disrupting my equilibrium. I shifted all my focus to breathing slowly. I breathed in through my nose and out through my mouth for a few breaths to help my body settle in. I began repeating my usual cold plunge mantra in my head, pairing it with my breath:

Inhale.

Let.

Exhale.

Go.

Let . . . Go . . .

Let . . . Go . . .

I quickly realized my normal ice bath rhythms weren't working. I looked at the timer sitting next to me.

It had been one minute, five seconds. Neither my body nor my mind were releasing to the water today.

Inhale.

Let.

Exhale.

Go.

Let . . . Go . . .

I looked at the timer again: one minute, eighteen seconds. Everything in me was resisting the cold, and I was far beyond the point where I typically started to welcome it. I fought to refocus on my breath and soften my locked jaw, yet my brow furrowed, my fists clenched, and my heart pounded. I knew this feeling. I recognized this emotion that had revealed itself in the water.

Rage.

My rage burned hot in me and refused to politely hide in the dark corners of my mind any longer. Fire coursed through my veins. It felt like the heat of my anger was powerful enough to boil the freezing water surrounding me.

Time: one minute, thirty-seven seconds. *What the hell is wrong with me?* I thought, knowing this question went far beyond the problem I was having settling into the ice bath. I felt the old, familiar urge to run. Tim wouldn't have thought anything of it if I'd just gotten up and said, "Screw it. I don't want to do this today." But something told me I needed the cold that day, so I stayed in and kept breathing.

I shivered on the outside and fumed on the inside, stewing in an angry contradiction. I was determined to fight through this. I would have at least one victory that week.

I closed my eyes and almost immediately visualized myself in the past, doing a bunch of different physical activities in a desperate attempt to move the emotion I felt in my body. I thought of all the times I had been certain the big emotions I was feeling would overtake me if I didn't outrun them.

I saw myself in Minnesota after my grandma passed, running in the corn fields outside of town, screaming as loudly and boisterously as I could. Then, I was on my grandma's front lawn, swinging an ax at a tree stump with all my might. Then, I was rolling around in the grass while it rained as I begged the earth to help me heal. Then, I was on a trail outside of Sedona, picking myself up off the ground after crashing my dirt bike. Then, I was back in Denver at my place, frantically calling Michelle, so she could talk me down from the suicidal ideation that had taken over. Then, I was on my first date with Emma, walking on the sidewalk in downtown Denver, holding her hand and imagining what our spark might become. Then, I was in the mountains with her on our second date, jumping in the mountain lake and cuddling in a hammock overlooking a small creek. Then, I was on the couch with her, crying as we broke up and said goodbye for the last time.

A guttural sound released from my lungs, and I yelled, "Damn it!" as the fury moved through my body. After it boiled over, the anger shifted to sorrow, and warm tears poured down my cheeks and swirled into the freezing water. Tim was concerned but understood my struggle. He sat with me as I let myself feel it all the way through. And then, eyes closed and still in the ice bath, the most interesting thing happened. I heard a voice—a memory replaying in my imagination.

"David, you have to let yourself collapse."

"What?" I replied.

I was in a therapy session with Syanna, and she repeated, "David, you are going to have to let yourself collapse. It's the only way."

I didn't know what she was talking about. It didn't make sense. The puzzled look on my face must've signaled that her words were not registering, because she continued, "There are three stages our nervous systems move through to help and protect us when we become dysregulated. In the first stage, things are generally good, and the nervous system is regulated. In the second stage, things are generally not good, and the nervous system is dysregulated. Then, in the third stage, the nervous system is heavily dysregulated and goes through a collapse in order to get back to stage one. Our bodies do this all the time when what we are going through in life is overburdening our system."

I nodded, slowly letting the information seep in. "The problem is, in our culture, we often get stuck in stage two because we are uncomfortable with collapse. The result of what can happen is that all these heavy emotions get stuck in our bodies because we don't fully surrender and feel our emotions all the way through."

She paused, and then continued, "You have to let yourself collapse, David. You can't stay in stage two and expect to get back to stage one. Collapse is the only way to heal."

This conversation had happened months ago, and I'd overlooked it until now. I had so much anger—anger that had been stuck in my body not just from the past few years, but from my childhood. All those big emotions I hadn't known what to do with had all been stuffed away and forced down into the cracks, crevices, and depths of my being. All because I hadn't known how to fully feel it and let it go.

I thought, *All this time, it's been about surrender. And yet, all this time, I've tried to control my healing and manage it on my terms. All the pain, like lions charging from multiple directions: my childhood anger, my ten-year marriage ending in divorce, dating again, my sex-drive shutdown, the suicidal ideation, and all the struggles I'd had for so long—it's all part of the portal to my deeper healing. If I resist death, I resist life. If I'm not willing to die, I'm not willing to live.*

I let it all in.

I kept breathing deeply and then opened my eyes and looked at the timer: nine minutes, fifty-five seconds. I inhaled deeply and dunked my head underwater. The rush of the ice-cold water around my head matched the piercingly painful truth that had just become so agonizingly clear: *efforting* would never get me back to stage one, back to a baseline of regulation and peace. There was no number of cold plunges, therapy sessions, breathwork exercises, or desperate prayers that would ever be enough to set me free.

Collapse and surrender was the only way.

TRACKER MANUAL

Step 12: Don't Run

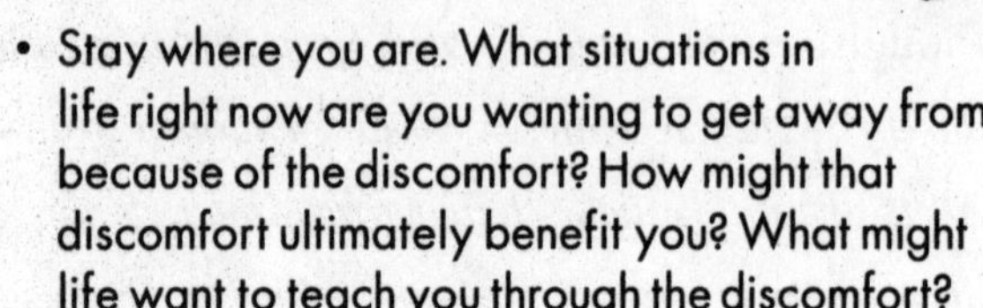

- Stay where you are. What situations in life right now are you wanting to get away from because of the discomfort? How might that discomfort ultimately benefit you? What might life want to teach you through the discomfort?
- Be present. Take five deep breaths. What does it feel like to be present?
- Surrender and let go. Where in your life are you being asked to let go of control and simply be still?

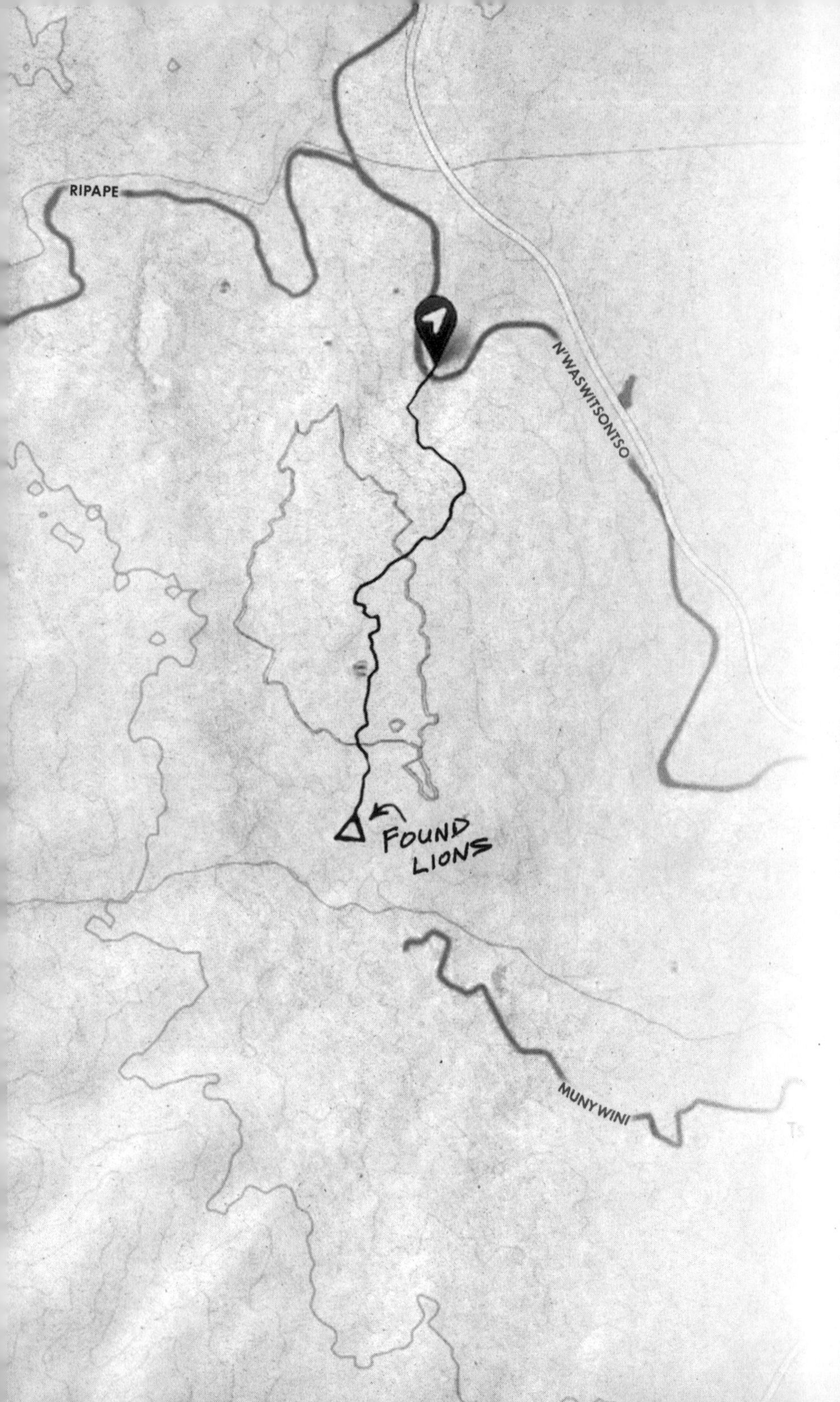
RIPAPE
N'WASWITSONTSO
FOUND
LIONS
MUNYWINI

CHAPTER 13

FACE THE LION

The wild isn't a place. It's who you become when you stop running from yourself.

ANONYMOUS

WE WERE ABOUT thirty meters from a pride of lions on a buffalo kill. They were preoccupied with eating, which had given us the opportunity to get so close. The terrain was thick with brush, so I had to crouch down low to get a good vantage point.

I could see seven lions feasting on their fresh kill. It was so *real*. Raw. Primal. Wild.

To call it one of the most amazing sights I've ever seen would be a massive understatement.

The lion closest to us was a young cub who was pulling small pieces of meat off the buffalo, which looked gigantic in comparison. Next to the cub stood a large male. I wondered if this was the cub's father who was showing his boy the ropes. On the other side of the buffalo were three lionesses—probably the mother and two doting aunts.

I could not believe how close I was to all this—close enough to hear the sound of wet buffalo flesh being torn from the kill and chewed by seven hungry lions. It was like I was watching a nature documentary on an IMAX screen. I could almost hear David Attenborough's voice whispering in my ear as these magnificent creatures feasted on the spoils of their hunt.

After I'd taken it in for about two minutes, something changed. Maybe the wind shifted and carried our scent to them. Maybe one of us adjusted our stance and rustled a leaf or branch beneath our foot. For whatever reason, the cub stopped munching and looked directly at us. I could see his little face peering intently at the bush we were crouched behind, his ears twitching as if trying to lock onto our position. He hopped to the side of the buffalo carcass to get a better look.

The three lionesses, sensing either the cub's curiosity or our presence behind the bush, immediately jumped up from their meal, dug their mighty paws into the dirt, and started growling—their eyes scanning the terrain and their nervous systems on full alert.

I'd received this message before: a lion's forceful, impatient way of saying, *"Go away. Now."* But I'd never gotten this message from *three* lionesses at one time—with an enormous male ready to back them up.

My heart felt like it was about to explode out of my chest, slamming against my rib cage with each rapid beat. My every instinct was to run. Every nerve, every muscle fiber in my body was tensed and ready to fly out of there like a bat out of hell. But if I moved as much as an inch—if any of us did—one of the lionesses would charge. I knew from experience (and from many, many warnings from my guides) that I must remain absolutely still.

Renias stood beside me, taking it all in.

"What do I do?" I whispered.

Without taking his eyes off the lions in front of us, Renias said three words that not only changed that encounter, but changed my life.

"Face the lion."

"I'm scared. I want to run," I admitted.

"Just stay still and face her, David. Trust me."

I stayed in my crouch, perfectly still, trying to control my breathing. My eyes remained fixed on the lions. Their eyes, I knew, remained fixed on me. Every second was an eternity. Who would flinch first?

Thirty seconds into the standoff, I felt a change in the air. I felt my heart rate and breathing begin to steady. My muscles slowly relaxed. I saw the same changes happening in the lionesses. It was as though all of us, man and beast alike, were releasing the tension in our bodies and acknowledging a mutual truce. At about the one-minute mark, two of the lionesses broke off their eye contact with us and returned to their kill as the third sauntered back and forth, casually keeping watch while her family finished their meal.

The standoff was over, and I'd managed to keep my cool. When everything in me wanted to run, I was able to tap into my breath, connect to my courage, remain calm, and face one of the most ferocious predators in the wilderness.

LOOKING FOR THE PEAK OF THE EMOTIONAL BELL CURVE

The months following my breakup with Emma and my "cold plunge surrender" moment weren't easy, but they were important. I continued meeting regularly with my therapist, Syanna, and I participated in a few therapeutic workshops and men's groups. Even though it may seem like I was still trying to control my healing journey, I kept leaning into the lesson that had become crystal clear in the icy waters of the cold plunge: I had to learn to surrender and not try to force things to happen when I wanted them to and how I wanted them to. I had to learn how to trust the tracks without *efforting* my healing to death.

I was making some progress, but I was bothered by the fact that I didn't really feel like I'd reached "the other side." In my mind, there would be a clear, unmistakable moment when I reached "peak pain" on the emotional bell curve Syanna had taught me. From then on, even on the hard days, at least I'd know I was on my way back down the curve toward whatever "new normal" my life would look like post-divorce. I had envisioned collapse as a specific moment in time, some big *aha* moment I could point to and say, "Right there! That's the moment when I totally collapsed! That's the moment when I turned the corner, when my cage was shattered, and when I finally started stepping into the truest, wildest, most untamed version of myself!"

I thought I'd hit that point when I crashed out during my cold plunge with my brother. *But*, I thought, *if I had really reached such a key milestone in my healing journey, wouldn't it be more obvious? Wouldn't I feel notably different? Wouldn't I feel . . . better?*

After all this time and effort, I really thought I should have found the wild creature moving at the end of the string by now.

But I hadn't.

So, I kept tracking.

And I booked another safari trip.

HOW DO YOU KNOW YOU LOVE SOMETHING?

May 2023

The wind whipped through my hair as the open-air Land Rover rumbled and jolted over the Mana Pools National Park's dirt roads. I closed my eyes and inhaled deeply—the mix of the dust swirling around and the musk of the wild filled my senses. I felt my nervous system settle in and relax a few more clicks.

I am here now in this.

I once heard someone say that Africa isn't a place; it's a way of being, an experience. That could not have been truer for me as we drove over the rough terrain with the sun on my face and my hand keeping a firm grip on the car's grab handle to brace myself. I feel as if I come to Africa to rediscover my soul.

Anticipation practically radiated from me, and I'm sure the smile stretching across my face communicated to anyone paying attention how excited I was to be back there. My mind raced as we cruised along: *What will I see this time? How close will I get to the lions, elephants, and hyenas? Will we have any close encounters like we did last time?* I deeply hoped so. I wasn't sure how the experiences I'd had on the safari in October could be topped, but my expectations were high as we arrived at the same campsite where I'd stayed just seven months prior.

We pulled into the camp, where I immediately spotted Stretch's unmistakable silhouette walking out to greet us.

"Welcome back, David!" he practically shouted in his warm Zimbabwean accent as we parked. He greeted me with his typical playful grin and a pat on the back with his enormous catcher's mitt of a hand. "Come have a drink with me!"

We strolled over to the deck overlooking the Zambezi River to have a beer and enjoy some snacks before going out for a short game drive before nightfall. Looking out over the river and full of a strange peace I seem to only feel in Africa, I thought, *There is literally nowhere else I'd rather be than right here.*

I meant where I was physically, of course, but even more so, I was thinking about the *state of being* I was in. I realized that the person I was while tracking in Africa was a different person from the guy I was back home. I liked the man I was in the wild, and I was ready to see him break through into the wilds of Denver, Colorado.

I woke up in my now-familiar tent at 5:00 a.m. Nothing topped this level of excitement. I was here. I was alive. I was living. I couldn't wait to get out and start tracking again.

Excited or not, I knew better than to leave my tent until the sun was up, so I got ready and then sat back down, waiting (not so patiently) for the early-morning sun to brighten the dark canvas walls that surrounded me. As soon as it seemed safe, I unzipped the door and looked in every direction for any hippos, snakes, or other animals that may have decided to bunk next to me for the night.

All clear.

I headed toward the deck for coffee and breakfast and was welcomed by the distinct glow of a glorious African sunrise. As I soaked in the warmth of the morning rays, my mind was at ease. *This is what peace feels like*, I thought.

A series of images flowed through my mind of the life I'd lived up to that very moment. These tracks, this string, had led me into and out of situations, relationships, and experiences I never could have imagined—many of which I never *wanted* to imagine. And now, the tracks had led me back here, to this place on the other side of the globe—nearly ten thousand miles from my front door—a foreign land that felt more like home than anywhere I'd ever been.

Of course, that wasn't what I felt the very first time I ventured out into the wild. Although this was only my second tracking safari, it was my sixth time in Africa. My very first safari, which I haven't mentioned yet, actually happened years before my divorce. Lisa and I had taken a safari trip together when we were married. It was much lower-risk and more of the typical safari tourist stuff, but it was still a pretty big deal at the time. I imagine my inner lion had been prowling around, sniffing around the edges of what would eventually become an important part of my life. But if "Wild David" was in me at all back then, he was pretty deeply buried beneath a mountain of worries, doubts, fears, and excuses. I had been so uptight, so stressed, so anxious, so *afraid*. Afraid that it would be a waste of money. Afraid it wouldn't live up to my expectations. Afraid that Lisa wouldn't enjoy it. Afraid that

I would get home and beat myself up for making such a foolish decision.

I realized I had been holding my breath as I thought about who I'd been back then. I exhaled and let my shoulders release downward. *Man*, I thought. *I used to live so much of my life that way. Guarded. Fearful. Avoiding risk at all costs. . . . What a miserable, caged way to live.*

I took another drink of my coffee and smiled with the pride that comes from wrestling through immense struggle, failure, and pain. *Yeah*, I thought, *but look how far I've come.*

"Let's get serious!"

Stretch's trademark morning greeting snapped me back into the present. "Let's get going!" he said, ushering our small group of explorers toward the Land Rover. He made sure he had everything he needed for the day—hat, sunglasses, binoculars, and keys—and then we were off to track. I climbed into the vehicle and began another African adventure, an adventure that I realized I'd completely fallen in love with.

Boyd Varty, author of *The Lion Tracker's Guide to Life*, says, "No one can tell you what your track will be or how to know what calls you and brings you to life. That's your work to do. But a great tracker can ask: How do you know you love something?"

I think you know you love something when you can feel it in the very fiber of your being, when every nerve ending in your body buzzes with energy and enthusiasm at the thought of it. It's when you feel perfectly attuned to something, a connection that feels hardwired into your body, mind, and spirit. It's inner harmony. It's confidence—a quiet confidence that's just for you and doesn't need to prove anything to anyone. It's the calm and clarity that comes with knowing for certain that something is *right*, that it fits, even if you can't articulate why or where the connection came from. Like your first few dates with someone magical. Like singing at the top of your lungs at a concert, surrounded by the unmatched energy of thousands of other people doing the same. Like finally quitting that job that's been sucking the life out of you. Like a dance party in your kitchen with music blasting. Like holding your newborn baby. Like a first kiss. It's your body, mind, and spirit being so in tune that the manifestation of it is—and can only be—gratitude reminding you that you are indeed alive and in love.

As I got into that Land Rover, my love for nature, animals, and what some might call "risky" adventures was visceral and undeniable. This was part of my path; I knew it in my bones. This was how I knew I was in love. All of me was dialed in. I'd felt something like this about a small handful of things before, but never like this. At thirty-nine, I had never felt such a clear and profound connection to anyone or anything as I felt here, bouncing around in a Land Rover, looking for lions.

The thought hit me not as a big revelation or dramatic, eye-opening realization but rather as a simple, calm, quiet, and clear acknowledgment: *I was made for this.*

Had all the tracking, following the string step after step, led me here? Was this the wild version of me I'd been searching for? Was this—this new passion for adventure and for tracking wild animals in Africa—part of the wild creature, the uncaged David, that was moving at the end of the string? I wasn't totally sure yet, but I did know, without a doubt, that I couldn't wait to get out of the vehicle and start tracking.

Early on that first day, we came across the distinctive tracks of a male lion. That presented us with a bit of a quandary. You see, when we're out tracking, we most often prefer tracking females. Lionesses are more predictable in their movements. If they're out and about, they are usually on a mission—either to hunt or to move their cubs from one place to another. So, if you don't catch up to them while they're on the move, you can usually find them wherever they end up, whether it's a watering hole or a new den. Males, on the other hand, wander all over the place. They aren't as predictable, and they double back on their tracks all the time. Their job is to protect the territory, so they are always moving around, investigating potential threats, and keeping an eye on everything. That makes tracking male lions much more difficult than tracking the females.

However, finding a male's unmistakable tracks is thrilling. Spotting a male in the wild is the big payoff for most lion trackers. The tracks practically beg you to follow them. You can't help but think, *Maybe this is the day I'll finally catch up to one.* It's like a fisherman throwing his line out again and again, certain the next throw will be the one that finally lands his trophy fish. Of course, that is rarely the case. There's a reason why most trackers prefer to track females—at least when they're responsible for entertaining a group of safari guests who spent a lot of money to get there. As Stretch often says: "Never follow a male lion. He'll make a fool out of you."

After we repeatedly discovered fresh male tracks that first day, we had a decision to make: ignore the male's tracks and look for some lionesses . . . or take a big risk and see if we could actually catch up to this guy.

Our group decided to go for it.

At one point that day, we were sure we'd made the right call. We came upon a large thicket in the afternoon.

Bushes, shrubs, and vines were all intertwined, which created a safe haven for wildlife—and a pretty scary place for a human to creep up on. There was no telling what might walk, run, pounce, jump, or slither out of there at any moment. But that's where the tracks were leading us. No turning back.

We reached the thicket and slowly peered around the corner of a large bush. Just then, about fifteen feet ahead of us, I saw a tail swish among some vines. He must have heard us at that point, though, because the tail was all we'd see. He took off almost immediately, disappearing deeper into the thicket. It was late afternoon by this point, so Stretch had to call an end to that day's tracking.

Finally, on the last day of tracking, we thought we'd give it one last effort. We headed out a little earlier in the afternoon than normal in the hopes of catching the lion napping—literally. Males often take early-afternoon naps, so we tried to use that to our advantage, hoping his fresh tracks would lead us to wherever he'd decided to rest. But the clock was ticking. It was only a few hours until sunset, so this really was our last-ditch effort to spot a lion before our safari ended.

We followed his tracks down into a sandy, dry riverbed about thirty feet wide with nearly ten-foot-high embankments along each side. For miles (and hours), we followed his tracks through and around the riverbed. We kept finding fresh tracks, so the whole time it felt like we'd look up and spot him at any second. Eventually, we came upon a spot near a fallen tree where Stretch could tell he'd laid down for an afternoon nap. But he was back on his feet. We'd missed naptime, but all the signs indicated he was still nearby. For all I knew, he'd been watching us the entire time, staying just out of our sight as we sauntered up and down the riverbed.

The bright afternoon sky was fading into a faint pink haze. I knew what that meant before Stretch said a word.

"That's it," he said. "I'm sorry, everyone, but sunset is almost here. We have to head back to camp."

Of course, I wanted to press on, just a little longer, certain we were only steps away from finding him. Stretch, however—as playful and excitable as he was—knew it would soon no longer be safe for us to be out. Our weeklong lion-tracking expedition was over.

Walking back to the Land Rover, I couldn't help but think about how familiar this mix of frustration and disappointment was for me. Then it hit me: Tracking this male lion the past few days was eerily similar to my healing journey of the past two years. Pursuing peace and recovery so often felt like tracking an elusive male lion through the jungle. I'd follow *this* path or try *that* tactic, always thinking I'd find what I was looking for just around the next bend. Then, I'd get there and realize my quarry was still ahead of me. I'd occasionally get a glimpse of healing for just a moment before it disappeared like a lion's tail swishing among the vines. I kept pushing forward, kept trying new things, kept clearing the ground ahead of me, but I kept coming up empty. I longed to know when I'd finally discover the creature at the end of the string.

If someone could have just told me how long it would take—whether it was two years or ten years—I think I might have handled myself better. I would have at least been able to keep my expectations in check and saved myself some self-inflicted disappointment every time I temporarily lost the track. But that's not how any of this worked. No one could tell us exactly where the lion was hiding that week, and no one could have told me when or where I'd finally find the healing I was pursuing. All I could do was follow the tracks, trust that *something* worth pursuing was still calling to me, and push forward one day at a time. I discovered in the process that emotional healing, like nature, has its own agenda.

Stretch and I shared a drink on the deck back at camp that night. "I'm sorry we weren't able to find that elusive male this week, David," he said. "I know it's been a bit of an anticlimactic trip this time around." His voice trailed off as he shook his head, clearly frustrated. Stretch took his job seriously, and he always did his best to ensure his guests had a good time, which usually directly correlated with the number of animals seen and exciting encounters experienced.

"I know you came here to see lions," Stretch said in an unusually somber tone. "I feel like I've let you down."

As Stretch apologized, I noticed something unexpected and uncharacteristic, given the situation: I wasn't that disappointed. In fact, I actually felt delighted. On one hand, I was a little bummed we didn't find the lion, but on the other hand, I was witnessing my transformation in real time. I was processing differently. The synapses were firing in my brain—connecting to the hours and hours of self-work I'd put into the last two and a half years.

"Stretch, thanks for saying that," I said. "But if I wanted some sort of guarantee of seeing a lion, I would have just gone to the zoo twenty minutes from my house. I don't come here for a guarantee. I come here for the mystery, the mysticism, and the wonder. I come here for the wild."

That response surprised me, but it was 100 percent authentic. The whole experience of being in the wild, unsure of what would happen and what I'd see, was the real payoff. It wasn't about seeing lions—although that is truly an amazing experience. The payoff is in seeing what this place, what this adventure, does to me and for me. It's seeing the person I become when I am here, and it's about finding ways to be that same adventurous, curious, and grateful person more often back home.

I used to be so afraid of the unknown. I'd trapped myself inside a cage as I tried to control things, *efforting* my way through life, which only further sealed my fate behind bars. It took me nearly twenty-five years to realize what that lion in the zoo was trying to tell me when I was fifteen. His message was a warning, an imploring: "*Don't end up like this.* Don't end up in an enclosure, in a cage. Go and live. Be wild. Trust your nervous system to take you toward aliveness and just go. Don't worry about how everything will work out. Just go." Here I was now, after living most of my adult life tame and confined, slowly and painstakingly cutting myself out of the cage.

The wild was teaching me to embrace uncertainty. There are no guarantees in the wild. Lions don't know where their next meal will come from. Over time, though, I'd made countless decisions in an attempt to trade uncertainty for some façade of a guarantee. In the process, I'd traded my truest nature for some pretense of comfort—my old "7 out of 10" way of life. But those guarantees weren't real, and neither was the empty satisfaction I felt in the cage I'd put myself in. My marriage was never guaranteed. My happiness was never guaranteed. My career, my relationships, my healing journey—none of it was ever guaranteed. They were all wild and unpredictable, no matter how "safe" I'd tried to make them. No wonder I failed to manage it all. You can't expect to manage things in the wild from the confines of a cage. It's like telling a lion in the zoo that he's the king of the jungle—he can't be the king of the wild if he's not out in it. The truth about our existence is that it's wonderfully messy and unpredictable. Any effort to believe otherwise is simply a protective mechanism, a false reality. The wild—the energy of the lion—was showing me what was real, what surrender looked like.

One of my therapists once asked me, "Have you ever wanted one thing but ended up getting something else, only to realize what you got was better than what you originally thought you wanted?"

Her question stopped me in my tracks. My mind was blank for a few seconds, but after sitting with the question for a moment, something clicked in my brain. I thought back on many of the surprising yet defining moments of my life when life or God had given me what I really needed, even when it wasn't what I really wanted.

That question echoed in my mind as I sat around the campfire in Zimbabwe with Stretch on the last night of my safari. I had come here only wanting to see lions, but *not* seeing them this week turned out to be the exact thing I needed. I wasn't just here for the lions after all. I was here for the adventure of it all, for the inherent mystery and exhilarating anticipation of every step, and for the way the wild demanded my complete presence.

The wild was teaching me to let the present moment be enough. It was teaching me that there was magic both in finding the lion and in searching for it. I was learning to let go and fall in love with the uncertainty of the wild.

Inhale.

Exhale.

I am here now in this.

As I sat with all of this, I wondered, *What if the lions leave the tracks for us, just so we can follow them? Maybe they want to hang out with us? Maybe they want to teach us?*

I paused, smiled, and let the joy and humor of that thought soak in before allowing my inner inquiry to continue.

What if life has always been laying these tracks for me to heal and find freedom and experience what it feels like to be fully and completely alive? What if the creature moving at the end of the string wasn't just about Africa and the wild "out there"? What if it was never just about how to keep the wild with me, but more importantly, how to find the wild inside of me? What if the point all along has been finding aliveness in and through ALL *the experiences—good and bad, fulfilling and frustrating—and being truly grateful for them all?*

What a beautiful thing that would be. To live every day, looking for the distinct magic in every moment. Rolling out of bed in the morning and planting my feet on the ground, conscious of the texture of the floor on my bare feet (gratitude). Getting in the car and realizing the gas tank is empty (gratitude). Dinner with a dear friend (gratitude). A breakup (gratitude). A growth opportunity at work (gratitude). Closing my eyes and taking a deep breath, filling my lungs with air, followed by a long, slow exhale (gratitude). What a beautiful thing that would be.

I wanted more of that in my life. More mystery. More magic. More gratitude. More curiosity. More inquiry.

And then, I realized this is what it felt like to collapse, to surrender—to finally let go and let life have me. It already does anyway.

I was free.

I *am* free.

TRACKER MANUAL

Step 13: Face the Lion

- Allow yourself to feel all of the emotions. All of them. What emotions do you most struggle to stay present with and feel fully?
- Realize your fear is lying to you. What are some fears you have had in the past that never came true? What fears do you currently have that might be lying to you?
- Face the lion and feel the rush of aliveness. When have you felt most alive in the past? What makes you feel the most alive today? How can you get more of it into your life?

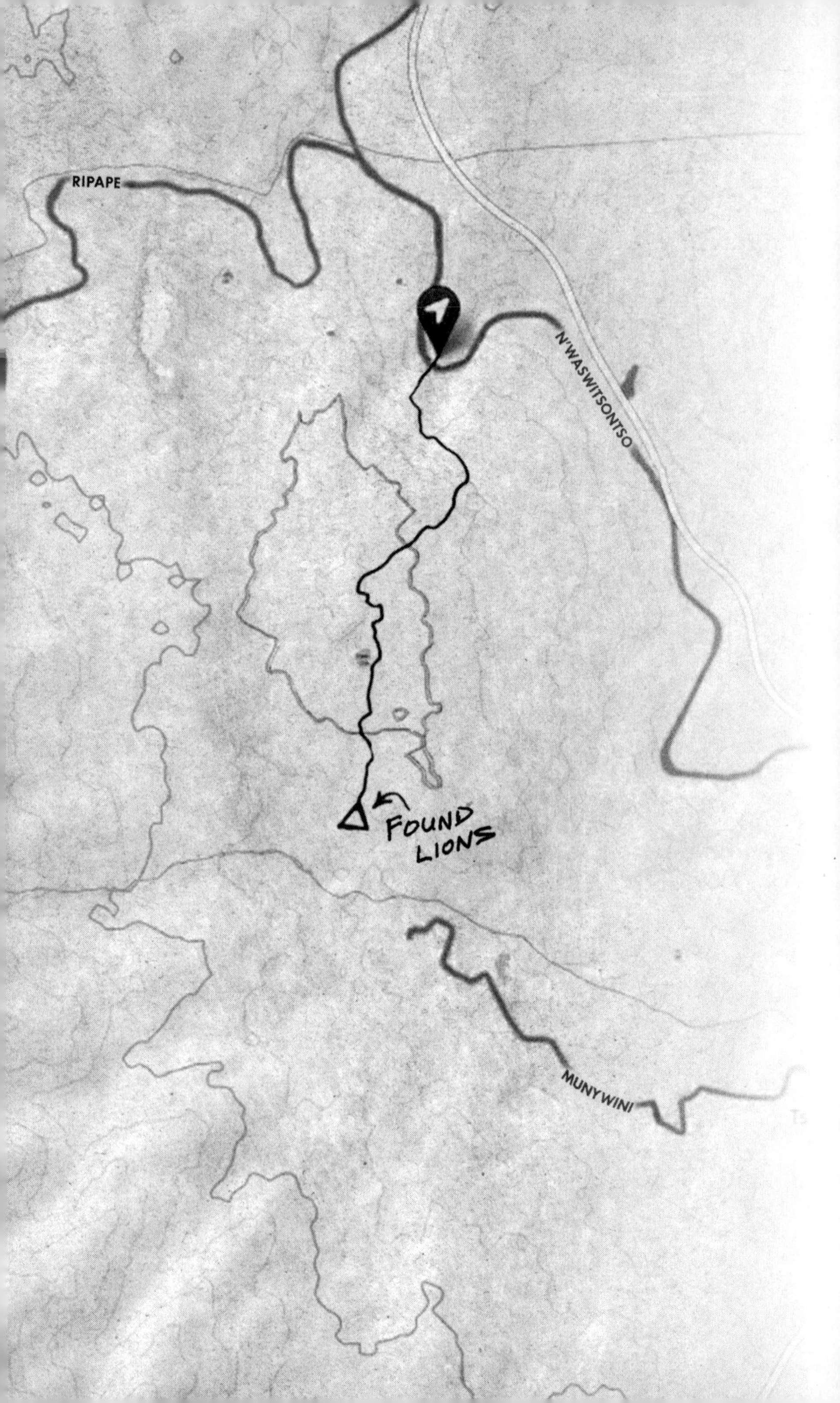
RIPAPE
N'WASWITSONTSO
FOUND LIONS
MUNYWINI

CHAPTER 14

THE LION IS YOU

The lion you're tracking is not only in the savanna—it's pacing inside your chest.

ANONYMOUS

HER GROWL CUT through the relative quiet of the jungle like a knife, splitting the veil between "We're not going to see any lions today" and "She sounds like she's right on top of us!" It was like standing right next to the biggest Harley-Davidson you've ever seen as the engine cranks and roars to life. I could feel the vibrations from her warning before my eyes finally spotted the lioness. Her tail was lashing back and forth, her ears were pinned back, and she was snarling with rage as she charged full speed directly at us.

Then, just as Renias had predicted the angry lioness came to a hard, immediate stop about six feet away from me.

I told this story in the introduction to this book, but there's a detail I didn't share then. It's something I wanted to hold back until we got here, to the end. Something I thought would make more sense once you'd gotten to know me and understood what all I had been through up to that point. As you know now, I'd spent years in the throes of grief. I'd spent every moment of every day drowning in fear, doubt, anxiety, uncertainty, and heartache. There were a lot of times when, if I'm being honest, I even wanted to die. But standing there, in the wilds of South Africa's Kruger National Park, with a two-hundred-fifty-pound lioness bearing down on me at about fifty miles per hour, all that emotional torture disappeared in an instant. When I saw her, something in my primal DNA switched on—something I'd never felt before. A flood of energy surged through my body. A cocktail of serotonin, dopamine, and adrenaline flooded my veins. My muscles tensed. Electricity crackled in every nerve ending. And then, the realization struck me. This feeling—my body's response to what could have been a life-threatening situation—it wasn't fear.

It was *presence*. It was like some part of me that I'd kept buried for most of my life had woken up in an instant. I felt truly, unmistakably . . . *alive*. It was something I hadn't felt in so long—maybe not even since that experience with the lion at the zoo at fifteen years old—but my body remembered the feeling. And it was glorious.

Not everyone who comes lion tracking comes just because they love adventure. Some come because something in them is hungry, and they don't know what to call it.

One man had been doing coaching work for a while. He'd made incredible progress. He could talk about growth. He could name his patterns. But there was still something missing—something he could feel but couldn't access. So, he made a decision that surprised even him: he decided to go to Africa with me to track lions on foot. He was not trying to escape his life; he was going to meet it, to stand in a place where the wild still has the right of way, and to see for himself what it feels like to look a lion in the eye.

The night before he left, as he was packing, his kids asked him the question that always lands deeper than it sounds: "Why do you have to leave us?"

He paused. He didn't give them a polished answer. He gave them the truth.

"Daddy is always telling you that you need to be brave," he said. "Well, Daddy has to be brave too."

Three days later, we were out in the bush with a small group. The light was soft and golden, the kind that makes everything feel close and ancient. We rounded a bend and found them—five lions, stretched out and still, as if they owned the air itself.

No one spoke.

And then the man leaned toward me, almost whispering, as if he didn't want to break whatever had opened inside him.

"I get it," he said.

He didn't say more. He didn't have to.

Because in that moment, bravery stopped being an idea he taught his children. It became something he practiced with his whole body. Something real. Something earned.

For the rest of the trip, his posture was different. Not louder. Not more confident. Just . . . more honest. Less defended. As if he had finally found the track again, not because everything was solved, but because he had met something true.

Lions have a way of bringing you into all your senses. The force and magnitude of a lion's presence are otherworldly. There have been many times since that first encounter in the wild when I have felt a nearby lion before I actually saw it. That's also how I felt at the zoo when I was fifteen. I felt the lion's eyes on me before I ever faced him. And as I stood there, staring into those powerful golden eyes for what felt like an hour, I could sense the enormity of his power—but it was constrained. He was locked away in his little cage: safe, controlled, domesticated. In our silent exchange, it's as though I could hear the lion's voice in my head, saying, "I don't belong in this cage, David. And neither do you. We are lions, and lions were meant to *live* . . . and *live free.*"

Realizing this changes how you move through the world, but it does not mean you do it alone. What I've learned is that staying connected to this version of yourself requires context and people who know how to hold it with you. In my life, that has meant continuing to surround myself with others who are committed to this kind of inner work and honest leadership. That is why my work alongside the community at Novus Global has remained such a meaningful part of my life, not as a role I play, but as a place where this way of being is continually practiced.

BURSTING OUT OF THE 1–10 SCALE

A solid 7 out of 10.

That's how I described my life, circa 2020, back in chapter 1. I'd checked all the boxes:

- College? *Check.*
- Career? *Check.*
- Wife? *Check.*
- Friends? *Check.*
- Relationship with God? *Check.*
- Own a home? *Check.*
- Good person? *Check.*
- Safe, stable, predictable life? *Check.*

See? An easy 7. Not perfect. Room for improvement. But thoroughly comfortable, like waking up in a warm, cozy bed on a cold winter morning.

So . . . why did I always feel like something was missing?

Looking back on those days, I can see how I had fooled myself into believing I was living the life of my dreams. Heck, maybe I was. Maybe the real problem back then was that my dreams were too small. I was striving for the life I thought I could attain without ever stopping to ask myself if that was the life I really wanted. It's not that I just wasn't listening to my inner voice; it's that my inner voice was locked inside the same glass cage I was. That's the problem with glass cages: sometimes, you can't see the walls that are closing in around you. Until, that is, the wall starts to crack—or someone throws a brick through it. For me, that moment came when Lisa drove a divorce-sized bulldozer right through the invisible confines of my enclosure. Once the walls around my safe, small, tidy life came crashing down, I was free to roam wild for the first time in my life. And that scared the hell out of me.

Those first couple of years after my divorce were hard. I've been pretty candid about that. I felt like I was in complete darkness for so long. I remember lying in my Airbnb in Napa Valley, a few hours after I'd told someone at that wine-tasting event that I wanted to track lions in Africa. That was the first time I'd said that out loud. It seemed absolutely ridiculous at the time. The guy I was talking to probably took it as seriously as he'd have taken a child telling him he wanted to grow up to be an astronaut. Sure, it's a fun dream, but there's a 0.00001 percent chance of it becoming a reality. But after I'd said it out loud, I couldn't get it out of my head.

I realized how desperately I didn't just want to heal, but to really live—to live big, to live a meaningful life full of risk and adventure. I didn't just want to rebuild a "7 out of 10" kind of life. I wanted to push the limits, to see how big a life I could live beyond the 1–10.

I didn't know how to get there, but I knew what I'd been doing up to that point wasn't getting me where my heart truly wanted to go. I realized at that moment that I could either run away from the darkness that was surrounding me, or I could run straight toward it. I knew all the time and effort I'd spent running away from it hadn't gotten me anywhere. What would happen, then, if I changed direction? I honestly didn't know, and that was terrifying—but it was also thrilling.

My whole adult life, I felt like I needed a guarantee before I'd do anything. I wouldn't—*I couldn't*—leap without seeing the patch of ground I'd land on. Maybe it was because I had to uproot my life and move every couple of years as a child. Maybe all the uncertainty and insecurity I had as a kid had burned through my lifetime supply of "blind faith" moments, leaving me unwilling and unable to take any leaps of faith as an adult. In some dark, lost part of my heart, I seemed to remember a love of mystery and a thrill at the unknown—but that part of me had become inaccessible in my twenties and thirties. Now, as a "grown-up," I felt like I needed certainty, control, and stability. Stable marriage. Stable career. Stable home. Reasonable expectations. Achievable goals. My perfect, safe, little 7. My cage.

But then, the glass walls of my enclosure were shattered, and the vast uncertainty of life flooded in, filling the void like air rushing into a broken vacuum. My meticulously ordered life was left in shambles. Everything I had bolted down was suddenly upended. I was left alone in the dark. The darkness, the unknown, had scared me for so long. I'd long been settled into very clear, black-and-white thinking: the light was good, and the dark was bad. But now, some hidden part of me was calling out, questioning what I thought I knew. As an executive coach, I've since watched this same moment show up in leaders, athletes, and executives whose lives looked nothing like mine, except for the sudden loss of certainty.

What if there are bad things the light blinds you from seeing? What if there are some good things you can only see in the dark? What if the only way to find the light again was to peer deeper into the darkness?

These questions eventually led me to a Byron Katie (BK) workshop in March 2023. Byron Katie (Byron Kathleen Mitchell) is a mental health speaker and author who teaches a powerful form of self-discovery called "The Work." Her therapeutic approach is built around four key questions:

1. Is your belief *true*?
2. Can you absolutely *know* that it is true?
3. What happens when you fully *believe* that thought?
4. Who would you be *without* that thought?

That may sound kind of simplistic, but it's amazing what happens when you really dig in, take these questions seriously, and do "The Work."

At that workshop, I met a woman who would quickly become one of the most significant people in my life: Sarah-Maya, who helped facilitate the event. I got to know her a bit that week, and I ultimately asked her to work with me one on one as a therapist/coach. I loved the BK framework and was experiencing some breakthroughs as Sarah-Maya and I worked together, but I never expected her to bridge the gap between my healing journey and my passion for tracking lions.

One of my heroes in the world of lion tracking is Boyd Varty, whom I have quoted throughout this book. Imagine my surprise, then, to discover one day that

Boyd followed Sarah-Maya on Instagram. I asked her if she really knew him (she did) and if she could make an introduction for me. She agreed, and I found myself on a Zoom call with Boyd a few weeks later. When his video popped up on my computer, I was a bit embarrassed to experience an unexpected flood of emotion. It was one of those rare times in my life when I knew—in that moment—I had just tripped over a significant track, one that would take me off in a new, exciting, and wild direction. And, as you've witnessed several times in this book, that emotion washed over me.

Boyd was patient and gracious with me, and we had a phenomenal thirty-minute conversation. By the time we ended it, I was certain that this was a track I *had* to follow. I asked Boyd if he would be willing to take me on as a coaching client and was thrilled when he said yes. Our friendship and mentoring relationship began on that call, and it has continued to this day. He has been instrumental in my growth not just as a lion tracker, but also as a stronger, healthier, and more uncaged human being.

All these incredible tracks—my BK experience, my ongoing therapy with Sarah-Maya, my love for lion tracking, and my coaching relationship with Boyd—converged unexpectedly in spring of 2024 when Sarah-Maya, in her loving but wonderfully direct manner, thought she caught a whiff of my bullshit during one of our calls. She said something to me that I've said to so many of my own clients in the past:

"I don't believe you."

It was April 2024, about a year into our counseling relationship. I'd been saying for months that I wanted to take another lion-tracking safari in South Africa, but I'd been way too busy with work and other commitments to make any headway at all on that goal. When I commented on that desire again in this call, Sarah-Maya wasn't having it.

"What do you mean, you don't believe me?" I asked, half-jokingly. "You know I love tracking in the wild! Of course, I want to go again!"

She replied bluntly, "Listen, I believe people *really want* something only when they're willing to take steps to move toward it. You've talked for months about wanting to take another trip, but David, you haven't taken even the smallest step toward it. So, how can I believe that you really want this?"

Ouch.

"It's not that I don't want it," I protested. "I'm just so busy! I don't know how to fit it into my schedule anytime soon!" I gave her a long list of excuses for why

I couldn't add a week of tracking to a business trip to South Africa I'd already planned for that fall.

She cut through the excuses gently but firmly. "You are getting way too far ahead of yourself, trying to figure out every detail all at once. Is that how you track lions? Do you just wait and wait and wait until the lions magically appear in front of you, or do you follow one track at a time until the tracks lead you to where the lions are?"

Leaning in closer, she said softly, "Let's just start with what you really want and what seems to be calling you, and then you can decide if you trust God enough to take the first step toward it and see what opens up."

She instructed me to close my eyes and search my mind and body for what I really, *really* wanted. Within a couple of minutes, I had a crystal clear, unmistakably specific vision for what I wanted. It was plain as day . . . but I still couldn't believe it.

"No way," I said out loud. "That can't be it. That is so irrational. How could I ever pull this off?"

As if she could see the shift in my physiology and energy, she said, "That! Whatever thought just came to your mind—that's what we're looking for."

"What do you mean?" I asked.

By this point, I'd spent more than a hundred hours in therapy with Sarah-Maya. She knew me incredibly well, and we'd built a huge amount of trust over the past year. She'd earned the right to call me out by then, and she was willing to do it.

"Come on, David. You obviously know what you *want* to do. The only question now is whether you want it badly enough to risk saying it out loud and putting in the work to make it happen."

Feeling a bit defensive, I started rattling off more excuses, but she cut me off. "I get it. You're busy. But there will always be excuses. There will never be a 'perfect' time to do something, and there will always be reasons for not listening to the call that's on your heart. But you've got to decide: Do you want to go for it or not?"

Somehow, I was terrified to speak the words out loud. It's like I knew that by speaking them, I would be fully acknowledging what I wanted to do. Giving voice to our deepest desires brings them out of the clouds and into our lives. It makes them real, even if we choose not to act on them. I knew that if I said what I really wanted to do, I'd immediately become responsible for either doing it or for *not* doing it.

"Okay, well . . . this is crazy . . . and I don't know how it could even be possible . . . but what I really want to do is fully immerse myself in the wild for an extended period of time. I don't just want to go for five days; I want to go all in on a long, uninterrupted, thirty-day tracking safari."

I could feel the impact of the words on my body as I spoke them aloud. I felt lightning in my veins. I felt fully alive as my dream was birthed into the world. It felt so good to experience myself saying what I really wanted out loud. To trust her with it. To trust myself with it. To trust life with it.

After sitting in the beauty of that moment for a few minutes, I fell back into activation mode and started trying to plan the whole thing out.

"Stop," she said. "Remember, David, this is like tracking. You don't go straight to the lion. You just look for the next track. Stop worrying about months down the road. Just focus on your next small step. That is all you need to worry about. Trust yourself and trust everything beyond you."

That reminder (plus a little intentional breathwork) helped calm my nervous system. And then, as I drew a big breath, I felt my whole mind and body relax in the assurance that I was finally acknowledging the tracks that had been right in front of me for a while, and that those tracks would lead me right into what would be a life-changing thirty-day adventure.

I didn't know the whole story yet, but I knew the next step: talk to my boss about taking the time off. I was nervous when I broached the subject with my CEO, but his whole face lit up as I told him about my vision for a monthlong tracking trip. "Yes!" he exclaimed. "That sounds amazing! I'm totally on board, David. Let's find a way to make this happen!"

To say I was shocked would be a massive understatement. I'd been worried about how my CEO would respond, but he actually became one of the biggest champions in helping me accomplish this huge goal.

My next track led me to Boyd, who I'd gotten to know well over the past several months of coaching calls. I asked him where I should go for such a long trip and how the planning would be different compared to what I'd done in the past. Boyd shocked me when he said, "David, you won't believe this, but the two trackers who taught me how to track just opened a camp in South Africa focused on lion tracking. I'll make a call to them, and we will get you all set up."

Unbelievable. Just a few tracks after having the audacity to say my dream out loud, and I already had the approval of my boss, the time off, a camp to go to, and time booked with Renias, one of the best, most experienced lion trackers in the world. Seeing it all fall perfectly into place, I couldn't help but think back to Sarah-Maya's wise words: "Let's just start with what you really want, and then you can decide if you trust God enough to take the first step toward it and see what opens up."

As scary as it had been to give voice to my deepest desire, God turned out to be pretty trustworthy after all. And that fall, less than six months after saying it out loud, I found myself on another small, dusty airstrip in South Africa, ready to begin the adventure of a lifetime.

That thirty-day safari fully blew the lid off my 1–10 thinking. I realized that the scale doesn't just go up to 10; it goes to infinity. There are no limits. There is no cap on life. If I was living a level-7 life before, it wasn't 7 out of 10. It was 7 out of 100 or 1,000. I was trapped in a little box of limited thinking. I thought a 10 was the best that life had to offer. What I've discovered since then is that a 10 was only as good as life could get within the confines of my little cage. Once I managed to break free, I realized there was no upper limit to the kind of life I could live.

From inside your enclosure, all you see are walls. Those walls tell you, "You can only grow *this* much.

You can only reach *this* far. You can only soar *this* high." But your cage is a lie. Imagine being born in a prison cell and spending every moment of your life in a little ten-by-ten-foot box. You look up at the ceiling and think that's the sky. You scan the walls to your left and right and think that's as far and wide as the world extends. You see the bland, beige-colored surfaces on all sides and think that's as colorful as the world gets. But then, you're suddenly dropped in the middle of the South African wildlands, and you *see*. Maybe for the first time. The horizon stretches forever, an unbroken canvas of endless sky meeting golden plains. Mountains rise in jagged majesty, their stone faces scarred and eternal, while rivers carve lifelines through a land both fierce and breathtaking. At dusk, the savanna ignites in fire and gold, every blade of grass catching the sun's last flame as lions stir in the gathering dark. *This* is life. *This* is the world you've been living in all this time—the world you could never see inside the "safe" and "comfortable," 7-out-of-10 way of living that you thought you were working for.

This is what it means to be fully, freely *alive*.

The Morgan Wallen song "Somebody's Problem" came on the radio the other day. I'd heard the song several times, but something about *that* day made the lyrics jump out at me in a whole new way. There's a line that goes, "Damn, I'd love to drown in them heartbreaker blue eyes."[16] The song tells the story of a guy who knows this woman could cause him a world of heartbreak, but he still wants to take his chances. There's something about her that is so alluring that he's willing to risk "drown(ing) in them heartbreaker blue eyes." I remember driving down the road, singing along, when it hit me: I want to live like that! I want to completely fall in love with life. I want to know how it feels to be so outrageously alive that I'm willing to take big swings and risk everything, even in the face of failure or heartbreak.

Life and love are full of risks. In fact, daring to love at all is the biggest risk, because you *know* that love will contain some heartbreak. As C.S. Lewis wrote:

> To love at all is to be vulnerable. Love anything and your heart will be wrung and possibly broken. If you want to make sure of keeping it intact you must give it to no one. Wrap it carefully round with hobbies and little luxuries; avoid all entanglements. Lock it up safe in the casket or coffin of your selfishness. But in that casket, safe, dark, motionless, airless, it will change. It will not be broken; it will become

> unbreakable, impenetrable, irredeemable. To love is to be vulnerable.[17]

There are no guarantees in life, whether you're tracking a lion through rough terrain or just trying to drum up the courage to ask a girl out on a date. There is very little certainty—and that's the shocking blessing of life in the wild! You discover that uncertainty is not a problem to manage but a catalyst for transformation. In our safe, predictable, "civilized" lives, we often yearn for guarantees because we're afraid of the unknown. We assume that what we *think* we want is better than what the wild might bring us. That's how I lived for so long. But once I surrendered to uncertainty, I opened myself to the indescribable joy of surprise, of adventure, of a more rewarding life than I ever could have dreamed of from behind the walls of my old cage! And once your eyes are opened to how big and beautiful the world can be, there is absolutely no going back.

TRACKING THE WILD WITHIN

Way back at the start of this book, I ended chapter 1 with these words: "This book is an invitation for you to track a lion. And that lion is you." Here's what I mean by that: This journey we're on isn't about finding the wild "out there." It's about finding the wild inside ourselves. It's about discovering the first track in your life that is leading you somewhere new, following that string wherever it leads, and finally finding the creature moving outside the confines of the life you've always known. It's about reconnecting with—or maybe even awakening for the first time—that part of you that yearns to feel truly alive, to bust out of the cage you've built around yourself and roam free. It's about tuning in to what your senses are telling you and trusting that your nervous system knows what it needs and where it needs to go. It's about waking up from the sleepwalking trance most of us stumble through life in and instead living purposefully, leaning into our whole, wild selves, no matter how crazy it seems.

But be warned: This journey is not for the faint of heart. It will push you to your limits and challenge your assumptions, and it will turn your paradigms on their head. It certainly did for me. I started out:

- Thinking "finding my person" would fix me, when the person I most needed to find was myself.

- Thinking something external would fill the void in my heart, when my real healing was waiting within.
- Wanting guarantees to loving mystery and adventure.
- Trying to force my healing to follow my plan instead of asking healing what it required of me.
- Rushing through my recovery as quickly as possible instead of slowing down to appreciate all the hidden gems at each step in the process.
- Resisting the flow of life instead of trusting it to carry me along.

Somehow, all those things I was so afraid of led me to the man I always wanted to become. It's like the great Ted Lasso, one of the best TV characters of all time, once said: "I think things come into our lives to help us get from one place to a better one." Those things could be big or small, victories or tragedies, loves or losses. They might even include something as difficult as divorce. But as Ted also says, "It may not work out how you think it will or how you hope it does. But believe me, it will all work out."[18]

Of course, "it will all work out" means something different for each of us. For me, it meant discovering a passion for nature, travel, exploration, and obviously tracking wild lions through the African savanna. That probably isn't what you'll find at the end of the string you're following—but don't totally count it out, either! Lion tracking is *my* thing; it's one of the things that makes *me* feel most alive. What's your thing? What is it that fills you with excitement? What activity seems to make time somehow stand still and fly by at the same time? What makes your heart skip a beat? What fills you with the kind of pure joy and anticipation that you used to feel as a child on Christmas Eve? If time and money were no object, what would you most want to spend your life doing? What makes you feel fully, freely, unashamedly *alive*?

Take these questions seriously. I mean it. Stop what you're doing right now and spend some time really thinking through these things. Fire up your phone or computer's Notes app or grab a notebook and pen, and really explore your heart, mind, and body. Look carefully for that first track. If you don't see it at first, do what my tracking guides taught me to do: slow down and move in ever-expanding concentric circles until you find it. In this context, that means taking a mental step back and asking yourself some broader questions. Don't stress about finding *the thing* that lights you up, especially if this is all new to you. Instead, try to circle the missing track by considering these questions:

- What do you enjoy doing?
- What part of your job do you find most fun and exciting?
- Who or what makes you feel most alive?
- What was the last thing you really got excited about?
- What dreams or desires are you scared to admit out loud but can't get out of your head?
- When in your life have you felt a palpable surge of energy in your body, even if it seemed irrational at the time?
- What is something you're curious about but never took the time to explore?
- Looking back at your childhood, what moment or activities made you feel most wild, free, and authentically yourself?
- What qualities do you secretly (or not so secretly) yearn to be known for? (Examples: courageous, bold, generous, compassionate, decisive)
- In what areas of your life are you currently settling for "tolerable despair" instead of truly going for what makes you giddy?

If "tracking lions in Africa" made your list, that's awesome! That's a dream I can definitely help make come true with you, and you can join me on one of the trips I lead. But chances are, you came up with one or two other things. I hesitate to make any suggestions; after all, I don't want to deprive you of the thrill of finding the track for yourself. However, after helping many other people through this exercise over the past few years, I know from experience that seeing some examples can help grease the mental gears and get the process running strong. So, with that in mind, here are some examples of the types of things people can come alive doing:

- Competitive fitness events, such as marathons, Hyrox, or Ironman events
- Sewing, knitting, or crocheting
- Gardening
- Computer programming
- Computer hardware
- Volunteering
- Running or bicycling
- Lifting weights
- Writing or blogging
- Collecting
- Traveling

- Skydiving
- Creating YouTube videos
- Outdoor adventuring
- Rafting
- Singing
- Playing an instrument
- Woodworking
- Dancing
- Spending quality time with your family and friends
- Championing issues that are important to you
- Crossing items off your bucket list
- Horseback riding
- Photography and/or videography

Whatever your "thing" is—whether it's on this list or something I've never heard of and would never think of—your job is to figure out what makes you feel most alive. That is the first track you need to discover. And then, when you've found the track, start following the string wherever it leads until you find that wild, free, fully alive version of yourself that's out there waiting for you.

Fair warning: This process won't happen overnight. It takes time to discover who you want to be and how you want to live, and it takes a lot more time to make the changes that are required to achieve that big goal. Cut yourself some slack if things don't come together as quickly as you'd like. My journey to aliveness took a lot longer than I would have liked . . . but I'm convinced it took exactly as long as it *needed* to take. So, don't try to rush it, and don't kick yourself if—actually, *when*—you screw up, fall down, take a wrong turn, and lose the track. This isn't a race, and we are not just looking for the meaning of life. We're searching for what makes us feel most alive.

For the first forty years of my life, I had no idea what this meant—but then, the lions showed me. And now, I'm learning to experience that same sense of aliveness in the comings and goings of everyday life that I once wrote off as boring or mundane. When you know what makes you come alive like never before, you'll discover that you can carry that feeling with you wherever you go and whatever you do. I might only spend a few weeks a year in Africa these days, but that doesn't mean I spend the other three hundred and thirty-five days a year *not* really living! I know what I love to do, what I'm passionate about, and what breathes life into me. And now, I've learned how to orient my life around that passion and that sense of aliveness even when I'm not out on a tracking safari. I can still be my most alive, fulfilled self when I'm working with my coaching clients, hanging out with my friends, or sitting all by myself in my Denver home. Again, I don't have to be tracking to feel alive; I just have to be living a life that's aligned with my truest self, with who I know the real David to be.

The same is true for you.

Life is and always has been leaving tracks for you to follow.

The version of you waiting at the other end of the string is begging you to follow the tracks of aliveness. Find others who are following *their* version of aliveness, and surround yourself with them. You may all be excited about different things, but if you're all tracking your best, truest selves and striving to live a life that is fully alive, then you'll be moving in the same direction.

Walk with them.

Run with them.

This is your pride.

TAKE A WALK ON THE WILD SIDE

So often in life, we get a quick flicker, a passing glance at the life that could be. Our heart rate quickens, and we feel tingles of excitement and electricity dancing along our nerve endings. It's as though, just for a moment, the path toward aliveness becomes crystal clear, the way the lights of an airport runway blaze brightly in the dark of night, showing the plane the exact path to take for a safe landing. But then, "reality" sets in. A lifetime of conditioning sounds the alarm. The zookeeper that's buried deep within us realizes we've caught a glimpse of something far outside our cage walls, and he sends out the voices to stop us:

- "You can't do *that*."
- "That's not reality."
- "You'll fail if you even think of trying that."
- "Who do you think you are?"
- "That's too big, too crazy for you."

I listened to those voices for forty years, but now, I do my best to ignore them.

The voices went crazy the first time I thought about building a business taking people lion tracking in Africa. It was so far outside my comfort zone that the old me would never have thought twice about it. The new me, though . . . he doesn't give up nearly as easily. Once that track presented itself, I *had* to follow it. It sounded absolutely crazy at the time. Heck, it still does. But guess what? I took my first group of clients to Kruger National Park in South Africa just last month, as I write this. I organized the trip, hired guides, coached my guests on what to expect, and I led them on the adventure of a lifetime. Was my new dream of building a business around tracking lions in South Africa *rational*? Probably not. But that doesn't mean it was impossible. I got to spend several days leading the tour with Renias, my friend and guide; I saw lions; I had a "too close for comfort" encounter with a black rhino; and I had a blast doing the thing I love most in the world. Most importantly, I helped a small group of clients discover a new sense of aliveness for themselves. This is so far outside the 1–10 scale I used to live by that I can't even measure it. How do you "rate" feeling more alive than you've ever felt? There isn't a number high enough to describe how much I love my life now.

This is what's waiting for you at the end of the string. This is the life you can experience for yourself—the fullest, freest, most alive kind of life you could possibly imagine! But that will only happen if you follow the tracks. So, start tracking. Get up. Look around. Find the first track. You don't have to figure out the rest of your life. You don't have to figure out the next ten years or even the next ten days. You've just got to find the next small step to take, moving forward one track at a time, following the wild creature who so desperately wants to be found.

I don't know what the map of your life looks like, but I know one thing for sure: If you can follow with childlike wonder the things that bring you to life, those are the tracks that will ultimately lead you back home… to yourself.

AFTERWORD

WHILE ON SAFARI in October 2022, I got the opportunity to have a profoundly intimate encounter with a lion in the wild. There was nothing standing between me and an enormous male lion but about thirty feet of air. I was in his world.

Fortunately, this didn't happen accidentally. I didn't round a corner in the brush one day and find myself face-to-face with a lion by surprise. While out tracking, we had found a male lion taking a nap, and for whatever reason, he was not disturbed by our presence. Stretch instructed me to sit about fifty feet from the lion and stay there a few minutes—time for me to get comfortable being that close to a lion and, more importantly, time for the lion to get comfortable having me that close. I controlled my breathing and even managed to get some amazing photos from close up.

The lion was resting in the heat of the day and didn't seem bothered by me being there, so Stretch told me I could inch closer if I wanted to. I put my camera in my lap and scooted forward a little bit, pausing to give the lion time to either approve or object. He was sitting upright now, fully awake and alert, but he didn't seem to care that we'd intruded on his naptime. He almost seemed to enjoy the company. Stretch told me I could move even closer if I wanted to, so I scooted forward a bit more. I did this "scoot and pause" maneuver a few times until I got about thirty feet away from him. That was close enough for me.

I sat there in the dirt taking in the strength of the creature in front of me, breathing in his pure, masculine, powerful energy. In my mind, I could feel myself reaching out to him, trying to pull his strength into myself. The other people in my party kind of faded into my periphery, and I really felt like it was just me and the lion.

Sitting there, looking up at him, I found myself thinking about my Grandpa Don. Then I remembered how alive I had felt when I was a kid, peddling my bike as fast as my little eight-year-old legs could go. That was the first time I can remember feeling fully free, fully alive. And now, here I was half a world away, experiencing that same sense of excitement and wonder in the face of this mighty lion. I named him Don, after my grandfather.

Don the Lion and I sat there in the dirt for several minutes. I was amazed by him, and I knew I'd be telling this story for the rest of my life. But part of me wondered what Don the Lion was thinking . . . about me. Was he as curious about me as I was about him? Was our afternoon together as meaningful to him as it was to me?

I believe he saw me that day—really saw me, and something in me that I was having trouble seeing in myself. I believe Don the Lion saw my courage, even when I couldn't.

Looking into those magical amber eyes, I felt the spirit of my Grandpa Don. I heard his voice calling out, encouraging me, welcoming me, and challenging me to keep going no matter how hard things were. I felt the energy of the lion join with Grandpa Don, as though together they were saying, "Keep tracking. Go and find the others who are tracking too. Follow the string, and you will find the creature moving at the end of it. And there, you'll realize that *you* are the lion you've been searching for all this time. It's been you all along."

ACKNOWLEDGMENTS

THIS BOOK WAS not written alone.

It was written in the quiet moments after conversations that cracked me open. It was written in airports, in African wilderness, in the space between who I was and who I was becoming. It was written because people refused to let me stay small when it would have been easier.

First, I owe my deepest gratitude to the trackers of the African Wilderness—especially **Renias Mhlongo**, **Stretch Ferreira**, and the men who walk the land with reverence and precision. You taught me that tracking is not about domination but about relationship. You showed me what it means to listen with your whole body, to slow down enough for truth to reveal itself, and to walk into uncertainty with calm eyes and a steady heart. Every page of this book carries your footprints.

To **Jason Jaggard** and the entire **Novus Global** community: this work would not exist without you. Novus Global gave me language for what I was already living but didn't yet know how to name. You challenged me to bring both strength and tenderness into my leadership. You gave me a place to belong while I was learning how to become. I am forever grateful for the way you walk with people through the hardest and most beautiful parts of their lives.

To **Dan Leffelaar**, thank you for opening the door to a world I didn't yet know I was meant for. You didn't just introduce me to coaching professional athletes; you invited me into a standard of excellence, presence, and emotional honesty that changed how I lead and how I live. You saw something in me before I could fully name it, and you gave me both opportunity and challenge in equal measure. Because of you, I learned what it means to stand in rooms of elite performers with confidence, humility, and real impact. This book and the work it represents carries your influence in every chapter.

To **Boyd Varty**, thank you for being the bridge between worlds. You helped me see that the wild is not somewhere we visit, it is something we experience. Your words, your presence, and your unwavering devotion to aliveness have shaped this book more than you know.

To the clients and athletes who trusted me with their stories—thank you. You let me witness your fears, your fire, your longing, and your becoming. You taught me that the lion lives in every human heart, just waiting to be remembered. This book is, in many ways, a reflection of your courage.

To my family, thank you for loving me through all the versions of myself. For your patience when I was restless. For your grace when I didn't have the words. For being my home when everything else felt uncertain.

To my friends, those who sat with me in the mess, those who asked the hard questions, those who refused to let me lie to myself, this book carries your fingerprints. You saw the lion before I did.

To my cowriters, **Mahla Hoffbeck and Allen Harris**: this book quite literally would not exist without you. You sat with me in the rawness of unfinished thoughts and half-formed stories and helped shape them into something real. You listened for the truth beneath my words, challenged me when I drifted from it, and kept calling me back to what mattered most. You held the tension between craft and soul, structure and wildness, until this book could stand on its own. I am profoundly grateful for your patience, your rigor, and your belief in what this story could become.

To **Allison Trowbridge**, thank you for seeing this book before it fully knew how to see itself. You believed in this project when it was still raw, wild, and unfinished, and you held a steady, grounded vision for what it could become. Your combination of editorial rigor and genuine care created a container where this story could mature without losing its soul. You didn't try to tame the lion—you helped it become clear. I am deeply grateful for your leadership, your patience, and the way you honored both the craft of publishing and the heart of this work.

And finally, to you, the reader: thank you for being brave enough to pick this up. Something in you already knows there is more. More life. More truth. More wildness. If these pages help you listen to that voice, even a little, then every mile, every doubt, every late night was worth it.

This book is an invitation. But it is also a thank you.

To everyone who walked with me while I learned how to walk with myself—this is for you.

APPENDIX

Here is a list of resources and people I worked with over the past several years that were incredibly helpful on my journey.

- Numerous people within my coaching firm at Novus Global (novus.global)
- Michelle Peterson: https://www.michelle-peterson.com/
- Sarah-Maya https://www.theworkwithsarahmaya.com/
- Syanna Wand https://www.syannawand.com/
- Boyd Varty https://boydvarty.com/
- Koelle Simpson https://koellesimpson.com/
- Dairek Morgan https://www.dairekmorgantherapy.com/
- Sarah Grieb https://www.breakthrough8.com/
- If you ever want to go track wild lions with me, details are on my website: www.davidagerber.com.

ENDNOTES

1 Trevor Hall, "The Fruitful Darkness," track 1 on *The Fruitful Darkness* (album), released June 1, 2018, digital audio, 3:36, by Trevor Hall, accessed via Spotify.

2 Tom Brown Jr., *The Tracker: The True Story of Tom Brown Jr.* (New York: Berkley Books, 1978), 20.

3 Brown Jr., *The Tracker*, 20.

4 Joseph Campbell, as quoted in numerous interviews and lectures (attribution commonly associated with Campbell's teachings on the hero's journey).

5 Boyd Varty, *The Lion Tracker's Guide to Life* (Boston: Houghton Mifflin Harcourt, 2016).

6 Matthew McConaughey, *Greenlights* (New York: Crown, 2020).

7 *Hacksaw Ridge*, directed by Mel Gibson, written by Andrew Knight and Robert Schenkkan, performance by Sam Worthington as Captain Glover, released November 4, 2016 (Los Angeles: Summit Entertainment), motion picture.

8 Rainer Maria Rilke, *Letters to a Young Poet*, trans. Stephen Mitchell (New York: Vintage International, 1986).

9 Chris Ferreiras, quotation attributed to Ferreiras in public writings and talks, often rendered as "Time won't heal what you don't make time to face."

10 Brianna Wiest, *The Mountain Is You: Transforming Self-Sabotage into Self-Mastery* (New York: Thought Catalog Books, 2020).

11 Peter Crone, quotation attributed to Crone in lectures and interviews on personal freedom and self-inquiry, often rendered as "Life will present us with people and circumstances to show us where we are not yet free."

12 Francis Weller, *The Wild Edge of Sorrow: Rituals of Renewal and the Sacred Work of Grief* (Berkeley, CA: North Atlantic Books, 2015).

13 Weller, *The Wild Edge of Sorrow*.

14 Varty, *The Lion Tracker's Guide to Life*.

15 Anthony de Mello, *Awareness: Conversations with the Masters* (New York: PRH Christian Publishing, 1992).

16 Morgan Wallen, "Somebody's Problem," on *Dangerous: The Double Album* (Big Loud Records, 2021).

17 C. S. Lewis, *The Four Loves* (New York: Harcourt, Brace & Company, 1960), 169.

18 *Ted Lasso*, season 2, episode 1, "Goodbye Earl," directed by Declan Lowney, written by Brendan Hunt and Phoebe Walsh, Apple TV+, aired July 23, 2021.